SERGEI VASIL'EVICH RACHMANINOFF

GARLAND COMPOSER
RESOURCE MANUALS
(Vol. 3)

GARLAND REFERENCE LIBRARY
OF THE HUMANITIES
(Vol. 471)

Volume 3

Garland Composer Resource Manuals

Advisory Editor:
Barry S. Brook

General Editor:
Guy A. Marco

SERGEI VASIL'EVICH RACHMANINOFF
A Guide to Research

Robert Palmieri

GARLAND PUBLISHING, INC. • NEW YORK & LONDON
1985

© 1985 Robert Palmieri
All rights reserved

220445
Library of Congress Cataloging in Publication Data
Palmieri, Robert, 1930–
   Sergei Vasil'evich Rachmaninoff.

   (Garland composer resource manuals ; v. 3)
(Garland reference library of the humanities ; v. 471)
   Bibliography: p.
   Discography: p.
   List of works: p.
   Repertoire: p.
   Includes indexes.
   1. Rachmaninoff, Sergei, 1873–1943—Bibliography.
I. Title. II. Series. III. Series: Garland reference
library of the humanities ; v. 471.
ML134.R12P3   1985   016.78'092'4   83-49315
ISBN 0-8240-8996-0

Printed on acid-free, 250-year-life paper
Manufactured in the United States of America

GARLAND
COMPOSER RESOURCE MANUALS

In response to the growing need for bibliographic guidance to the vast literature on significant composers, Garland is publishing an extensive series of Resource Manuals. It is expected that this series, which will appear over a ten-year period, will encompass more than a hundred composers; they will represent Western musical tradition from the Renaissance to recent times.

Each Resource Manual will offer a selective, annotated list of writings—in all European languages—about one or more composers. There will also be lists of works by the composers, unless these are available elsewhere. Biographical sketches and guides to library resources, organizations, and specialists will be presented. As appropriate to the individual composers, there will be maps, photographs or other illustrative matter, and glossaries and indexes of various sorts. These volumes are being compiled by musical and bibliographical specialists, under the general editorial direction of Dr. Guy A. Marco. Advisory editor for the series is Dr. Barry S. Brook.

CONTENTS

Preface ix
Introduction xiii

I. Rachmaninoff's Compositions
  1. Rachmaninoff's Publishers 3
  2. Works for Piano and Orchestra 4
  3. Works for Piano 7
  4. Transcriptions and Arrangements for Piano by Rachmaninoff 17
  5. Works for Orchestra 23
  6. Chamber Music 28
  7. Operas 31
  8. Works for Chorus 33
  9. Songs 36
  10. Selection of Arrangements and Transcriptions of Rachmaninoff's Works Written by Others 60

II. The Rachmaninoff Repertoire
  1. Introduction to Rachmaninoff's Repertoire 67
  2. Rachmaninoff's Repertoire as Pianist 69
  3. Rachmaninoff's Repertoire as Conductor 84

III. Rachmaninoff Discography
  1. Introduction to Rachmaninoff's Recordings 93
  2. Recordings Made by Rachmaninoff 95

IV. Rachmaninoff Bibliography 119

References 295

Illustrations	299
Author Index	303
Index of Proper Names	309
Index of Rachmaninoff's Compositions	321
Subject Index	333

PREFACE

In compiling a substantive bibliography on a subject, the difficulty of selectivity exists both as to quality and quantity of material. The limits of search and comprehensiveness are in the hands of the bibliographer. The primary concern here has been to include only those works that delve into detail or present unique concepts or historical impressions of Rachmaninoff. Not all concert reviews, obituaries, musical dictionary (encyclopedia) entries, and works in all languages are present herein. The inclusion of reviews is important, for they reveal the contemporary critical climate regarding Rachmaninoff. Only those reviews that pertain to premieres or are historically significant are included in the bibliography. Obituaries are kept to a minimum, entering only those written by authorities or those contributing informative data.

Innumerable Rachmaninoff bibliographic lists, as well as many annual and periodic lists have been scrutinized. Those foreign language works entered in *The Music Index* and *Répertoire international de littérature musicale* (RILM Abstracts) and those appearing in diverse Rachmaninoff bibliographies have been sought and reviewed when available. Theses and dissertations concerning Rachmaninoff also were examined when available. The majority of items listed in the present bibliography are available in this country, including the Russian books and periodicals. The usual bibliographic information is supplied with each entry; when available, the International Standard Book Number (ISBN) has been incorporated. Heralding in the computer age, the On-line Computer Library Center, Inc. (OCLC) number has also been included when available. OCLC is an on-line bibliographic data base constituting one of the largest cataloging records in the world. There are well over 10 million records, representing books and other publications in over 3,000 libraries. Information can be directly accessed via the OCLC computer. This formidable link of library holdings and speed of retrieving data greatly facilitates the search process.

The Library of Congress system of transliterating modern Russian with diacritical marks has been utilized. Consistency in transliteration of Russian names is difficult. In the spelling of the names of the more common Russian musicians and composers, I have adopted the accepted Western spelling. Therefore, the names of Chaĭkovskiĭ, Shaliapin, Skriabin, Stravinskiĭ, Musorgskiĭ, Rimskiĭ-Korsakov, Prokof'ev, Kusevitskiĭ and Rakhmaninov, are spelled in the Western manner: Tchaikovsky, Chaliapin, Scriabin, Stravinsky, Mussorgsky, Rimsky-Korsakov, Prokofiev, Koussevitzky and Rachmaninoff. Otherwise, all other Russian language citations have been transliterated using the Library of Congress transliteration system.

Generally, dates referred to in Russian works and reviews prior to the end of January 1918 are in the Old Style (Julian) calendar; to convert to the New Style (Gregorian) calendar add 12 days if the event is during the nineteenth century or 13 days if the event is in the twentieth century. Example: Rachmaninoff was born on 20 March 1873 in the Old Style (Julian) calendar, but on 1 April 1873 using the New Style (Gregorian) calendar.

The photographs have been reproduced with the kind permission of L.S. Sidel'nikov, director of Izdatel'stvo *Muzyka*, and the representatives of the Rachmaninoff estate.

Numerous libraries were visited in the quest for material on Rachmaninoff. I would like to thank the staffs of the following institutions for their assistance: The Library of Congress Music Division, including Charles Sens, Elizabeth Auman, Elmer Booze, and Wayne Shirley; Cleveland Public Library, Ohio State University Library, New York Public Library Slavonic Division, New York University Library, University of Chicago Library, Northwestern University Library, and the University of Wisconsin (Milwaukee) Library. The Kent State University Library was most helpful, and I would like to thank its efficient Interlibrary Loan staff, especially Michael R. Cole for his expeditious assistance. My gratitude also to Larry R. Andrews, Richard W. Shindle, Adriaan and Berendina de Vries, Martin K. Nurmi, and Sylvia DeCapite, all of Kent State University, as well as to master bibliographer Guy A. Marco, and to Margaret, Nora, and Nancy Palmieri. In addition my thanks go to the Kent State University Division of Research for granting me a Summer Research Appointment to work on this project. Finally, to my Russian friend and colleague Michael A. Rogers of the Kent State University Germanic and Slavic Language Department I express my sincerest gratitude for his Russian translations. His knowledge, interest, and enthusiasm are greatly appreciated.

INTRODUCTION

Since the publication of the meager Rachmaninoff entry in the 5th edition of Sir George *Grove's Dictionary of Music and Musicians* in 1955 (certainly a catalyst for further inquiry), musicians and scholars have endeavored to re-examine this richly endowed composer–pianist. Rightly so, for throughout his lifetime Rachmaninoff endured demeaning critical remarks similar to those made by Rosa Newmarch in the above-mentioned *Grove's*, and although the scholarly consensus is now based predominantly on the man and his total output, previously such consensus was based on a comparative criticism, usually with his less traditional contemporaries and on a partial examination of his works. Rachmaninoff's music has survived the crucial period: after his death, his music was expected to fade from the musical repertoire because of the absence of its prime propagator. However, his works have not disappeared from the musical environment as prophesied; in fact, the popularity of his piano works, as seen in contest repertoire, heard in recitals, and noted in the ever-increasing recordings of the complete piano works, has gained greatly in appreciation. Even the new generation of pianists, upon hearing Rachmaninoff's recordings, marvel at his pianistic wizardry. His gift and mastery of melodic lyricism are paramount; Rachmaninoff represents the culmination of the wonderfully rich Russian lyric epic-dramatic style.

Those attempting to unlock the mystery of Rachmaninoff's inner being will have a difficult venture. The man rarely discussed his desires, fears, and values, although he did convey some of these emotions to his intimate friends (e.g., "Re" Marietta Sergeevna Shaginîan) in letters and reminiscences but even these disclosures are guarded.

Many of the early concert reviews in the West are preoccupied with the exterior appearance of the new musical celebrity on the scene. His unique stage demeanor, dour facial expression, lack of exaggerated mannerisms (there was a mania for the mannered style at the time), and his self-imposed exile from his homeland were colorful enough to satisfy the curiosity of the reader. Critics were unanimous in their approval of the pianist Rachmaninoff, and that positive acclaim helped him endure the tribulations resulting from this self-imposed exile from his native Russia. This career choice interfered with his compositional creativity, but that is only part of the reason for his decreased productivity following his departure to the West. The reasons are too convoluted and complex for explanation although some have attempted to propose a rationale. Rachmaninoff's simple answers, when approached about the scarcity of new compositions, were that he longed for his homeland and without this environmental stimulus he could no longer write, or that he could only do one thing at a time—when he performed he could not write, and when he wrote he could not perform. These were expeditious answers to a complex dilemma that continually perplexed him.

The *New Grove Dictionary of Music and Musicians* (1980) makes restitution for its past paltry representation of Rachmaninoff by seriously examining the composer's life and creativity. *Musical Times* critic Geoffrey Norris wrote the Rachmaninoff chapter for the New Grove's 1980 edition, a chapter that truly represents the composer.

Scholarly examination of Rachmaninoff, both in the USSR and in the West, has increased, especially after the 1973 centenary anniversary of his birth, when a flood of material on the composer appeared. Recent important works added to the literature on Rachmaninoff which offer valuable general information are: Zarui Apetîan's monumental work *S. Rakhmaninov: literaturnoe nasledie* [S. Rachmaninoff: literary heritage] (1978–80), a three-volume collection of letters, reminiscences, articles, interviews, etc.; Robert Threlfall and Geoffrey Norris' *Catalogue of the Compositions of S. Rachmaninoff* (1982), which provides copious details on the works of Rachmaninoff; and Sergei Bertensson and Jay Leyda's *Sergei Rachmaninoff: A Lifetime in Music* (1956), with data supplied by Sofîa Satina. This last-mentioned volume still remains the definitive biographical study of Rachmaninoff.

Introduction xv

There are many fine specialized works on the composer, too many to enumerate here, but a few that are of special interest are: the five monographs presented in *Tempo* 22 (Winter 1951–52); the four articles in *Sovetskaia muzyka*, sbornik chetvertyĭ, (April 1945); the studies contained in Tamara E. Tsytovich's *S.V. Rakhmaninov*, sbornik stateĭ i materĭalov (1947), and in Igor F. Belza's *S.V. Rakhmaninov i russkaia opera* (1947); the five articles in the Rachmaninoff centenary anniversary issue of *Muzykal'naia zhizn'* No. 6 (March 1973). The numerous articles on Rachmaninoff appearing in *Sovetskaia muzyka* are historically informative, whereas those appearing in *Muzykal'naia zhizn'* are less scholarly and formal. The important Soviet journal *Sovetskaia muzyka*, established in 1933 and published monthly, is the organ of the Soiuz Sovetskikh Kompozitorov SSSR [USSR Union of Composers] and the Ministerstvo Kul'tury SSSR [USSR Ministry of Culture]. *Muzykal'naia zhizn'* was established in 1957 and is published bi-monthly. The numerous Rachmaninoff interviews in the American magazine *Etude* are also enlightening.

The two major Rachmaninoff archives containing diverse materials on the composer are the Gosudarstvennyĭ Tsentral'nyĭ Muzeĭ Muzykal'noĭ Kul'tury Imeni M.I. Glinki [State Central Glinka Museum of Musical Culture] located in Moscow, and the Library of Congress in Washington, D.C. The Soviet Rachmaninoff Archive holdings are cataloged in M.G. Rytsareva's (ed.) *Avtografy S.V. Rakhmaninova* (1980). The Library of Congress Rachmaninoff Archive holdings are not cataloged; instead, major categories of material contained therein are listed in *Music and Books on Music* (Subject Cataloging Division Processing Department Class M) Library of Congress (1978); the Archive's Rachmaninoff autographs are listed in Edward Waters' article "Music" in the *United States Library of Congress Quarterly Journal of Current Acquisitions* 9 (November 1951); and a partial inventory of letters contained in the Archive is listed in *National Union Catalog of Manuscript Collections* (Catalog 1973–74) Library of Congress (1975).

Soviet Rachmaninoff scholar Zarui Apetian spent some time in the Music Division of the Library of Congress compiling material from the Rachmaninoff Archive for incorporation in her major corpus, *S.V. Rakhmaninov: literaturnoe nasledie*, 3 vols.

(1978–80). There have been several historical works on Rachmaninoff that contain elements and sources derived from both the Soviet and American archives, but the inclusion of materials such as letters and articles from the Library of Congress in Apetîan's book is an initial attempt to at least partially consolidate items from the two major Rachmaninoff archives.

The literature on Rachmaninoff is richly endowed with reminiscences. The Alfred and Katherine Swan "Rachmaninoff Personal Reminiscences," in the *Musical Quarterly* 30 (January and April 1944) is vividly related; the two works of Zarui Apetîan that contain reminiscences written by Rachmaninoff's close friends and colleagues are *S. Rakhmaninov: literaturnoe nasledie*, Vol. 1 (1978), and *Vospominaniîa o Rakhmaninove* (1974). Rachmaninoff's wife Natalîa Aleksandrovna Rakhmaninova offers an intimate narrative of her husband's life and career in *New Review (Novyĭ zhurnal)* Nos. 100 and 103 (1970), titled "S.V. Rakhmaninov." These are but a few of the many interesting and colorful reminiscences about Rachmaninoff. When searching for a specific aspect of the composer contained in recollections, it is suggested that the reader explore more than one reminiscence or another source, for information contained therein is liable to be biased from the writer's viewpoint and emotionally colored.

The state of research on Rachmaninoff is now at the point where investigative focus is on particular aspects of the composer's life and work. The long-range overview of Rachmaninoff, which was a common subject shortly after his death, is no longer essential. This present bibliography reflects these two investigative practices: the examination of a specific subject and the presentation of a broad overview. The mix is slowly and steadily reaching a balance.

Rachmaninoff as a person and creative artist is gradually becoming more understood; his talent and genius are recognized and are no longer compromised because of comparison with his more innovative contemporaries. The label of traditionalist is no longer used with demeaning implications as it was in the past. Rachmaninoff's diverse musical talents as composer, pianist, and conductor demonstrate superior qualities. His skill and craftsmanship as a composer are undeniable; as a pianist he remains one of the finest ever known; and, unfortunately, Russia lost its most promising conductor when Rachmaninoff left his homeland in 1917. Rachmaninoff is indeed a fascinating, intriguing, colorful, though enigmatic, musician to investigate.

Sergei Vasil'evich Rachmaninoff

I

RACHMANINOFF'S COMPOSITIONS

Rachmaninoff's Publishers

Karl Aleksandrovich Gutkheil' [Gutheil] approached Rachmaninoff about publishing his first opera *Aleko*. The young composer was delighted and astonished at the offer and readily accepted Gutheil's proposal to publish the new opera. *Aleko* was published by the Gutheil publishing house in 1892. This marked the beginning of a long association, for Rachmaninoff remained with Gutheil until he left Russia in 1917. The Gutheil firm was eventually acquired by Sergeĭ Aleksandrovich Kusevitskiĭ [Koussevitzky] (purportedly for 300,000 rubles) in 1914 (Gutheil/Koussevitzky). Since Russia was not a signator to the Universal Copyright Convention until 27 May 1973, the Gutheil publishing firm worked in conjunction with Breitkopf und Härtel, in order to take advantage of their international copyright protection. In this way, Russian works were published under both names (Gutheil/Breitkopf) and protected by copyright laws. Edition Russe de Musique was established in 1909 by Koussevitzky, as a firm to publish works of young Russian composers.

Rachmaninoff's works written after he settled in the USA were published by Carl Fischer, TAIR (Paris), and Charles Foley. Rachmaninoff founded TAIR (the logos was derived from the names of his daughters, TAtiana and IRina) in 1925; TAIR was to be used primarily to publish Russian works that warranted distribution. He used TAIR in publishing his later works.

Current editions acquiring material from the above publishers are: Belwin-Mills, International, Boosey & Hawkes, and the Soviet editions Muzgiz (derived from MUZykal'noye Gosudarstvennoye IZdatel'stvo [State Music Publication]), Muzyka, and Mezhdunarodnīa Kniga (Mez Kniga) [International Book], their export edition. "Sovetskiĭ Kompozitor" [Soviet Composer], a publishing division that did not publish Rachmaninoff's music, but appears often in the bibliography, was initiated in 1956 and was dedicated to publishing contemporary works of Soviet composers and authors. In 1964, the divisions Muzgiz and "Sovetskiĭ Kompozitor" merged to create one encompassing music publishing house called Muzyka. In the USSR, all music publication by any name is controlled by the mighty Muzykal'noye Gosudarstvennoye Izdatel'stvo.

Symbols

Date- date of completion

Ded- name of dedicatee

Perf- date of first performance; performers; location

Pub- first publisher; other publishers; most recent publishers

---

Works for Piano and Orchestra

Kontsert [*Concerto*]

> *Allegro molto, C Minor (unfinished two piano score of first movement)*

    Date- November 1889

Concert pour le piano avec accompagnement d'orchestre [*Concerto for Piano and Orchestra*] *No.1 in F-sharp Minor Op.1*

Date- original version 6 July 1891, revised edition 10 November 1917

Ded- Aleksandr Il'ich Ziloti

Perf- first movement only 17 March 1892 Rachmaninoff-Safonov, Moscow Conservatory; revised version 29 January 1919 Rachmaninoff-Altschuler, Russian Symphony Orchestra in New York

Pub- Gutheil/Breitkopf (1892,1919), Schirmer (1943), Boosey & Hawkes (1947), Leeds, International, Kalmus, Foley, Muzyka (1971), Belwin-Mills

 1. *Vivace, F-sharp Minor*
 2. *Andante, D Major*
 3. *Allegro vivace, F-sharp Minor*

2-me Concert pour le piano avec accompagnement d'orchestre [Second Concerto for Piano and Orchestra] *in C Minor Op.18*

Date- 21 April 1901

Ded- Nikolaĭ Dahl

Perf- second and third movements (which were written first) 2 December 1900 Rachmaninoff-Ziloti, Moscow Conservatory; complete concerto 27 October 1901 Rachmaninoff-Ziloti Moscow Philharmonic Society Orchestra

Pub- Gutheil/Breitkopf (1901), Macmillan (1938), Schirmer (c.1939), Broude Brothers (1944), Kalmus (1946), C. Fischer (1946), Boosey & Hawkes (1947), Leeds, International (1954), Belwin-Mills, Mez Kniga

 1. *Moderato, C Minor*
 2. *Adagio sostenuto, E Major*
 3. *Allegro scherzando, C Minor*

3-me Concert pour le piano avec orchestre [Third Concerto for Piano and Orchestra] in D Minor Op.30

    <u>Date</u>- 23 September 1909

    <u>Ded</u>- Josef Hofmann

    <u>Perf</u>- 28 November 1909 Rachmaninoff-Damrosch, New York Symphony Orchestra

    <u>Pub</u>- Gutheil/Breitkopf (1910), Schirmer (c.1939), Leeds, Kalmus, International (1941), C. Fischer/Foley (1946), Boosey & Hawkes (1947), Belwin-Mills, Mez Kniga

        1. *Allegro ma non tanto,* D Minor
        2. *Intermezzo, Adagio,* A Major, D-flat Major
        3. *Finale. Alla breve,* D Minor

4-me Concert pour le piano et orchestre [Fourth Concerto for Piano and Orchestra] in G Minor Op.40

    <u>Date</u>- original version 25 August 1926; final version 1941

    <u>Ded</u>- Nikolaĭ Karlovich Medtner

    <u>Perf</u>- 18 March 1927 Rachmaninoff-Stokowski, Philadelphia Orchestra, Philadelphia

    <u>Pub</u>- TAIR (1928), Foley (1944), Belwin-Mills (1934), Eulenberg, Schott, Muzgiz (1954)

        1. *Allegro vivace,* G Minor
        2. *Largo,* C Major
        3. *Allegro vivace,* G Minor

Rapsodie sur un thème de Paganini pour piano et orchestre [Rhapsody on a Theme of Paganini for Piano and Orchestra] Op.43

Rachmaninoff's Compositions

    Date- 18 August 1934

    Ded- none

    Perf- 7 November 1934 Rachmaninoff-Stokowski Philadelphia Orchestra, Baltimore, Md.

    Pub- TAIR (1934), C. Fischer/Foley (1934) Eulenberg, Schott, Muzgiz (1957), Belwin-Mills

---

Works for Piano

Chetyre p'esy [*Four Pieces*]

    Date- c.1887

    Pub - Muzgiz (1948)

        1. *Romans, F-sharp Minor*
        2. *Preliud, E-flat Minor*
        3. *Melodiia, E Major*
        4. *Gavot, D Major*

Tri nokturna [*Three Nocturnes*]

    Date- 1887-88

    Pub- Muzgiz (1949), Belwin-Mills/Marks (1973)

        1. *Andante cantabile, F-sharp Minor*
        2. *Andante maestoso-Allegro assai, F Major*
        3. *Andante, C Minor*

[*Fugetta (Fughetta)*], *F Major (untitled)*

    Date- 4 February 1899

    Pub- unpublished

[*P'esa (Piece)*] (*canonic style, originally untitled*), D Minor

    Date- c.1890

    Pub- Muzgiz (1949), Leeds (1951; in *Two Fantasy Pieces*)

Prelíudiía [*Prelude*]

    Date- 1891

    Pub- Muzgiz (1949)

        Commodo, F Major

Morceaux de fantaisie Op. 3

    Date- 1892

    Ded- Anton Stepanovich Arenskiĭ

    Perf- complete 28 December 1892 Rachmaninoff, Kharkov

    Pub- Gutheil/Breitkopf (1893), Ditson (1910; nos.3 [original],4), Macmillan (1938; nos.2,3,4,5), Foley (1910; no.3 [revised]), Hamelle, Muzgiz, Mez Kniga (nos.1,3,5), Boosey & Hawkes, Bosworth, Belwin-Mills

        1. *Elégie, E-flat Minor*
        2. *Prélude, C-sharp Minor*
        3. *Mélodie, E Major* (revised in 1940)
        4. *Polichinelle, F-sharp Minor*
        5. *Sérénade, B-flat Minor* (revised in 1940

Russkaía rapsodiía (*Rapsodie russe pour deux pianos*) [*Russian Rhapsody* (*Russian Rhapsody for Two Pianos*)]

Date- 1891

Perf- 17 October 1891 Rachmaninoff and Josef Lhévinne, Moscow

Pub- Muzgiz (1951), Leeds (1955)

    1. *Moderato-Vivace-Meno mosso, E Minor*
    2. *Andante-Con moto, G Major*

Val's [*Valse*] *and Romance*
(for one piano, six hands)

Date- 1890-91

Ded- Natalīa, Līudmila, and Vera Skalon

Pub- Muzgiz (1948), Leeds (1960)

    1. *Valse, A Major*
    2. *Romance, A Major*

Fantaziīa. Sīuita No.1 (Fantaisie pour deux pianos)
[*Fantasia. Suite No.1 (Fantasy for Two Pianos)*] Op.5

Date- 1893

Ded- Peter Ilich Tchaikovsky

Perf- 30 November 1893 Rachmaninoff and Pavel Avgustovich Pabst, Moscow

Pub- Gutheil/Breitkopf (c.1894), International (1943), Boosey & Hawkes (1947), Muzgiz

    1. *Barkarola (Barcarolle), G Minor*
    2. *"I noch', i līubov'" (La nuit, l'amour)* [*Oh Night, Oh Love*] *D Major*
    3. *Slezy (Les larmes)* [*Tears*], *G Minor*
    4. *Svetlyĭ prazdnik (Pâques)* [*Easter*], *G Minor*

Romans [*Romance*]
   (duet)

      Date- c.1894

      Pub- Muzgiz (1950)

Sem' p'es [*Seven Pieces*] *(Morceaux de salon) Op.10*

      Date- 1894

      Ded- Pavel Avgustovich Pabst

      Perf- 31 January 1894 Rachmaninoff, Moscow

      Pub- Gutheil/Breitkopf (1894), Bosworth (1896), Schott (1912), Ditson (1910; nos.1,2), Muz Sektor (1923), Macmillan (1938; nos.1,2,3,5), Hansen, Foley (1940), Muzgiz (1948), Kalmus (1965), Willis, Mez Kniga (nos.5,6), Belwin-Mills

         1. *Noktiurn* [*Nocturne*], *A Minor*
         2. *Val's* [*Valse*], *A Major*
         3. *Barkarola* [*Barcarolle*], *G Minor*
         4. *Melodiia* [*Mélodie*], *E Minor*
         5. *Iumoreska* [*Humoreske*], *G Major* (revised in 1940)
         6. *Romans* [*Romance*], *F Minor*
         7. *Mazurka, D-flat Major*

Shest' p'es (Six morceaux) Op.11
   (for one piano, four-hands)

      Date- 1894

      Pub- Gutheil/Breitkopf (1894), Macmillan (1938; nos.3,6), Boosey & Hawkes (1947), Muzgiz (1950), International (1951), Muzyka (1968)

         1. *Barkarolla (Barcarolle), G Minor*
         2. *Skertso (Scherzo), D Major*

3. Russkaiā pesniā (Thème russe), B Minor
4. Val's (Valse), A Major
5. Romans (Romance), C Minor
6. Slava, C Major

Shest' muzykal'nykh momentov (Six moments musicaux)
Op. 16

Date- 1896

Ded- Aleksandr Viktorovich Zataevich

Pub- Jurgenson (1896), A.J. Benjamin (1925), Macmillan (1938; no.3), Foley (1940), International (1942,1950), Muzgiz (1948), Schauer, Simrock, Muzyka (1967), Mez Kniga, Belwin-Mills

1. Andantino, B-flat Minor
2. Allegretto, E-flat Minor (revised in 1940)
3. Andante cantabile, B Minor
4. Presto, E Minor
5. Adagio sostenuto, D-flat Major
6. Maestoso, C Major

Chetyre improvizatsiĭ [Four Improvisations]
(collaborative work by Arenskiĭ, Glazunov, Rachmaninoff, and Taneev)

Date- 1896

Pub- Muz Sektor (1925), Muzgiz (1950)

Fantasticheskaiā p'esa (Morceau de fantaisie) in G Minor

Date- 1899

Pub- Muzgiz (1949), Leeds (1951)

Vtoraĩa sĩuita (2-me Suite pour deux pianos)
[*Suite No.2 for Two Pianos*] Op.17

> Date- 1901
>
> Ded- Aleksandr Borisovich Gol'denveizer
>
> Perf- 24 November 1901 Rachmaninoff and Ziloti, Moscow
>
> Pub- Gutheil/Breitkopf (1901,1910), Macmillan (1938; nos.2,3), International (1941), Boosey & Hawkes, Muzgiz (1951)
>
>> 1. *Vstuplenie (Introduction)*
>> 2. *Val's (Valse)*
>> 3. *Romans (Romance)*
>> 4. *Tarantella*

Variãtsiĩ na temu Shopena (Variations sur un thème de F. Chopin) [*Variations on a Theme of Chopin*] Op.22

> Date- 1903
>
> Ded- Theodor Leschetizky
>
> Perf- 10 February 1903 Rachmaninoff, Moscow
>
> Pub- Gutheil/Breitkopf (1904), Macmillan (1938), Boosey & Hawkes, Muzgiz, International (1945,1960)

Desĩat' preliũdiĩ (10 Préludes pour piano)
[*Ten Preludes for Piano*] Op.23

> Date- 1903
>
> Ded- Aleksandr Il'ich Ziloti
>
> Perf- 10 February 1903 Rachmaninoff, Moscow
>
> Pub- Gutheil/Breitkopf (1903), Macmillan (1938; nos.4,5), Marks (1940), Schirmer (1942), Boosey & Hawkes (1947),

Muzgiz (1948), Kalmus, International
(1954), Peters (in preparation)

1. *Largo, F-sharp Minor*
2. *Maestoso, B-flat Major*
3. *Tempo di minuetto, D Minor*
4. *Andante cantabile, D Major*
5. *Alla marcia, G Minor* (written in 1901)
6. *Andante, E-flat Major*
7. *Allegro, C Minor*
8. *Allegro vivace, A-flat Major*
9. *Presto, E-flat Minor*
10. *Largo, G-flat Major*

Polka italienne [Italian Polka]
    (duet)

   Date- c.1906

   Ded- Sergeĭ Ziloti

   Pub- Jurgenson (c.1906), C. Fischer/Foley (1938), Muzgiz (1950), Belwin-Mills

Sonate für Pianoforte [*Sonata for Piano*] *No.1 in D Minor* Op.28

   Date- 14 May 1907

   Perf- 17 October 1908 Konstantin Nikolaevich Igumnov, Moscow

   Pub- Gutheil/Breitkopf (1908), Boosey & Hawkes, Kalmus, Muzgiz (1948), International (1944)

   1. *Allegro moderato, D Minor*
   2. *Lento, F Major*
   3. *Allegro molto, D Minor*

Trinadtsat' preliūdiĭ (13 Préludes pour piano)
[*Thirteen Preludes for Piano*] Op.32

Date- 1910

Perf- 5 December 1911 Rachmaninoff, St. Petersburg

Pub- Gutheil/Breitkopf (1911), Marks (1941), Schirmer (1942), Boosey & Hawkes, Kalmus, Muzgiz (1948), International (1954), Belwin-Mills, Peters (in preparation

1. *Allegro vivace, C Major* (30 August 1910)
2. *Allegretto, B-flat Minor* (2 September 1910)
3. *Allegro vivace, E Major* (3 September 1910)
4. *Allegro con brio, E Minor* (28 August 1910)
5. *Moderato, G Major* (25 August 1910)
6. *Allegro appassionato, F Minor* (25 August 1910)
7. *Moderato, F Major* (25 August 1910)
8. *Vivo, A Minor* (24 August 1910)
9. *Allegro moderato, A Major* (26 August 1910)
10. *Lento, B Minor* (6 September 1910)
11. *Allegretto, B Major* (23 August 1910)
12. *Allegro, G-sharp Minor* (23 August 1910)
13. *Grave, D-flat Major* (10 September 1910)

Polka de W.R.
(a transcription of a Scherzpolka by Franz Behr)

Date- 1911

Ded- Leopold Godowsky

Perf- 23 November 1913 Rachmaninoff, St. Petersburg

Pub- Edition Russe de Musique (1911), Boston Music (1919), Boosey & Hawkes (1947), Muzgiz (1950)

Rachmaninoff's Compositions

Etiudy-kartiny (Etudes-tableaux) Op.33

    Date- 1911

    Perf- c.November 1911 Rachmaninoff, UK

    Pub- Gutheil/Breitkopf (1912), International (1941), Muzgiz (1948), Leeds 1950), Music Corp. of America, Boosey & Hawkes (1969), Muzyka (1969), Kalmus (1965), Belwin-Mills

1. *Allegro non troppo, F Minor* (11 August 1911)
2. *Allegro, C Major* (16 August 1911)
3. *Non-allegro-Presto, E-flat Minor* (23 August 1911)
4. *Allegro con fuoco, E-flat Major* (17 August 1911)
5. *Moderato, G Minor* (15 August 1911)
6. *Grave, C-sharp Minor* (13 August 1911)

(There were originally three other études in this collection; one was emended and placed in Op.39 [no.6], and the other two [C Minor and D Minor] were published posthumously)

Deuxième Sonate pour piano [*Second Sonata for Piano*] *in B-flat Minor Op.36*

    Date- original version 1913, revised edition 1931

    Ded- Matveĭ Leont'evich Presman

    Perf- 3 December 1913 Rachmaninoff, Moscow

    Pub- Gutheil/Breitkopf (1914; original version), Gutheil/Koussevitzky (1931; revised edition), Muzgiz (1950; both versions), Boosey & Hawkes (revised version), International (1944; revised version)

16   *Rachmaninoff's Compositions*

                1. *Allegro agitato, B-flat Minor*
                2. *Non allegro-Lento, E Minor*
                3. *Allegro molto, B-flat Major*

Deviat' Etiudov-kartin (Neuf Etudes-tableaux)
Nine Etudes-tableaux Op.39

        Date- 1916-17

        Perf- 21 February 1917 Rachmaninoff, Petrograd

        Pub- Editions Russe de Musique (1917), Muzgiz (1948), International (1948), Boosey & Hawkes, Leeds (1950), Music Corp. of America, Kalmus (1969)

                1. *Allegro agitato, C Minor* (5 October 1916)
                2. *Lento assai, A Minor*
                3. *Allegro molto, F-sharp Minor* (14 October 1916)
                4. *Allegro assai, B Minor* (24 September 1916)
                5. *Appassionato, E-flat Minor* (17 February 1917)
                6. *Allegro, A Minor* (8 September 1917)
                7. *Lento lugubre, C Minor*
                8. *Allegro moderato, D Minor*
                9. *Allegro moderato, Tempo di marcia, D Major* (2 February 1917)

[*Prelude in D Minor*]
    (posthumous; originally untitled)

        Date- 1917

        Pub- Belwin-Mills (1973)

[*Oriental Sketch*]
    (originally untitled)

Rachmaninoff's Compositions 17

    Date- 1917

    Pub- Muzgiz, C. Fischer/Foley (1938), Belwin-Mills (1973)

[*Fragments*]
    (originally untitled)

    Date- 1917

    Pub- T. Presser (1919), Belwin-Mills (1973)

Variations on a Theme of Corelli Op.42

    Date- 1931

    Ded- Fritz Kreisler

    Perf- 12 October 1931 Rachmaninoff, Montreal

    Pub- TAIR (1931), C. Fischer/Foley (1931), Belwin-Mills (1931), Muzgiz (1948)

Transcriptions and Arrangements for Piano by Rachmaninoff

Bach, Johann Sebastian

    Suite in E Major (the *Prelude, Gavotte,* and *Gigue* from the *Violin Partita in E Major* [BWV 1006] transcribed for piano solo)

    Date- 1933

    Perf- 9 November 1933 Rachmaninoff, Harrisburg, Pa.

    Pub- C. Fischer (1933), Foley (1941), Belwin-Mills (1943), Muzgiz (1950)

Bizet, Georges

> *Minuet from L'Arlesienne suite No.1* (orchestral work transcribed for piano solo), [two versions in the P. Lamm edition (Muzgiz)]
>
>> Date- 13 September 1900
>>
>> Perf- 19 January 1922 Rachmaninoff, Tulsa, Okla.
>>
>> Pub- C. Fischer/Foley (1923), J.B. Cramer, Muzgiz (1950), Belwin-Mills

Glazunov, Aleksandr Konstantinovich

> *Symphony No.6 in D Minor Op.58* (arranged for piano duet)
>
>> Date- 1896
>>
>> Pub- Belaiev (1898)

Kreisler, Fritz

> *Liebesleid* (violin composition transcribed for piano solo)
>
>> Date- c.1921
>>
>> Perf- 20 November 1921 Rachmaninoff, Chicago, Ill.
>>
>> Pub- C. Fischer/Foley (1923), Schott, Muzgiz (1950), Belwin-Mills (1973)

> *Liebesfreud* (violin composition transcribed for piano solo)
>
>> Date- 1925
>>
>> Perf- 29 October 1925 Rachmaninoff, Stamford, Conn.

Pub- C. Fischer/Foley (1926), Schott, Muzgiz (1950), Belwin-Mills (1973)

Liszt, Franz

Cadenza to the Hungarian Rhapsody No.2

Date- c.1919

Perf- 10 January 1919 Rachmaninoff, Boston, Mass.

Pub- Mercury (c.1945; no manuscript exists, cadenza was reconstructed from the Edison recording [no.82169-70] made in 1919)

Mendelssohn, Felix

Scherzo from a Midsummer Night's Dream (orchestral work transcribed for piano solo)

Date- 1933

Perf- 23 January 1933 Rachmaninoff, San Antonio, Tex.

Pub- C. Fischer/Foley (1933), Muzgiz (1950), Belwin-Mills (1973)

Mussorgsky, Modest Petrovich

Gopak [*Hopak*](from *Sorochinskaĩa ĩarmarka* [Sorochintzi Fair])

Date- 1924

Perf- 13 November 1923 Rachmaninoff, Scranton, Penn.

Pub- C. Fischer/Foley (1924), Muzgiz (1950), Belwin-Mills (1973)

_____ (arranged for violin and piano)

    Date- 11 May 1925

    Pub- C. Fischer (1926)

Rachmaninoff, Sergei Vasil'evich

   Caprice bohémien Op.12 (orchestral work arranged for piano duet)

    Date- c.1892

    Pub- Gutheil/Breitkopf (c.1895)

   Utes [*The Rock*] Op.7 (Fantasy for orchestra arranged for piano duet)

    Date- 1894

    Pub- Jurgenson (1894), Gos. Izd-vo (1928)

   Symphony No.1 in D Minor Op.13 (symphony arranged for piano duet)

    Date- c.1895

    Pub- Muzgiz (1950)

   Siren' [*Lilacs*] Op.21, No.5 (song arranged for piano solo)

    Date- c.1913

    Perf- 23 November 1913 Rachmaninoff, St. Petersburg

    Pub- Gutheil/Breitkopf (c.1919), Macmillan (1938), Foley (1941)

   Margaritki [*Daisies*] Op.38, No.3 (song arranged for piano solo)

Date- ?

Perf- 5 March 1922 Rachmaninoff, Montreal

Pub- TAIR/Foley (1940), Muzgiz (1950)

Prelude in C-sharp Minor Op.3, No.2 (arranged for two pianos)

Date- ?

Pub- C. Fischer/Foley (1938)

Symphonic Dances Op.45 (arranged for two pianos)

Date- 1942

Pub- Foley (1942), Muzgiz (1951)

Noch' pechal'na [*Night is Mournful*] Op.26, No.12 (song arranged for voice, piano and cello)

Date- ?

Pub- unpublished

Rimsky-Korsakov, Nikolaĭ Andreevich

The Bumble Bee (from *Tsar Saltan* transcribed for piano solo)

Date- c.1929

Perf- 13 March 1937 Rachmaninoff, London

Schubert, Franz

Wohin? [*The Brooklet*] (song from *Die schöne Müllerin* transcribed for piano solo)

Date- 1925

Perf- 29 October 1925 Rachmaninoff, Stamford, Conn.

Pub- C. Fischer/Foley (1929), Muzgiz (1950) Belwin-Mills (1973)

Smith, John S.

The Star Spangled Banner (transcribed for piano solo)

Date- c.1918

Perf- 15 December 1918 Rachmaninoff, Boston, Mass.

Pub- (no manuscript exists; recorded on Ampico piano roll [no.57282] in 1919)

Tchaikovsky, Peter Ilich

Spi͡ashchai͡a krasavit͡sa [*The Sleeping Beauty*] (suite from the ballet arranged for piano duet)

Date- 1891

Pub- Jurgenson (1892)

Manfred Symphony (arranged for piano duet)

Date- 1886

Pub- (no manuscript exists; Rachmaninoff and Matveĭ Leont'evich Presman performed this arrangement for Tchaikovsky in c.December 1886)

Kolybel'nai͡a pesni͡a [*Lullaby*] (song Op.16, No.1 transcribed for piano solo)

Date- 1941

Perf- 14 October 1941 Rachmaninoff, Syracuse, N.Y.

Pub- Foley (1941), Belwin-Mills (1943), Muzgiz (1950)

Works for Orchestra

Skertso [*Scherzo*]

    Date- 21 February 1887

    Perf- 2 November 1945 N. Anosov, Moscow

    Pub- Muzgiz (1947)

        1. *Allegro, D Minor*

Simfoniia d-moll, 1-ia chast' (*Symphonie d-moll 1-re partie*) [*Symphony in D Minor, first movement*] (no relation to Op.13)

    Date- 28 September 1891

    Pub- Muzgiz (1947), Mez Kniga

        1. *Grave-Allegro molto, D Minor*

Kniaz' Rostislav [*Prince Rostislav*] (symphonic poem based on Aleksei Konstantinovich Tolstoi's ballad)

    Date- 15 December 1891

    Ded- Anton Stepanovich Arenskii

    Perf- 2 November 1945 N. Anosov, Moscow

    Pub- Muzgiz (1947), Mez Kniga

Utes. Fantaziia dlia simfonicheskogo orkestra [The Rock. Fantasy for Symphony Orchestra] Op.7

    Date- 1893

    Ded- Nikolaĭ Andreevich Rimsky-Korsakov

    Perf- 20 March 1894 Vasily Il'ich Safonov, Russian Music Society, Moscow

    Pub- Jurgenson (1895), Muzgiz (1955), Foley/Belwin-Mills, C.F. Peters, Kalmus, Forberg, Mez Kniga

Kaprichchio na tsyganskie temy dlia orkestra [Capriccio on Gypsy Themes for Orchestra] *(Capriccio bohémien)* Op.12

    Date- September 1894

    Ded- Pyotr Viktorovich Lodyzhenskiĭ

    Perf- 22 November 1895 Rachmaninoff, Moscow

    Pub- Gutheil/Breitkopf (1894), Boosey & Hawkes, Kalmus, Muzyka (1966)

Simfoniia No.1 [Symphony No.1] in D Minor Op.13

    Date- August 1895

    Ded- A.L. (Anna Aleksandrovna Lodyzhenskaia)

    Perf- 15 March 1897 Glazunov, Russian Symphony Concert, St Petersburg

    Pub- Breitkopf, Muzgiz (1947), Boosey & Hawkes, Mez Kniga

  (manuscript of the full score has not been found; score was reconstructed from the four-hand piano version and from orchestral parts found in the Leningrad Conservatory in 1946)

1. Grave-Allegro ma non troppo,
   D Minor
2. Allegro animato, F Major
3. Larghetto, B-flat Major
4. Allegro con fuoco, D Major

Vesna. Kantata dli͡a baritona, khora i orkestra
[Spring. Cantata for baritone, chorus and orchestra]
Op.20; listed under Choral Works

Simfonii͡a No.2 [Symphony No.2] in E Minor Op.27

    <u>Date</u>- April 1907

    <u>Ded</u>- Sergei Ivanovich Taneev

    <u>Perf</u>- 26 January 1908, Rachmaninoff, St. Petersburg

    <u>Pub</u>- Gutheil/Breitkopf (1908), Kalmus (1950), Muzyka (1960), Boosey & Hawkes (1967), Foley/Belwin-Mills

1. Largo-Allegro moderato, E Minor
2. Allegro molto, A Minor
3. Adagio, A Major
4. Allegro vivace, E Major

Ostrov mertvykh (Die Toteninsel) [The Isle of the Dead] Op.29
   (symphonic poem based on Swiss artist Arnold
   Böcklin's work of the same name [Die Todteninsel])

    <u>Date</u>- 17 April 1909

    <u>Ded</u>- Nikolaĭ Georgievich Struve (Nicolas von Struve)

    <u>Perf</u>- 18 April 1909 Rachmaninoff, Philharminic Society Moscow

    <u>Pub</u>- Gutheil/Breitkopf (1909), Boosey & Hawkes (1947), International (1943), Muzyka (1973), Foley, Kalmus/Belwin-Mills

Kolokola [*The Bells*] Op.35
   (choral symphony for orchestra, chorus, and solo
   soprano, tenor, and baritone; based on Edgar
   Allan Poe's poem)

   Date- 27 July 1913; partial revision in 1936

   Ded- Josef Willem Mengelberg and the Concert-
        gebouw Orchestra of Amsterdam

   Perf- 30 November 1913 Rachmaninoff, St.
         Petersburg

   Pub- Gutheil/Breitkopf (1920), Muzyka (1967),
        Boosey & Hawkes (1979), Mez Kniga

        1. *Allegro ma non tanto, A-flat Major*
        2. *Lento, D Major*
        3. *Presto, F Minor*
        4. *Lento lugubre, C-sharp Minor*

Vokaliz [*Vocalise*] Op.34, No.14
   (the song arranged for orchestra by Rachmaninoff)

   Date- c.1919

   Perf- April 1920 Damrosch, New York Music
         Festival

   Pub- Gutheil/Breitkopf (1919), Boosey &
        Hawkes (1960), Foley/Belwin-mills

Vokaliz [*Vocalise*] Op.34, No.14
   (the song arranged for soprano and orchestra)

   Pub- Edition Russe de Musique/Chester (1916)

Tri russkie pesni (Trois chansons russe) [*Three
Russian Songs*] Op.41
   (for chorus and orchestra) listed under Choral
   Works

Rachmaninoff's Compositions

Symphony No.3 in A Minor Op.44

    Date- 30 June 1936

    Perf- 6 November 1936 Stokowski, Philadelphia Orchestra, Philadelphia

    Pub- TAIR/Foley (1937; revised score edition 1939), Muzgiz (1954), Muzyka (1960, 1975), Belwin-Mills (1973)

        1. *Lento-Allegro moderato, A Minor*
        2. *Adagio ma non troppo-Allegro vivace-Tempo come prima, C-sharp Minor*
        3. *Allegro, A Major*

Symphonic Dances Op.45

    Date- 29 October 1940

    Ded- Eugene Ormandy and The Philadelphia Orchestra, Philadelphia

    Pub- TAIR/Foley (1941), Belwin-Mills (1941), Muzgiz (1953)

        1. *Non allegro-Lento-Tempo I, C Minor*
        2. *Andante con moto (Tempo di valse), G Minor*
        3. *Lento assai-Allegro vivace, D Minor*

The following orchestral works are mentioned in Rachmaninoff's letters but no manuscripts exist:

Manfred
    (for orchestra)

        Date- c.1890 (unfinished; no manuscript)

Two episodes à la Liszt
    (for orchestra)

        Date- summer 1894 (unfinished; no manuscript)

Neosushchestvlennaĩa simfoniĩa [an unrealized symphony]
    (sketches only)

      Date- 5 April 1897

Chamber Music

Dve chasti iz kvarteta dlĩa dvukh skripok, al'ta i violoncheli [Two movements from Quartet for two violins, viola and violoncello] String Quartet No.1
    (an unfinished work; only two movements exist)

      Date- c.1889

      Perf- October 1945 Beethoven Quartet, Moscow

      Pub- Muzgiz (1947)

          2. *Romance, G Minor*
          3. *Scherzo, D Major*

Romance in A Minor
    (for violin and piano)

      Date- c.1880

      Pub- Leeds (1951)

Pesnĩa (Lied) [*Romance*] *in F Minor*
    (for cello and piano)

      Date- August 1890

      Ded- Vera Dmitrievna Skalon

      Pub- Muzgiz (1948)

Melody on a theme by S. Rachmaninoff
    (for cello or violin and piano)

Rachmaninoff's Compositions

    Date- c.1890

    Pub- Composers Press (1947; edited by Modest Isaakovich Altschuler who states he copied the manuscript before it became lost in the 1920s)

Elegicheskoe trio (Trio élégiaque)
    (for violin, cello, and piano)

    Date- 21 January 1892

    Perf- 30 January 1892 Rachmaninoff, David Krein, and Anatoli Andreevich Brandukov, Moscow

    Pub- Muzgiz (1947), Boosey & Hawkes

Preliūdiia i vostochnyĭ tanet͡s (dli͡a violoncheli s akkompanenmentom fortepi͡ano) [*Prélude et Danse oriental (for violoncello with piano accompaniment)*] Op.2

    Date- 1892

    Ded- Anatoli Andreevich Brandukov

    Perf- 30 January 1892 Rachmaninoff and Brandukov, Moscow

    Pub- Gutheil/Koussevitzky (c.1892), Muz Sektor (1930), Boosey & Hawkes (1947)

        1. *Prélude,* F Major
        2. *Danse orientale,* A Minor

Dve p'esy [*Two Pieces*] Op.6
    (for violin and piano)

    Date- summer 1893

    Ded- I͡uliĭ Eduardovich Koni͡us [Julius Conus]

Rachmaninoff's Compositions

    Pub- Gutheil/Breitkopf (c.1894), Augener (1902), Muz Sektor (1924), Kalmus/Belwin-Mills

        1. *Romans* [*Romance*], *D Minor*
        2. *Tanets vengerskii* [*Danse hongroise*] *D Minor*

Elegicheskoe trio (Trio élégiaque pour piano, violin et violoncelle) in D Minor Op.9

    Date- 15 December 1893

    Ded- Peter Ilich Tchaikovsky

    Perf- 31 January 1894 Rachmaninoff, Conus, and Brandukov, Moscow

    Pub- Gutheil (1894), Gutheil/Breitkopf (1907; revised edition), Muzgiz (1950; further revised edition), International (1943; revised edition), Mez Kniga

        1. *Moderato-Allegro vivace, D Minor*
        2. *Quasi variazione, F Major*
        3. *Allegro risoluto-Moderato, D Minor*

Kvartet dlia dvukh skripok, al'ta i violoncheli [*Quartet for two violins, viola and violoncello*] *String Quartet No.2* (unfinished work; two movements exist)

    Date- c.1896

    Perf- October 1945 Beethoven Quartet, Moscow

    Pub- Muzgiz (1947)

        1. *Allegro moderato, G Minor*
        2. *Andante molto sostenuto, C Minor*

Sonate pour piano et violoncelle [*Sonata for Piano and Violoncello*] *in G Minor Op.19*

Date- 12 December 1901

Ded- Anatoli Andreevich Brandukov

Perf- 2 December 1901 Rachmaninoff and Brandukov, Moscow

Pub- Gutheil/Breitkopf (1902), Boosey & Hawkes (1947), International (1943,1964), Gos. Muz. Izd-vo (1950)

1. *Lento-Allegro moderato, G Minor*
2. *Allegro scherzando, C Minor*
3. *Andante, E-flat Major*
4. *Allegro mosso, G Major*

Oh, Cease Thy Singing, Maiden Fair
(song *Op.4, No.4*; English text by John McCormack, violin obbligato by Fritz Kreisler; new edition by Rachmaninoff)

Pub- C. Fischer (1922)

When Night Descends in Silence
(song *Op.4, No.3*; English text by Edwin Schneider, violin obbligato by Fritz Kreisler; new edition by Rachmaninoff)

Pub- Foley/C. Fischer (1930)

Operas

Aleko
(opera in one act; libretto by Vladimir Ivanovich Nemirovich-Danchenko based on Aleksandr Sergeevich Pushkin's narrative poem *Tsygany* [Gypsies])

Date- 13 April 1892

Perf- (complete) 27 April 1893 Ippolit Altani, Bol'shoĭ Theater, Moscow

Pub- Gutheil (1892), Muzgiz (1948,1953),
       Mez Kniga

Skupoĭ ry͡tsar' [*The Miserly Knight*] *Op.24*
(opera in three scenes; libretto from Aleksandr
Sergeevich Pushkin's short play *Skupoĭ ry͡tsar'*;
title sometimes translated as *The Avaricious
Knight*)

    Date- June 1905

    Perf- 11 January 1906 Rachmaninoff, Bol'shoĭ
           Theater

    Pub- Gutheil/Breitkopf (1905), Muzyka (1968,
           1972)

Francheska da Rimini [*Francesca da Rimini*] *Op.25*
(opera in two scenes with prologue and epilogue;
libretto by Modest Il'ich Tchaikovsky based on
Dante's *La divina commedia* [*The Divine Comedy*]
inferno, canto V)

    Date- August 1905

    Perf- 11 January 1906 Rachmaninoff, Bol'shoĭ
           Theater, Moscow

    Pub- Gutheil/Breitkopf (1905), Muzyka (1974),
           Mez Kniga

Monna Vanna
(unfinished opera; libretto by Mikhail Akimovich
Slonov based on the play by Maurice Maeterlinck)

    Date- 15 August 1907 (vocal score of Act I)

    Perf- 11 August 1984 (vocal score of Act I)
           orchestrated and conducted by Igor
           Buketoff, Philadelphia Orchestra,
           Saratoga Springs, N.Y.

Esmeralda
(opera sketch, fragments only; based on Victor
Hugo's *Notre Dame de Paris*)

    Date- 17 October 1888

Works for Chorus

Deus meus
(motet for six-part unaccompanied mixed chorus)

Date- Spring 1890

Perf- 24 February 1891 Rachmaninoff, Moscow Conservatory Chorus

Pub- Muzyka (1972,1976)

V Molitvakh neusypaiushchuiu Bogoroditsu (O Mother of God Perpetually Praying) G Minor
(motet for four-part unaccompanied mixed chorus)

Date- summer 1893

Perf- 12 December 1893 Orlev, Synodical Choir, Moscow

Pub- Muzgiz (1972)

Khor dukhov [*Chorus of Spirits*]
(for four-part unaccompanied chorus; from Aleksei Konstantinovich Tolstoi's poem *Don Zhuan* [*Don Juan*])

Date- c.1894

Pub- Muzyka (1972,1976)

Shest' khorov [*Six Choruses*] Op.15
(for women or children's voices and piano)

Date- 1895-96

Pub- Jurgenson (1896), Boston Music (1913),

C. Fischer (1915; no.1 only), Galexy (1933; no.4 only), Marks (1946; no.3 only), Muzyka (1976)

1. *Slav'sīa͡ [Be Praised]* (text by Nikolaĭ Alekseevich Nekrasov), *G Major*
2. *Nochka [The Night]* (Vladimir Lodyzhenskiĭ), *F Major*
3. *Sosna [The Pine Tree]* (Mikhail I͡ur'evich Lermontov), *A Minor*
4. *Zadremali volny [The Waves Slumbered] [Dreaming Waves]* (Konstantin Konstantinovich Romanov), *D Major*
5. *Nevolīa͡ [Captivity][Slavery]* (Nikolaĭ Grigor'evich T͡syganov), *F Major*
6. *Angel [The Angel]* (Mikhail I͡ur'evich Lermontov), *E Major*

Panteleĭ-t͡selitel' [Panteley the Healer]
 (for four-part unaccompanied mixed chorus; based on Alekseĭ Konstantinovich Tolstoĭ's poem), *E Minor*

    Date- c.1901

    Perf- 1901 Synodical Choir, Moscow

    Pub- Gutheil (1901), Muzyka (1976)

Vesna. Kantata dli͡a baritona, khora i orkestra *[Spring.* Cantata for baritone, chorus and orchestra] *Op.20*
 (based on Nikolaĭ Alekseevich Nekrasov's poem *Zelyony shum*)

    Date- January-February 1902

    Ded- Nikita Semenovich Morozov

    Perf- 11 March 1902 Ziloti, Moscow Philharmonic Society

Pub-   Gutheil/Breitkopf (1902), Boosey &
       Hawkes, Schirmer (1910,1938). Muzyka
       (1964), Mez Kniga

Liturgiĩa Sviãtogo Ioanna Zlatousta [*Liturgy of
Saint John Chrysostom*] Op.31
    (for four-part unaccompanied mixed chorus)

   Date- 30 July 1910

   Perf- 25 November 1910 Nikolaĭ Danilin,
          Synodical Choir, Moscow

   Pub-   Gutheil (1910), Boosey & Hawkes (1911),
          Baley and Ferguson (1915), Muzyka
          (1976)

Kolokola [*The Bells*] Op.35
    (choral symphony for orchestra, chorus, and solo
    soprano, tenor and baritone) Listed under Works
    for Orchestra

Vsenoshchnoe bdenie [*All-Night Vigil (Vespers)*] Op.37
    (for four-part unaccompanied mixed chorus)

   Date- January-February 1915

   Ded-   memory of Stepan Vasil'evich Smolenskiĭ

   Perf- 10 March 1915 Nikolaĭ Danilin, Synodical
          Choir, Moscow

   Pub-   Rossiiskoe Muzykal'noe Izd-vo (1915),
          Gray Co. (1920), Boosey & Hawkes (1978),
          Belwin-Mills

Tri russkie pesnĭ (Trois chansons russe) [*Three Russian Songs*] Op.41
    (for orchestra and chorus)

Date- 1926

Ded- Leopold Stokowski

Perf- 18 March 1927 Stokowski, Philadelphia Chorus and Orchestra

Pub- TAIR (1928), Foley/Belwin-Mills, Muzyka (1959)

1. *Cherez rechku* [*Over the Little River*] E Minor
2. *Akh, ty, Van'ka* [*Oh, Vanka, You Bold Fellow*], D Minor
3. *Belilitsy, rumianitsy vy moĭ* [*Quickly, Quickly, From My Cheeks*], B Minor

(English translations by Kurt Schindler TAIR edition)

Songs (translations in brackets are the published titles of the English editions)

U vrat obiteli sviatoĭ [*At the Gate of Holy Abode*] (for low voice; text by Mikhail Iur'evich Lermontov), *G Minor*

Date- 29 April 1890

Ded- Mikhail Akimovich Slonov

Pub- Muzgiz (1947)

Ia tebe nichego ne skazhu [*I Shall Tell Nothing*] (for low voice; text by Afanasy Afanas'evich Shenshin [pseud. Afanasy Fet]), *C Major*

Date- 1 May 1890

Pub- Muzgiz (1947)

Opi͡at' vstrepenulos' ty serdt͡se [*Again You Leapt, My Heart*]
    (for high voice; text by Nikolaĭ Grekov), *G Minor*

    Date- c.1890

    Pub- Muzgiz (1947)

C'etait en avril
    (for high voice; text by Edouard Pailleron), *E-flat Major*

    Date- 1 April 1891

    Pub- Muzgiz (1947)

Smerkalos' [*Twilight Has Fallen (Dusk)*]
    (for high voice; text by Alekseĭ Konstantinovich Tolstoĭ)

    Date- 22 April 1891

    Pub- Muzgiz (1947)

Monologi [*Monologues*]

    Borisa [*Boris'*] (three versions written; for low voice; text based on Pushkin's *Boris Godunov*), *D Minor*

    Pimena [*Pimen's*] (two versions written; for high voice; text on Pushkin's *Boris Godunov*), *D Minor*

    Arbenina [*Arbenin's*] (for low voice; text on Lermontov's *Maskarad* [Masquerade], *D Minor*

    Date- c.1891

    Pub- Muzgiz (1947; one version of each monologue)

Grīanem-ukhnem
   (Russian boatmen's song arranged for voice and
   piano)

   Date- c.1891

   Ded- Adol'f Adol'fovich Īaroshevskiĭ
        [Yaroshevsky]

   Pub- Muzgiz (1944)

Pesnīa razocharovannogo [*Song of the Disillusioned*]
   (for low voice; text by Daniil Maksimovich
   Ratgauz [Rathaus]), *A-flat Major*

   Date- 1893

   Pub- Muzgiz (1947)

Uvīal tsvetok [*The Flower Has Faded*]
   (for high voice; text by Daniil Maksimovich
   Ratgauz [Rathaus]), *A Minor*

   Date- 1893

   Pub- Muzgiz (1947)

Ty Pomnish' li vecher [*Do You Remember This Evening?*]
   (for high voice; text by Alekseĭ Konstantinovich
   Tolstoĭ), *E Major*

   Date- 17 July 1891

   Pub- Muzgiz (1947)

Shest' romansov [*Six Songs*] *Op.4*

   1. *O net, moliū, ne ukhodi* [*Oh No, I Beg You,
      Forsake Me Not (Oh Stay, My Love, Forsake
      Me Not)*]

(for medium voice; text by Dmitriĭ
Sergeevich Merezhkovskiĭ), *C-sharp
Minor*

Date- 26 February 1892

Ded- Anna Aleksandrovna Lodyzhenskai͡a

Perf- 27 January 1893 Mikhail Akimovich
Slonov and Rachmaninoff, Kharkov

Pub- Gutheil (1893), Ditson (1921; as "Oh,
No, I Pray, Do Not Depart" in e, Eng.
and Ger.), Boosey & Hawkes (1947; in
e and d, Eng., Fr., and Ger.), Schirmer (1960; as "Forsake Me Not, My Love,
I Pray" in e), Muzgiz (1957,1974),
Mez Kniga

2. *Utro* [*Morning*]
   (for low voice; text by M. I͡anova),
   F Major

Date- 1892

Ded- I͡uriĭ Sergeevich Sakhnovskiĭ

Pub- Gutheil (1893;1921), Schirmer (1910;
Eng., in G), Boston Music (in B-flat
and G), C. Fischer (1923; Eng., Fr.,
and Ger., in B-flat, D-flat, and F),
Paxton (1949; in B-flat and G), Muzgiz
(1957), Mez Kniga, Belwin Mills

3. *V molchan'i nochi tainoĭ* [*In the Silence
   of the Secret Night (In the Silent Night)*]
   (for medium voice; text by Afanasy
   Afanas'evich Shenshin [pseud. Afanasy
   Fet]), *D Major*

Date- 17 October 1890

Ded- Vera Dmitrievna Skalon

Perf- 27 January 1893 Mikhail Akimovich Slonov
and Rachmaninoff, Kharkov

Pub- Gutheil (1893,1921), Chester 1916, 1923), Schirmer (1917,1939; as "In the Silence of Night" In F), Boston Music (1919; as "In the Silent Night"), Ditson (1927), Foley/C. Fischer (1930; as "When Night Descends in Silence" with violin obbligato by Fritz Kreisler, in F), Boosey & Hawkes (1947; in Eng., Fr., Ger., and Russ., in D and F), Paxton (1949; in D and F), Muzgiz (1957,1973), Mez Kniga

4. *Ne poĭ, krasavitsa* [*Sing Not to Me, Beautiful Maiden (Oh, Never Sing to me Again)*] (for high voice; text by Aleksandr Sergeevich Pushkin), *A Minor*

Date- c.1892

Ded- Natalia Aleksandrovna Satina

Pub- Gutheil (1893,1921), Chester (1916), C. Fischer (1922; as "Oh, Cease Thy Singing Maiden Fair" with violin obbligato by Fritz Kreisler), Boosey & Hawkes (1947; in Eng., Fr., Ger., and Russ., in f-sharp and a), Paxton (1949; in e and g), Muzgiz (1957), Mez Kniga

5. *Uzh ty, niva moia* [*Oh Thou, My Field (The Harvest of Sorrow)*] (for high voice; text by Alekseĭ Konstantinovich Tolstoĭ), *D Minor*

Date- 1893

Ded- E.N. Lysikova

Pub- Gutheil (1893,1921), Schirmer (1911; as "Oh Thou Billowy Harvest-Field" in b), Ditson (1921; as "Field Beloved" Ger., in b), C. Fischer (1922; as "Drooping Corn" Eng., in b and a), Boosey & Hawkes (1947; Eng., Fr., Ger., and Russ., in d and b), Paxton (1949, in b and a), Chester (1916,1923; in b),

Muzgiz (1957), Mez Kniga, Belwin-Mills
(as "Oh, Thou Waving Field of Golden
Corn")

6. *Davno l', moĭ drug* [*How Long My Friend
   (So Many Hours)*]
   (for high voice; text by Arensiĭ
   Arkad'evich Golenishchev-Kutuzov),
   G Minor

   Date- 1893

   Ded- Ol'ga Andreevna Golenishcheva-Kutuzova

   Perf- 31 January 1894 Elizaveta Andreevna
   Lavrovskaia and Rachmaninoff, Moscow

   Pub- Gutheil (1893,1921), Boosey & Hawkes
   (1947), Muzgiz (1957), Mez Kniga

Shest' romansov [*Six Songs*] Op.8
(German and Ukrainian texts translated into Russian by Alekseĭ Nikolaevich Pleshcheev)

1. *Rechnaia liliia* [*The Water Lily*]
   (for medium voice; text by Heinrich
   Heine), *G Major*

   Date- October 1893

   Ded- Adol'f Adol'fovich Iaroshchevskiĭ
   [Yaroshevsky]

   Pub- Gutheil (1894,1906,1921), Boosey &
   Hawkes (1947), Muzgiz (1957), Mez Kniga

2. *Ditia, kak tsvetok, ty prekrasna* [*Child,
   Thou Art as Beautiful as a Flower (Like
   Blossom Dew-Freshen'd)*]
   (for medium voice; text by Heinrich
   Heine), *E-flat Major*

   Date- October 1893

   Ded- Mikhail Akimovich Slonov

Pub- Gutheil (1894,1906,1921), Boosey &
Hawkes (1947; F and E-flat), Muzgiz
(1957), Mez Kniga

3. *Duma* [*Brooding*]
(for medium voice; text by Taras
Grigor'evich Shevchenko), *D Minor*

Date- October 1893

Ded- L.G. I͡akovlev

Pub- Gutheil (1894,1906,1921), Boosey &
Hawkes (1947), Muzgiz (1957), Mez Kniga

4. *Poli͡ubila i͡a na pechal' svoi͡u* [*I Have
Grown Fond of Sorrow (The Soldier's Wife)*]
(for medium voice; text by Taras
Grigor'evich Shevchenko), *G Minor*

Date- October 1893

Ded- M.V. Olfer'eva

Perf- 31 January 1894 Elizaveta Andreevna
Lavroskai͡a and Rachmaninoff, Moscow

Pub- Gutheil (1894,1906,1921), Chester (1915,
1923), Boosey & Hawkes (1947; Eng., Fr.,
Ger., and Russ., in a and g), Paxton
(1949; in g and f), Muzgiz (1957), Mez
Kniga

5. *Son* [*The Dream*]
(for high voice; text by Heinrich
Heine), *E-flat Major*

Date- October 1893

Ded- Natali͡a Dmitrievna Skalon

Pub- Gutheil (1894,1906,1921), Boosey &
Hawkes (1947), Muzgiz (1957), Foley,
Mez Kniga, Belwin-Mills

6. *Molitva* [*A Prayer*]
   (for high voice; text by Johann Wolfgang von Goethe), *C Minor*

Date- October 1893

Ded- Mariia Deisha-Sionitzkaia

Pub- Gutheil (1894,1906,1921), Boosey & Hawkes (1947), Muzgiz (1957), Mez Kniga

Dvenadtsat' romansov [*Twelve Songs*] Op.14

1. *Ia zhdu tebia* [*I Wait For Thee*]
   (for high voice; text by Mariia Davidova), *E-flat Major*

Date- 1894

Ded- Liudmila Dmitrievna Skalon

Pub- Gutheil (1896,1906,1921), Boosey & Hawkes (1947), Muzyka (1957), Mez Kniga

2. *Ostorovok* [*The Isle*]
   (for high voice; text by Percy Bysshe Shelley, translated by Konstantin Dmitrievich Bal'mont), *D Major*

Date- 1896

Ded- Sof'ia Aleksandrovna Satina

Pub- Gutheil (1896,1906,1921), C. Fischer (1922; in Eng.), Schirmer (1939; in F), Boston Music (in F and D), Boosey & Hawkes (1947; Eng., Fr., Ger., and Russ., in E and D), Muzyka (1957), Mez Kniga

3. *Davno v liubvi* [*For Long Love Has Brought Little Consolation (How Few the Joys)*]
   (for low voice; text by Afanasy Afanas'evich Shenshin [pseud. Afanasy Fet]), *F-sharp Minor*

Date- October 1896

Ded- Zoi͡a Arkad'evna Pribytkova

Pub- Gutheil (1896,1906,1921), Boosey & Hawkes (1947,1950), Muzyka (1957), Mez Kniga

4. *I͡a byl u neĭ* [*I Came to Her*]
(for medium voice; text by Alekseĭ Vasil'evich Kol't͡sov), *F Major*

Date- October 1896

Ded- I͡uriĭ Sergeevich Sakhnovskiĭ

Pub- Gutheil (1896,1906,1921), Boosey & Hawkes (1947), Muzyka (1957), Mez Kniga

5. *Eti letnie nochi* [*These Summer Nights (Midsummer Nights)*]
(for high voice; text by Daniil Maksimovich Ratgauz [Rathaus]), *E Major*

Date- October 1896

Ded- Marii͡a Ivanovna Gutkheil' [Gutheil]

Pub- Gutheil (1896,1906,1921), Boosey & Hawkes (1947), Muzyka (1957), Mez Kniga

6. *Tebi͡a tak li͡ubi͡at vse* [*How Everyone Loves Thee (The World Would See Thee Smile)*]
(for medium voice; text by Alekseĭ Konstantinovich Tolstoĭ), *G Minor*

Date- 1896

Ded- A.N. Ivanovskiĭ

Pub- Gutheil (1896,1906,1921), Boosey & Hawkes (1947), Muzyka (1957), Mez Kniga

7. *Ne ver' mne drug* [*Believe Me Not, Friend (Believe It Not)*]

(for high voice; text by Alekseĭ
Konstantinovich Tolstoĭ), *C Major*

Date- 1896

Ded- Anna Georgievna Klokacheva

Pub- Gutheil (1896,1906,1921), Boosey &
Hawkes (1947; in Eng., Fr., Ger., and
Russ.), Muzyka (1957), Mez Kniga

8. *O ne grusti* [*Oh, Do Not Grieve*]
(for medium voice; text by Alekseĭ
Nikolaevich Apukhtin), *F Minor*

Date- 1896

Ded- Nadezhda Aleksandrovna Aleksandrova

Pub- Gutheil (1896,1906,1921), Boosey &
Hawkes (1947; Eng., Fr., and Ger., in
a and f), Muzyka (1957), Mez Kniga

9. *Ona, kak polden', khorosha* [*She Is Lovely
As the Noon*]
(for medium voice; text by Nikolaĭ
Maksimovich Minskiĭ [Vilenkin]), *E-flat
Major*

Date- 1896

Ded- Elizaveta Andreevna Lavrovskaía

Pub- Gutheil (1896,1906,1921), Boosey &
Hawkes (1947), Muzyka (1957), Mez Kniga

10. *V moeĭ dushe* [*In My Soul (Love's Flame)*]
(for low voice; text by Nikolaĭ
Maksimovich Minskiĭ [Vilenkin]), *D
Major*

Date- 1896

Ded- Elizaveta Andreevna Lavrovskaía

Pub- Gutheil (1896,1906,1921), Boosey &
Hawkes (1947), Muzyka (1957), Mez Kniga

11. *Vesennie vody* [*Spring Waters (Floods of Spring)*]
    (for high voice; text by Fedor Ivanovich Tiutchev), *D-flat Major*

    Date- 1896

    Ded- Anna D. Ornatskaia

    Pub- Gutheil (1896,1906,1921), Schirmer (1906; as "Floods of Spring" in E-flat), J. Church (1914; as "Floods of Spring"), Chester (1916,1923; in D-flat), Hamelle (as "Le printemps" in D-flat), Ditson (1921; as "Floods of Spring" in Eng., and Ger., in D-flat), C. Fischer (1922; as "Ecstasy of Spring"), Schott (Eng. and Ger., in D-flat), Boosey & Hawkes (1947; Eng., Fr., Ger., and Russ., in E-flat and D-flat), Paxton (1949; in D-flat and B-flat), Muzyka (1957), Mez Kniga

12. *Pora!* [*'Tis Time*]
    (for low voice; text by Semen Iakovlevich Nadson), *E-flat Minor*

    Date- 1896

    Ded- none

    Pub- Gutheil (1896,1906,1921), Boosey & Hawkes (1947; Eng., Fr., Ger., and Russ., in f), Muzyka (1957), Mez Kniga

Ikalos' li tebe [*Were You Hiccupping?*]
   (for low voice; based on text by Petr Andreevich Viazemskii), *F Major*

   Date- 17 May 1899

   Ded- Natalia Aleksandrovna Satina

   Pub- Muzyka (1957)

Rachmaninoff's Compositions 47

Noch' [*Night*]
 (for medium voice; text by Daniil Maksimovich Ratgauz [Rathaus]), *A Minor*

    Date- 1900

    Pub- Jurgenson (1904), Muzyka (1957)

Dvenadt͡sat' romansov [*Twelve Songs*] Op.21

    1. *Sud'ba* [*Fate*]
       (for low voice; text by Aleksei̯ Nikolaevich Apukhtin), *C Minor*

    Date- 18 February 1900

    Ded- Fedor Ivanovich Chaliapin

    Perf- 9 March 1900 Chaliapin and Rachmaninoff, Moscow

    Pub- Gutheil (1900,1902,1921), Boosey & Hawkes (1947), Muzgiz (1957,1973), Mez Kniga

    2. *Nad svezhei̯ mogiloi̯* [*By the Grave*]
       (for low voice; text by Semen I͡akovlevich Nadson)

    Date- April 1902

    Pub- Gutheil (1902,1921), Ditson (1921; as "By a New-Made Grave" in g), C. Fischer (1922; as "The New Grave" in a and f-sharp), Boosey & Hawkes (1950), Muzgiz (1957,1973), Mez Kniga

    3. *Sumerki* [*Twilight*]
       (for high voice; text by Zhan-Mari Gi͡uio [Jean-Marie Guyot], translated by M. Tkhorzhevskii̯), *E Minor*

    Date- April 1902

Ded- Nadezhda Ivanovna Vrubel'

Pub- Gutheil (1902,1921), Boosey & Hawkes (1947), Muzgiz (1957,1973), Mez Kniga

4. *Oni otvechali* [*They Answered (The Answer)*]
(for high voice; text by Victor Hugo, translated by Lev Aleksandrovich Meĭ), *D-flat Major*

Date- April 1902

Ded- Elena Ĭul'evna Kreit͡ser

Pub- Gutheil (1902,1921), Boosey & Hawkes (1947; Eng., Fr., and Russ., in D-flat and B-flat), Muzgiz (1957,1973)

5. *Siren'* [*Lilacs*]
(for high voice; text by Ekaterina A. Beketova), *A-flat Major*

Date- April 1902

Ded- none

Pub- Gutheil (1902,1921), Schirmer (1910; in Eng. and Ger.), Chester (1916; in Eng. and Fr.), Boston Music (in A-flat and E), C. Fischer (1922; as "The Tryst"), Boosey & Hawkes (1947; Eng., Fr., Ger., and Russ., in A-flat and G-flat), Leeds (1951), Muzgiz (1957,1973), Mez Kniga

6. *Otryvok iz Miǔsse* [*Fragments from de Musset (Loneliness)*]
(for high voice; text by Alfred de Musset, translated by Aleksei Nikolaevich Apukhtin), *F-sharp Minor*

Date- April 1902

Ded- Aleksandra Andreevna Liven

Pub- Gutheil (1902,1921), Boosey & Hawkes (1947), Muzgiz (1957,1973), Mez Kniga

7. *Zdes' khorosho* [*How Fair This Spot*]
   (for high voice; text by G. Galina
   [pseud. for A. Einerling]), *A Major*

   Date- April 1902

   Ded- N[ataliâ Aleksandrovna Rakhmaninova]

   Pub- Gutheil (1902,1921), Schirmer (1910;
   as "How Sweet the Place" in F), Chester
   (1916), C. Fischer (1922; as "Here
   Beauty Dwells"), Boosey & Hawkes (1947,
   1952; Eng., Fr., Ger., and Russ., in A
   and F), Muzgiz (1957,1973), Mez Kniga

8. *Na smert' chizhika* [*On the Death of a Linnet*]
   (for medium voice; text by Vasiliĭ
   Andreevich Zhukovskiĭ), *D Minor*

   Date- April 1902

   Ded- Ol'ga Andreevna Trubnikova

   Pub- Gutheil (1902,1921), Boosey & Hawkes
   (1947), Muzgiz (1957,1973), Mez Kniga

9. *Melodiîa* [*Melody*]
   (for high voice; text by Semen Îakovle-
   vich Nadson), *B-flat Major*

   Date- April 1902

   Ded- Nataliâ Nikolaevna Lanting

   Pub- Gutheil (1902,1921), Boosey & Hawkes
   (1947), Muzgiz (1957,1973), Mez Kniga

10. *Pered ikonoĭ* [*Before the Image*]
    (for medium voice; text by Arensiĭ
    Arkad'evich Golenishchev-Kutuzov),
    E-flat Minor

    Date- April 1902

    Ded- Mariâ Aleksandrovna Ivanova

    Pub-   Gutheil (1902,1921), Boosey & Hawkes
            (1947; Eng., Fr., Ger., and Russ., in
            f-sharp and e-flat), Muzgiz (1957,1973),
            Mez Kniga

11. *I͡a ne prorok* [*No Prophet I*]
    (for high voice; text by Aleksandr
    Kruglov), *E-flat Major*

    Date- April 1902

    Ded- none

    Pub-   Gutheil (1902,1921), Boosey & Hawkes
            (1947; Eng., Fr., Ger., and Russ., in
            E-flat and D-flat), Muzgiz (1957,1973),
            Mez Kniga

12. *Kak mne bol'no* [*How Painful for Me (Sorrow in Springtime)*]
    (for high voice; text by G. Galina
    [pseud. for A. Einerling]), *G Minor*

    Date- April 1902

    Ded- Vladimir Aleksandrovich Satin

    Pub-   Gutheil (1902,1921), Ditson (1921; as
            "Sorrow in Spring"), Boosey & Hawkes
            (1947; Eng., Fr., Ger., and Russ., in
            g and e), Muzgiz (1957,1973), Mez Kniga

Pi͡atnadt͡sat' romansov [*Fifteen Songs*] Op.26
    (dedicated to María Semenovna Kerzina and Arkady
    Mikhailovich Kerzin; first complete performance,
    12 February 1907, Kerzin Concerts in Moscow)

    1. *Est' mnogo zvukov* [*There Are Many Sounds (The Heart's Secret)*]
       (for medium voice; text by Alekseĭ
       Konstantinovich Tolstoĭ), *D-flat Major*

    Date- 14 August 1906

Pub- Gutheil (1907,1921), Boosey & Hawkes
(1947; Eng., Fr., Ger., and Russ., in
D-flat and F), Muzgiz (1957,1973), Mez
Kniga

2. *Vse otnĩal u menĩa* [*He Took All from Me
(All Once I Gladly Owned)*]
(for medium voice; text by Fedor Ivanovich Tĩutchev), *F-sharp Minor*

Date- 15 August 1906

Pub- Gutheil (1907,1921), Boosey & Hawkes
(1947; Eng., Fr., Ger., and Russ., in
f-sharp and a), Muzgiz (1957,1973),
Mez Kniga

3. *My otdokhnem* [*Let Us Rest (Come Let Us
Rest)*]
(for low voice; text by Anton Pavlovich
Chekhov), *G Minor*

Date- 14 August 1906

Pub- Gutheil (1907,1921), Boosey & Hawkes
(1947), Leeds (1951; as "We Shall Have
Reason" in f), Muzgiz (1957,1973), Mez
Kniga

4. *Dva proshchanĩa* [*Two Partings*]
(duet [dialogue] for soprano and baritone; text by Aleksei Vasil'evich
Kol'tsov), *C Minor*

Date- 22 August 1906

Pub- Gutheil (1907,1921), Boosey & Hawkes
(1947), Muzgiz (1957,1973), Mez Kniga

5. *Pokinem* [*Beloved, Let Us Fly (Let Us Leave
My Dear)*]
(for high voice; text by Arensiĭ
Arkad'evich Golenishchev-Kutuzov),
A-flat Major

Date— 22 August 1906

Pub— Gutheil (1907,1921), Boosey & Hawkes
(1947), Muzgiz (1957,1973), Mez Kniga

6. *Khristos* [*Christ Is Risen*]
(for medium voice; text by Dmitriĭ
Sergeevich Merezhkovskiĭ), *F Minor*

Date— 23 August 1906

Pub— Gutheil (1907,1921), Boosey & Hawkes
(1947; Eng., Fr., Ger., and Russ., in
f and g), Chester (1917), Muzgiz (1957,
1973), Mez Kniga

7. *K detiâm* [*To the Children*]
(for medium voice; text by Alekseĭ
Stepanovich Khomiâkov), *F Major*

Date— 9 September 1906

Pub— Gutheil (1907,1921), Ditson (1921),
Boosey & Hawkes (1947; Eng., Fr., Ger.,
and Russ., in F and G), Schirmer (1960;
in G), Muzgiz (1957,1973), Mez Kniga

8. *Poshchady iâ moliû* [*Thy Pity I Implore
(I Implore Pity)*]
(for high voice; text by Dmitriĭ Sergeevich Merezhkovskiĭ), *A Minor*

Date— 25 August 1906

Pub— Gutheil (1907,1921), Boosey & Hawkes
(1947), Muzgiz (1957,1973), Mez Kniga

9. *Iâ opiât' odinok* [*Again I Am Along (Let
Me Rest Alone)*]
(for high voice; text by Taras Grigor'-
evich Shevchenko, translated by Ivan
Alekseevich Bunin), *D Minor*

Date— 4 September 1906

Pub- Gutheil (1907,1921), Boosey & Hawkes
      (1947), Muzgiz (1957,1973), Mez Kniga

10. *U moego okna* [*Before My Window*]
    (for high voice; text by G. Galina
    [pseud. for A. Einerling]), *A Major*

Date- 17 September 1906

Pub- Gutheil (1907,1921), Schirmer (1910;
      Eng., in G), Ditson (1921), C. Fischer/
      Foley (1923; as "The Alder Tree" in G),
      Boosey & Hawkes (1947; Eng., Fr., Ger.,
      and Russ., in A and G-flat), Muzgiz
      (1957,1973), Mez Kniga, Belwin-Mills

11. *Fontan* [*The Fountain*]
    (for high voice; text by Fedor Ivano-
    vich Tiutchev), *D Major*

Date- 6 September 1906

Pub- Gutheil (1907,1921), C. Fischer (1923),
      Boosey & Hawkes (1947), Muzgiz (1957,
      1973), Mez Kniga, Belwin-Mills

12. *Noch' pechal'na* [*Night Is Mournful*]
    (for high voice; text by Ivan Aleksee-
    vich Bunin), *B Minor*

Date- 3 September 1906

Pub- Gutheil (1907,1921), Boosey & Hawkes
      (1951; in Eng. and Fr.), Muzgiz (1957,
      (1973), Mez Kniga

13. *Vchera my vstretilis* [*When Yesterday We
    Met*]
        (for medium voice; text by Iakov Petro-
        vich Polonskii), *D Minor*

Date- 3 September 1906

Pub- Gutheil (1907,1921), Boosey & Hawkes
      (1951; in Eng. and Fr.), Muzgiz (1957,
      1973), Mez Kniga

14. *Kol'tso* [*The Ring*]
(for medium voice; text by Aleksei̯
Vasil'evich Kol'tsov), *B Minor*

<u>Date</u>- 10 September 1906

<u>Pub</u>- Gutheil (1907,1921), Boosey & Hawkes
(1947), Muzgiz (1957,1973), Mez Kniga

15. *Prokhodit vse* [*All Things Depart*]
(for low voice; text by Daniil Maksimovich Ratgauz [Rathaus]), *E-flat
Minor*

<u>Date</u>- 8 September 1906

<u>Pub</u>- Gutheil (1907,1921), Boosey & Hawkes
(1947; Eng., Fr., Ger., and Russ., in
e-flat and f), Muzgiz (1957,1973), Mez
Kniga

*Pis'mo Konstantinu Sergeevichu Stanislavskomu (k 10-
letnemu iubileiu Khudozhestvennogo Teatra)* [(musical)
*Letter to Konstantin Sergeevich Stanislavskii̯ on the
10th anniversary of the (Moscow) Arts Theater*]
(for low voice, *E-flat Major*)

<u>Date</u>- October 1908

<u>Perf</u>- 14 October 1908 Chaliapin, Moscow Arts
Theater

<u>Pub</u>- Gutheil (c.1908), Muzgiz (1957,1973),
also in Bertensson and Leyda's <u>Sergei
Rachmaninoff</u>, New York: New York University Press, 1956, p. 148-51.

Chetyrnadtsat' romansov [*Fourteen Songs*] *Op.34*

1. *Muza* [*The Muse*]
(for high voice; text by Aleksandr
Sergeevich Pushkin), *E Minor*

Date- 6 June 1912

Ded- 'Re' [Marietta Sergeevna Shaginían]

Pub- Gutheil (1913,1922), Boosey & Hawkes
(1947), Muzgiz (1957,1973), Mez Kniga

2. *V dushe u kazhogo iz nas* [*In the Soul of Each of Us (The Soul's Concealment)*]
(for low voice; text by Apollon Apollonovich Korinfskiĭ), *C Major*

Date- 5 June 1912

Ded- Fedor Ivanovich Chaliapin

Pub- Gutheil (1913,1921), Boosey & Hawkes
(1947), Muzgiz (1957,1973), Mez Kniga

3. *Buría* [*The Storm*]
(for high voice; text by Aleksandr Sergeevich Pushkin), *E Minor*

Date- 7 June 1912

Ded- Leonid Vital'evich Sobinov

Pub- Gutheil (1913,1921), Boosey & Hawkes
(1947), Muzgiz (1957,1973), Mez Kniga

4. *Veter pereletnyĭ* [*The Migrant Wind (Day to Night Comparing Went the Wind Her Way)*]
(for high voice; text by Konstantin Dmitrievich Bal'mont), *C Major*

Date- 9 June 1912

Ded- Leonid Vital'evich Sobinov

Pub- Gutheil (1913,1921), Boosey & Hawkes
(1947), Muzgiz (1957,1973), Mez Kniga

5. *Arion*
(for high voice; text by Aleksandr Sergeevich Pushkin), *D Minor*

Date- 8 June 1912

Ded- Leonid Vital'evich Sobinov

Pub- Gutheil (1913,1921), Boosey & Hawkes (1947), Muzgiz (1957,1973), Mez Kniga

6. *Voskresenie Lazaria* [*The Raising of Lazarus*]
    (for low voice; text by Alekseĭ Stepanovich Khomiakov), *F Minor*

Date- 4 June 1912

Ded- Fedor Ivanovich Chaliapin

Pub- Gutheil (1913,1921), C. Fischer (1922; Eng. and Russ., in g and e), Boosey & Hawkes (1947), Muzgiz (1957,1973), Mez Kniga

7. *Ne mozhet byt'* [*It Cannot Be (So Dread a Fate I'll Ne'er Believe)*]
    (for medium voice; text by Apollon Nikolaevich Maikov), *E-flat Minor*

Date- 7 March 1910, revised 13 June 1912

Ded- memory of Vera Fedorovna Komissarzhevskaia

Pub- Gutheil (1913,1922), Boosey & Hawkes (1947), Muzgiz (1957,1973), Mez Kniga

8. *Muzyka* [*Music*]
    (for medium voice; text by Iakov Petrovich Polonskiĭ), *E-flat Minor*

Date- 12 June 1912

Ded- P. Ch. [?P. Chaĭkovskiĭ (Tchaikovsky)]

Pub- Gutheil (1913,1923), Boosey & Hawkes (1947), Muzgiz (1957,1973), Mez Kniga

9. *Ty znal ego* [*You Knew Him (The Poet)*]
     (for medium voice; text by Fedor Ivanovich Tiutchev), *D Major*

   Date- 12 June 1912

   Ded- Fedor Ivanovich Chaliapin

   Pub- Gutheil (1913,1922), Boosey & Hawkes (1947), Muzgiz (1957,1973), Mez Kniga

10. *Seĭ den' i͡a pomni͡u* [*I Remember That Day (The Mourn of Life)*]
     (for high voice; text by Fedor Ivanovich Tiutchev), *A-flat Major*

   Date- 10 June 1912

   Ded- Leonid Vital'evich Sobinov

   Pub- Gutheil (1913,1922), Boosey & Hawkes (1947), Muzgiz (1957,1973), Mez Kniga

11. *Obrochnik* [*The Peasant (With Holy Banner Firmly Held)*]
     (for low voice; text by Afanasy Afanas'evich Shenshin [pseud. Afanasy Fet]), *C-sharp Minor*

   Date- 11 June 1912

   Ded- Fedor Ivanovich Chaliapin

   Pub- Gutheil (1913,1922), Boosey & Hawkes (1947), Muzgiz (1957,1973), Mez Kniga

12. *Kakoe schast'e* [*What Happiness (What Wealth of Rapture)*]
     (for high voice; text by Afanasy Afanas'evich Shenshin [pseud. Afanasy Fet]), *A Major*

   Date- 19 June 1912

   Ded- Leonid Vital'evich Sobinov

Pub-　Gutheil (1913,1922), Boosey & Hawkes
　　　　　　(1947), Muzgiz (1957,1973), Mez Kniga

13. *Dissonans* [*Dissonance (Discord)*]
　　　(for high voice; text by I͡akov Petro-
　　　vich Polonskiĭ), *E-flat Minor*

　　　Date-　17 June 1912

　　　Ded-　Feliı͡a Vasil'evna Litvin

　　　Pub-　Gutheil (1913,1922), Boosey & Hawkes
　　　　　　(1947), Muzgiz (1957,1973), Mez Kniga

14. *Vokaliz* [*Vocalise*]
　　　(for high voice), *C-sharp Minor*

　　　Date-　21 September 1915

　　　Ded-　Antonina Vasil'evna Nezhdanova

　　　Perf-　24 January 1916 Nezhdanova and Rach-
　　　　　　maninoff, Moscow

　　　Pub-　Gutheil (1913,1916,1922), Edition Russe
　　　　　　de Musique (1916), Chester (1916),
　　　　　　Boosey & Hawkes (1947; in c-sharp and
　　　　　　a), Schirmer (1944,1960, in c-sharp and
　　　　　　a), Muzgiz (1957,1973), Mez Kniga

Shest' stikhotvoreniĭ [*Six poems*] *Six Songs Op.38*
　For all songs of Op.38:
　　(for high voice)

　　　Ded-　Nina Pavlovna Koshits [Koshetz]

　　　Per-　24 October 1916 Koshetz and Rachmaninoff,
　　　　　　Moscow

　　　Pub-　Edition Russe de Musique (1916), Russ-
　　　　　　ischer Musikverlag (1922), Muz Sektor
　　　　　　(1923), Boosey & Hawkes (1947), Muzgiz
　　　　　　(1957,1973), Mez Kniga

1. *Noch'iu v sadu u menia* [*In My Garden*]
   (text by Avetik Isaakian, translated by Aleksandr Aleksandrovich Blok],
   G Minor

   Date- 12 September 1916

2. *K neĭ* [*To Her*]
   (text by Andreĭ Belyĭ [pseud. of Boris Bugayev]), *F Major*

   Date- 12 September 1916

3. *Margaritki* [*Daisies*]
   (text by Igor' Severianin [pseud. of Igor' Vasil'evich Lotarev]), *F Major*

   Date- undated

4. *Krysolov* [*The Rat-Catcher (The Pied Piper)*]
   (text by Valeri Iakovlevich Briusov),
   C Major

   Date- 12 September 1916

5. *Son* [*The Dream (Dreams)*]
   (text by Fedor Kuz'mich Sologub [pseud. of Fedor Teternikov]), *D-flat Major*

   Date- 2 November 1916

6. *Au (The Quest)*
   (text by Konstantin Dmitrievich Bal'mont), *D-flat Major*

   Date- 14 September 1916

Apple Tree, O Apple Tree
   (for low voice; Russian folk-song arranged by Rachmaninoff for Alfred Swan), *B-flat Major*

Date- 1920

Pub-   Enoch and Sons, London (1923)

Iz evangeliĩa ot Ioanna [*From the Gospel of St. John*]
(for low voice; text from St. John XV,13),
A Major

Date- 16 February 1915

Pub-   Jurgenson (1915), Muzgiz (1957,1973)

Belilitsy rumenitsy vy moĭ [*Powder and Paint*]
(Russian folk-song arranged for voice and piano
by Rachmaninoff; song also used in Op.41)

Date- 1925

A Selection of Arrangements and Transcriptions of
Rachmaninoff's Works Written by Others

Orchestral Arrangements

Andante cantabile
  (*piano piece Op.16, No.3* arranged for string
  orchestra by Alexander Reisman)

Pub-   Western International Music (1965)

Chanson Géorgienne
  (*song Op.4, No.4* arranged for solo voice and
  orchestra by L. Leonardi)

Pub-   Gutheil/Breitkopf (1922), Boosey &
       Hawkes

Cinq études-tableaux
  (*five Etudes-tableaux* arranged
  for full orchestra by Ottorino Respighi)

Date- 1930

Perf- December 1931 Koussevitzky

Pub- Edition Russe de Musique (1931),
Muzyka (1973)

1. *La mer et les mouettes (Op.39, No.2)*
2. *La foire (Op.33, No.7)*
3. *Marche funèbre (Op.39, No.7)*
4. *Le Chaperon rouge et le Loup (Op.39, No.6)*
5. *Marche (Op.39, No.9)*

Polka de W.R.
(arranged for orchestra by Harold Perry)

Pub- Boosey & Hawkes (1955)

Polichinelle
(*piano solo Op.3, No.4* arranged for orchestra by H. Maurice Jacquet)

Pub- Schirmer (1928)

Prelude in G Minor
(*piano solo Op.23, No.5* arranged for orchestra by Charles J. Roberts)

Pub- C. Fischer (1920)

Prelude in C-sharp Minor
(*Op.3, No.2* arranged for orchestra by Henry J. Wood)

Pub- Novello (1914)

Three Preludes
(piano solos arranged for full orchestra by Lucien Cailliet)

Pub- Foley/Belwin-Mills

1. *Prelude in C-sharp Minor Op.3, No.2*
2. *Prelude in G Major Op.32, No.5*
3. *Prelude in G Minor Op.23, No.5*

Suite No.2
(*two-piano Suite Op.17* arranged for piano and orchestra by Lee Holby)

Pub- Boosey & Hawkes

Vocalise
(*song Op.34, No.14* arranged for string orchestra by Arkady Dubensky)

Pub- Colombo

Ziguernertanz
(*violin piece Op.6, No.2* arranged for orchestra by M. Schonherr)

Pub- Krenn

Arrangements for Diverse Instruments

Daisies
(*song Op.38, No.3* arranged for violin and piano by Jascha Heifetz)

Pub- C. Fischer (1947)

Etiūd-kartina
(*Etude-tableau Op.33, No.5* arranged for violin, cello, and piano by V. Kriūkova)

Pub- Muzsektor Gos. (1930)

Rachmaninoff's Compositions

Etude-tableau No.2
    (*Op.33, No.2* arranged for violin and piano by Jascha Heifetz)

        Date- 1945

        Pub- C. Fischer (1947)

In the Silence of the Night
    (*song Op.4, No.3* arranged for cello and piano by Aleksandr Ziloti; cello part revised by Pablo Casals)

        Pub- C. Fischer (1929)

Italian Polka
    (the piano duet arranged for violin and piano by Fritz Kreisler)

        Pub- Foley (1949)

Marguerite (Albumleaf)
    (*Daises Op.38, No.3* arranged for violin and piano by Fritz Kreisler)

        Pub- C. Fischer (1926)

Melodiîa
    (*piano solo Op.3, No.3* arranged for violin, cello, and piano by V. Kriukova)

        Pub- Gos. Muzykal'noe Izd-vo (1931)

Oriental Sketch
    (piano solo arranged for violin and piano by Jascha Heifetz)

        Date 3 November 1945

        Pub- C. Fischer (1947)

Preliūdiīa
    (*Prelude Op.23, No.10* arranged for violin, cello and piano by V. Kriūkova)

        Pub- Muz Sektor (1930)

Prelude in G Minor
    (arranged for violin and piano by Fritz Kreizler)

        Pub- Foley (1946)

Reverie
    (*piano solo Op.3, No.3* words and arrangement for voice and piano by Geraldine Farrar)

        Pub- C. Fischer (1937)

Romance
    (*song Op.4, No.3* arranged for cello and piano by Aleksandr Ziloti; cello part revised by Pablo Casals)

        Pub- C. Fischer (1929)

Serenade
    (*piano solo Op.3, No.5* arranged for violin and piano by Mischa Elman)

        Pub- C. Fischer (1917)

Siren
    (*song Op.21, No.5* arranged for violin, cello, and piano by A.N. Shefer')

        Pub- Gos. Izd-vo (1928)

Rachmaninoff's Compositions

Vocalise de S. Rachmaninoff
   (*song Op.34, No.14* arranged for violin, cello, and piano by Iulii Eduardovich Konius [Julius Conus])

   Pub-   Gutheil/Koussevitzky (1928), Boosey & Hawkes, International

Vocalise
   (*song Op.34, No.14* arranged for violin and piano, edited by Josef Gingold)

   Pub-   Boosey & Hawkes, International (1958)

Vocalise
   (*song Op.34, No.14* arranged for cello and piano by Leonard Rose)

   Pub-   Boosey & Hawkes, International (1960)

Arrangements for Piano

The Isle of the Dead Op.29
   (orchestral work arranged for piano duet by Otto Taubmann)

   Date- 1910

   Pub-   Gutheil (1910)

Italian Polka
   (piano duet arranged for two pianos by Ada Brant)

   Pub-   Foley (1946)

Italian Polka
   (the piano duet arranged for solo piano by Felix Gunther)

   Pub-   Marks (1941)

Polka italienne
   (duet arranged for solo piano by Aleksandr
   Ziloti)

   <u>Pub</u>-   Gutheil (1925), Boosey & Hawkes

Prelude in G Minor
   (*Op.23, No.5* arranged for two pianos eight-hands
   by Wolfgang Rebner)

   <u>Pub</u>-   Schirmer (1939)

Romance
   (*song Op.8, No.2* arranged for piano solo by Aleksandr Ziloti)

   <u>Pub</u>-   Gutheil (1899), Macmillan (1938)

Symphony in E Minor Op.27
   (arranged for piano duet by Vladimir Vil'shau
   [Wilshaw])

   <u>Date</u>   1910

   <u>Pub</u>-   Gutheil/Breitkopf (1910)

Three Songs
   (*Vocalise, It's Lovely Here* [*Op.21, No.7*], and
   Floods of Spring arranged for two pianos by
   Victor Babin)

   <u>Pub</u>-   Universal Music Co. [Chicago] (1949)

Tret'ia simfonia
   (*Third Symphony Op.44* arranged for piano duet by
   G. Kirkora)

   <u>Pub</u>-   Gos. Muzykal'noe Izd-vo (1949)

II

THE RACHMANINOFF REPERTOIRE

Introduction to

Rachmaninoff's Repertoire

Rachmaninoff's repertoire as pianist demonstrates a herculean achievement, considering that the years he spent in Russia (until 1917) were principally occupied with being composer and conductor. As pianist at this time, he primarily performed his own works, with the exception of the years 1915-16 when he toured performing works of Scriabin, in memory of his friend and colleague who had died on 14 April 1915.

It is difficult to believe that Rachmaninoff's first solo piano recital occurred as late as 4 November 1909 during his first American tour, in Northampton, Mass. Programs previous to this (in Russia) were either joint recitals, chamber music programs, or as soloist in concerti. His first solo piano recital in Russia was in Kazan on 17 December 1910. As expected, the Northampton and Kazan recitals consisted only of Rachmaninoff works. This does not imply that he knew no other music than his own, for as early as 17 October 1891, upon graduation from the piano division of the Moskovskaía Konservatoriía [Moscow Conservatory], and through 1895, Rachmaninoff publicly performed short groups of works by Chopin, Schumann, Liszt, Arenskiĭ, and Tchaikovsky. After this brief period of performing works by other composers, he evidently confined himself to his own works until after he fled Russia. The next time he programmed works of others was in Lund, Sweden on 18 September 1918, when he performed Mozart's "Variations in A Major" (first movement of *Sonata in A Major* KV331), two *Moments musicaux Op.94, Nos.3 and 4* (D780) by Schubert, three Chopin works, and two compositions by Tchaikovsky, the *Romance Op.5* and *Trepak Op.72, No.18* (from *Dixhuit morceaux*). From this time on Rachmaninoff performed recitals that consisted predominantly of works by other composers, though he always included a group of his own compositions. This marked the beginning of his career as international concert pianist. At the age of 45 the composer chose to pursue this career path, to become one of the finest pianists ever known. Rachmaninoff worked hard (five hours a day) at the piano during his brief stay in Scandinavia, 24 December 1917-1 November 1918, before sailing for the USA. One can only conjecture on whether he learned this apparently new repertoire during this period; his conservatory training undoubtedly developed a repertoire for the young Rachmaninoff but what type or extent of extra-Russian literature he studied is not known. Surely he knew more of the literature than shown by the meager representation performed in 1891-95; or did he assimilate new literature rapidly, since he had a keen musical intellect and aptitude? Regardless whether newly-mastered or revived and refurbished, his active repertoire grew rapidly; this is a testament to the artistic achievement of Rachmaninoff the pianist.

The first time Rachmaninoff conducted professionally was with Savva Ivanovich Mamontov's Moskovskaia Chastnaia Russkaia Opera [Moscow Private Russian Opera] in October 1897-98, when he directed seven operas in twenty-six performances. In 1904 Rachmaninoff signed a contract to direct opera at the Bol'shoi Imperial Theater. He resigned from that position in 1906 after directing some twelve operas in over ninety performances. In 1911-14 Rachmaninoff directed the Moscow Russkoye Muzikal'noye Obshchestvo [Russian Musical Society] orchestra where he developed a sizable orchestral repertoire. There were many other engagements to conduct orchestras in Russia and elsewhere in the years prior to the Revolution. Rachmaninoff directed orchestras in London (1899), Paris (1907), Antwerp (1908), Boston, Philadelphia, and Chicago (1909), as well as in Russia. Unfortunately, Rachmaninoff's successful career as conductor virtually came to a close when he left Russia in 1917. After he settled in the USA there were only a few times when he conducted his own works, in New York and Philadelphia in 1939, and Chicago in 1941. He evidently chose to forgo his promising career as conductor in favor of his other two musical vocations, that of composer and pianist.

Rachmaninoff's Repertoire as Pianist

Alkan, Charles Valentin

> *Marche funèbre Op.26*
> *Etude, "Comme le vent"* ("As the Wind," from *Douze études Op.39, No.1)*

Arenskiĭ, Anton Stepanovich

> *Two sketches, F Major and A-Flat Major*

Bach, Johann Sebastian

> *English Suite No.2 in A Minor* BWV 807
> *French Suite No.6 in E Major* BWV 817
> *Italian Concerto* BWV 971
> *Partita No.4 in D Major* BWV 828
> *Prelude in Fugue in D Minor* (WTC Bk?)
> *Toccata in E Minor* BWV 914
>
> ### Busoni Transcriptions
>
> > *Chaconne in D Minor* (from *Partita for solo violin No.2* BWV 1004)
> > *Organ Prelude, "Nun kommt der Heiden Heiland"* (BWV 659)
> > *Organ Prelude, "Nun freut euch, lieben Christen"* (BWV 734)
> > *Organ Prelude and Fugue in G Minor* (BWV 535)

Liszt Transcriptions

Organ Fantasy and Fugue in G Minor (BWV 542)
Organ Prelude and Fugue in A Minor (BWV 551)
Praeludium on, "Weinen, Klagen, Sorgen, Zagen" (BWV 12)

Rachmaninoff Transcription

Prelude, Gavotte and Gigue from Partita for solo violin No.3 in E Major (BWV 1006)

Tausig Transcriptions

Organ Choral in A Minor
Toccata and Fugue in D Minor (BWV 565)

Balakirev, Mily Alekseevich

Islamei
(see also transcription of work by Glinka)

Beethoven, Ludwig van

Concerto for Piano and Orchestra No.1 in C Major Op.15
Sonata in D Major Op.10, No.3
Sonata in C Minor Op.13 (Pathetique)
Sonata in A-flat Major Op.26
Sonata in C-sharp Minor Op.27, No.2 (Moonlight)
Sonata in G Major Op.31, No.1
Sonata in D Minor Op.31, No.2 (Tempest)
Sonata in F Minor Op.57 (Appassionata)
Sonata in F-sharp Major Op.78
Sonata in E-flat Major Op.81a
Sonata in E Minor Op.90
Sonata in E Major Op.109
Sonata in C Minor Op.111
Sonata for Violin and Piano in G Major Op.30, No.3
Thirty-two Variations in C Minor

Anton Rubinstein-(Rachmaninoff) Transcription

Turkish March from the *Ruins of Athens*

Rachmaninoff's Repertoire   71

Bizet, Georges

    Rachmaninoff Transcription

        Minuet from L'Arlésienne suite No.1 in
        C Minor

Borodin, Aleksandr Porfir'evich

    Skertso [Scherzo] in A-flat Major

Brahms, Johannes

    Ballade in D Minor Op.10, No.1
    Ballade in D Major Op.10, No.2
    Ballade in G Minor Op.118, No.3
    Intermezzo in E-flat Minor Op.118, No.6

Chopin, Frédéric François

    Ballades Opp.23(g), 38(F), 47(A-flat), 52(f)
    Barcarolle in F-sharp Major Op.60
    Berceuse in D-flat Major Op.57
    Etudes Op.10, Nos.1(C), 3(E), 5(G-flat),
      10(A-flat)
    Etudes Op.25, Nos.1(A-flat), 4(a), 5(e),
      7(c-sharp), 9(G-flat), 12(c)
    Fantasy in F Minor Op.49
    Fantaisie-Impromptu in C-sharp Minor Op.66
    Impromptus Opp.29(A-flat), 36(F-sharp)
    Mazurkas Op.6, Nos.1(f-sharp), 3(E)
    Mazurkas Op.7, Nos.2(a), 3(f)
    Mazurka in A Minor Op.17, No.4
    Mazurkas Op.59, Nos.2(A-flat), 3(f-sharp)
    Mazurkas Op.63, Nos.2(f), 3(c-sharp)
    Mazurkas Op.67, Nos.1(G), 4(a)
    Mazurka in A Minor Op.68, No.2
    Nocturne in E-flat Major Op.9, No.2
    Nocturnes Op.15, Nos.1(F), 2(F-sharp)
    Nocturnes Op.27, Nos.1(c-sharp), 2(D-flat)
    Nocturne in B Major Op.32, No.1
    Nocturne in G Major Op.37, No.2
    Nocturne in F-sharp Minor Op.48, No.2
    Nocturne in F Minor Op.55, No.1
    Nocturne in E Major Op.62, No.2

Nocturne in C-sharp Minor Op.63, No.3
Nocturne in E Minor Op.72, No.1
Polonaises Op.26, Nos.1(c-sharp), 2(e-flat)
Polonaises Op.40, Nos.1(A), 2(c)
Polonaise in F-sharp Minor Op.44
Polonaise in A-flat Major Op.53
Préludes Op.28, Nos.1(C), 2(a), 3(G), 4(e),
 5(D), 6(b), 11(B), 12(g-sharp), 16(b-flat),
 19(E-flat), 22(g), 23(F)
Rondo in E-flat Major Op.16
Scherzi Opp.20(b), 31(b-flat), 39(c-sharp)
 54(E)
Sonatas Opp.35(b-flat), 58(b)
Tarantella in A-flat Major Op.43
Waltz in E-flat Major Op.18
Waltz in F Major Op.34, No.3
Waltz in A-flat Major Op.42
Waltzes Op.64, Nos.1(D-flat), 2(c-sharp),
 3(A-flat)
Waltzes Op.69, Nos.1(A-flat), 2(b)
Waltzes Op.70, Nos.1(G-flat), 3(D-flat)
Waltz in E Minor (Op. posth.)

Liszt Transcriptions

Zyezenie ("Maiden's Wish," from *Polish Songs Op.74)*·
Narzeczony ("Bridegroom" or "The Return," from *Polish Songs Op.74)*

Dandrieu, Jean-François

Godowsky Transcription

Caprice, "Le caquet"

Daquin, Louis Claude

Le coucou (from *Pièces pour le clavecin*)

Debussy, Claude

Children's Corner (Dr. Gradus ad Parnassum, Serenade for the Doll, The Little Shepherd, Golliwogg's Cake-Walk)

Jardin sous la pluie (Estampes)
Pour le piano
Prélude, Bk.1, No.8 "La fille aux cheveau de lin"
Suite bergamasque

Delibes, Leo

    Dohnányi Transcription

        Valse, "Naila"

Dohnányi, Ernst von

    Etude-caprice in F Minor Op.28
    (see also transcription of work by Delibes)

Field, John

    Nocturne in G Major
    Nocturne in E Major ("Noontide")

Glinka, Mikhail Ivanovich

    Balakirev Transcription

        Zhavoronok [The Lark]

Gluck, Christoph Willibald

    Pauer Transcription

        Gavotte from the opera, *Paride ed Elena*

    Saint-Saëns Transcription

        Caprice from *Air de ballet, Alcesta*

    Sgambatti Transcription

        Melody in D Minor from the ballet of the blessed spirits, *Orfeo ed Euridice*

Godard, Benjamin
"*En courant*"

Gounod, Charles
Liszt Transcription
Faust Waltz

Grieg, Edvard
Ballade in G Minor Op.24
Elfentanz Op.12, No.4 (Lyric Pieces)
Sonata for Violin and Piano in C Minor Op.45
Valse Op.12, No.2 (Lyric Pieces)
Valse, "On the Mountain," Op.19, No.1

Handel, George Frideric
Air and Variations in E Major ("Harmonious Blacksmith") from Suite No.5 in E Major

Haydn, Josef
Fantasia in C Major   Hob.XVII:4
Variationen [Variations] in F Minor Hob.XVII:6

Henselt, Adolf
Etude in F-sharp Major Op.2, No.6 "Si oiseau j'étais" ["Were I a Bird"]

Kreisler, Fritz
Rachmaninoff Transcriptions
Liebesfreud (originally for violin and piano)
Liebesleid (originally for violin and piano)

Liadov, Anatol Konstantinovich
  Muzykal'naia tabakerka [Musical Snuffbox] Op.32

Liszt, Franz
  Au bord d'une source (from Première années
    de pèlerinage)
  Ballade No.2 in B Minor
  Concerto for Piano and Orchestra No.1 in
    E-flat Major
  Etude de concert No.1 in A-flat Major
  Etude de concert No.3 in D-flat Major
  Gnomenreigen
  Grandes études de Paganini Nos.2(E-flat),
    3(g-sharp), 5(E), 6(a)
  Fantasia quasi sonata (apres une lecture de
    Dante, from Deuzième années de pèlerinage)
  Funérailles (from Harmonies poétiques et
    religieuses)
  Grand galop chromatique
  Hungarian Rhapsodies nos.2(c-sharp; with
    cadenza by Rachmaninoff), 9(E-flat), 11(a),
    12(c-sharp), 14(f), 15(a)
  Liebestraum No.3 in A-flat Major
  Polonaise No.2 in E Major
  Rapsodie espagnole
  Sonata in B Minor
  Sonetto 104 di Petrarca in E Major (from
    Deuzième années de pèlerinage)
  Sonetto 123 di Petrarca in A-flat Major (from
    Deuzième années de pèlerinage)
  Tarantella (from Années de pèlerinage,
    "Venezia e Napoli")
  Totentanz for Piano and Orchestra
  Transcendental études No.7 in E-flat Major
    (Eroica), and No.11 in D-flat Major (Har-
    monies du soir)
  Valse impromptu
  Valses oubliées No.1(F-sharp), 3(D-flat)
  Waldesrauschen
  (see also transcriptions of works by Bach,
    Chopin, Gounod, Schubert, Schumann, and
    Wagner)

Loeilly, Jean Baptiste

Godowsky Arrangement

Gigue in E Minor

Medtner, Nikolaĭ Karlovich

Skazki [Fairy Tales] Op.14, No.2(e); Op.20, No.1(b-flat); Op.26, No.3(f); Op.34, Nos.1(b), 2(e); Op.51, No.1(d)
Fragment tragique Op.7
Improvizat͡sii͡a (from Tri p'esy Op.31)
Novelli Op.17, Nos.1(G), 2(c)
Sonata-Skazka [Sonata-Fairy Tale] in C Minor Op.25, No.1
Traurnyĭ marsh (from Tri p'esy Op.31)
Tri gimna trudu [Three Hymns in Praise of of Toil] Op.49 1.Gimn pered rabotoĭ [before work] 2. Gimn "U nakoval'ni" [at the anvil] 3. Gimn posle raboty [after work]

Mendelssohn, Felix

Etudes Op.104, Nos.2(F), 3(a)
Rondo Capriccioso Op.14
Songs Without Words Op.19, Nos.3(A), 4(A); Op.30, Nos.4(b), 5(D); Op.38, Nos.1(E-flat), 5(a); Op.67, Nos.2(f-sharp), 4(C); Op.85, No.1(F); Op.102, No.5(A)
Variations sérieuses in D Minor Op.54

Rachmaninoff Transcription

Scherzo from *Midsummer Night's Dream*

Moskowskiĭ, Moritz

Jongleurin Op.52, No.4

Mussorgsky, Modest Petrovich

Rachmaninoff Transcription

Gopak [Hopak] (from *Sorochinskai͡a i͡armarka [Sorochintzi Fair]*)

Rachmaninoff's Repertoire

Mozart, Wolfgang Amadeus
- Sonata in D Major   KV 311
- Sonata in A Major   KV 331
- Sonata in D Major   KV 576

Pauer, Ernst
- *Old French gavotte, "Ce sont les amours"* in F Major
  (see also transcription of work by Gluck)

Poulenc, Francis
- *Novelette in C Major*
- *Toccata* (from *Trois pièces pour piano*)

Rachmaninoff, Sergei Vasil'evich

Rachmaninoff performed all his solo piano literature, the concerti, and the *Rhapsody on a Theme of Paganini* at one time or another. Some works were primarily performed in Russia, especially immediately after completion and in complete sets, as the *Preludes* or *Etudes-tableaux* for example. He was of course partial to his favorites and these are the compositions he programmed often during his performing career in the Western world. Some of his works he never publically played again after the initial performance. The piano works listed here are the compositions that remained active in his repertoire and received numerous performances.

- *Barcarolle in G Minor Op.10, No.3* (played very often)
- *Concert pour le piano avec accompagnement d'orchestre* [*Concerto for Piano and Orchestra*] *No.1 in F-sharp Minor Op.1*
- *2-me Concert pour le piano avec accompagnement d'orchestre* [*Second Concerto for Piano and Orchestra*] *in C Minor Op.18*
- *3-me Concert pour le piano avec orchestre* [*Third Concerto for Piano and Orchestra*] *in in D Minor Op.30*

4-me Concert pour le piano et orchestre
[*Fourth Concerto for Piano and Orchestra*]
in G Minor Op.40
Margaritki [*Daisies*] in F Major op.38, No.3
Elégie in E-flat Minor Op.3, No.1 (played
very often)
Etudes-tableaux Op.33, Nos.1(f), 2(C),
3(e-flat), 4(E-flat), 5(g), 6(c-sharp),
7(E-flat)
Etudes-tableaux Op.39, Nos.4(b), 5(e-flat),
6(a), 9(D)
*Fantaziĩa. Siũita No.1 (Fantasie pour deux
pianos)* [*Fantasia. Suite No.1*] (*Fantasy for
Two Pianos*) Op.5 (played often in Russia)
Humoresque in G Major Op.10, No.5 (played
very often)
Siren' [*Lilacs*] Op.21, No.5
Mélodie in E Major Op.3, No.3 (played very
often)
Moment musicale in E-flat Minor Op.16, No.2
Oriental Sketch in B-flat Major
Polichinelle in F-sharp Minor Op.3, No.4
(played very often)
Polka de W.R. in A-flat Major
Prelude in C-sharp Minor Op.3, No.2 (played
most often)
Preludes Op.23, Nos.1(f-sharp), 2(B-flat),
3(d), 4(D), 5(g), 10(G-flat)
Preludes Op.32, Nos.3(E), 5(G), 6(f), 8(a),
10(b), 12(g-sharp)
*Rapsodie sur un thème de Paganini pour piano
et orchestre* [*Rhapsody on a Theme of Paganini
for Piano and Orchestra*] Op.43
Sérénade in B-flat Major Op.3, No.5 (played
often)
Sonate für Pianoforte [*Sonata for Piano*] No.1
in D Minor Op.28 (played principally in
Russia)
Sonate pour piano et violoncelle (in G Minor
Op.19) (played often in Russia)
Deuxième Sonate pour piano [*Second Sonata for
Piano*] in B-flat Minor Op.36
Vtoraĩa siũita (2-em Suite pour deux pianos)
[*Suite No.2 for Two Pianos*] Op.17 (played
in Russia)
*Elegicheskoe trio (Trio élégiaque pour piano,
violon et violoncelle)* in D Minor Op.9
(played often in Russia)

Rachmaninoff's Repertoire 79

    Valse in A Major Op.10, No.2
    Variatsiĭ na temu Shopena (Variations sur un thème de F. Chopin) [*Variations on a Theme of Chopin*] Op.22
    Variations on a Theme of Corelli Op.42
    (see also transcriptions of works by Bach, Bizet, Kreisler, Mendelssohn, Mussorgsky, Rimsky-Korsakov, Schubert, and Tchaikovsky)

Rameau, Jean-Phillippe

    Gavotte avec 6 doubles

Ravel, Maurice

    Toccata (from *Le tombeau de Couperin*)

Rimsky-Korsakov, Nikolaĭ Andreevich

    Rachmaninoff Transcription

        The Bumble Bee (from *Tsar Saltan*)

Rubinstein, Anton Grigor'evich

    Ball Masquerade [*Bal costumé*] for piano duet Op.103 (performed with Leonid Aleksandrovich Maximov in 1890)
    Barcarolla in A Minor Op.45
    Kontsert No.4 d-moll dlia f-no s orkestrom [*Concerto No.4 in D Minor for Piano and Orchestra*] Op.70
    Etude Op.81
    Polka bohème Op.82, No.7
    (see also transcription of work by Beethoven)

Rubinstein, Nikolaĭ Grigor'evich

    Valse and Tarantella (arr. for two pianos by E. Langer; with Aleksandr Borisovich Gol'denveizer in 1900)

Saint-Saëns, Camille

> Caprice on a Theme by Gluck (Alceste)
> Dance macabre (arr. for two pianos; with Aleksandr Borisovich Gol'denveizer in 1900)
> Le cygne [The Swan] (arranged by Aleksandr Il'ich Ziloti)

Scarlatti, Domenico

> Sonata in D Minor (no identifying numbers indicated for these three sonatas)
> Sonata in G Minor
> Sonata in D Major
>
> Tausig Arrangements
>
>> Sonata Pastorelle in D Minor (K9)
>> Sonata Capriccio in E Major (K20)

Schlözer, Paul de

> Etude de concert in A-flat Major Op.1, No.2

Schubert, Franz

> Duo [Sonata "Duo"] for Piano and Violin in A Major (D 574)
> Impromptu in A-flat Major Op.90, No.4 (D 899)
> Impromptus Op.142, Nos.1(f), 4(f) (D 935)
> Moments musicaux Op.94, Nos.3(f), 4(c-sharp) (D 780)
> Rondo for Piano and Violin in B Minor (D 895)
> Sonata in D Major (Rondo) Op.53 (D 850)
>
> Liszt Transcriptions
>
>> Ave Maria (D 839)
>> Das Wandern (D 795)
>> Der Wanderer (D 489)
>> Die Forelle (D 550)
>> Ständchen (D 957)
>> Wandererfantasie (D 760)

Rachmaninoff Transcription

Wohin? [The Brooklet] (song from Die schöne Müllerin [D 795] transcribed for piano solo)

Tausig Transcriptions

Andantino and Variations in B Minor (D 823?)
Marche militaire in D Major (D 733)

Schumann, Robert

Albumblätter Op.124, Nos.1(d), 2(a), 3(F)
Andante and Variations for two pianos Op.46
  (with Leonid Aleksandrovich Maximov in 1888)
Arabesque Op.18
Carnival Op.9
Concerto for Piano and Orchestra Op.54
Davidsbündlertanze Op.6
Etudes symphoniques Op.13
Faschingsschwank aus Wien Op.26
Kreisleriana Op.16
Nachtstücke Op.23, No.4 (F)
Novelletten Op.21, Nos.5(D), 8(f-sharp)
Papillons Op.2
Phantasiestücke Op.12, Nos.1(D-flat), 2(f), 4(D-flat), 5(f), 6(C)
Sonata in G Minor Op.22
Studien nach Capricen von Paganini Op.3, No.2(E)
Vogel als Prophet (from Waldscenen Op.82)

Liszt Transcription

Widmung (from Myrten Op.25)

Tausig Transcription

Der Kontrabandiste (Op.74, No.9)

Scriabin, Aleksandr Nikolaevich

Etudes Op.8, Nos.10(D-flat), 12(d-sharp)
Etudes Op.42, Nos.1(D-flat), 3(f-sharp), 5(c-sharp)
Fantasia Op.28
Kontsert fis-moll dlia f-no e orkestrom
  [Concerto in F-sharp Minor for Piano and Orchestra] Op.20

Poème in F-sharp Major Op.32, No.1
Poème satinique Op.36
Préludes Op.11, Nos.1(C), 3(G), 6(b),
  8(f-sharp), 14(e-flat), 20(c), 21(B-flat),
  23(F), also possibly *nos.5(D), 16(B-flat),*
  18(f), 24(d)
Sonatu-fantaisie in G-sharp Minor Op.19
Sonata in F-sharp Major Op.30
Sonata in F-sharp Major Op.53

Strauss, Johann

Godowsky Transcription

Valse "Künstlerleben" (Op.316)

Schulz-Evler Transcription

An der schönen blauen Donau [On the Beautiful Blue Danube] *(Op.314)*

Tausig Transcriptions

Valse caprice No.1 "Nachtfalter" [the moth] *(Op.157)*
Valse caprice No.2 "Man lebt nur einmal" [One lives but once] *(Op.167)*
Valse caprice No.3 "Waldstimmen" [Voices of the forest] *(Op.250)*

Taneev, Sergeǐ Ivanovich

Prelude and Fugue in G-sharp Minor Op.29

Tausig, Carl

Ziegeunerweisen
(see also transcriptions of works by Bach, Scarlatti, Schubert, Schumann, Strauss, and Weber)

Tchaikovsky, Peter Ilich

Humoresque Op.10, No.2
Kontsert dlia f-no s orkestrom No.1 [Concerto for Piano and Orchestra No.1] in B-flat Minor Op.23
Les saisons Op.37, Nos.3(g), 6(g), 10(d), 11(E)
Nocturne (?, possibly *Op.19, No.4)*
Romance in F Minor Op.5
Thème original et variations Op.19, No.6 (from Six morceaux)
Trepak Op.72, No.18 (from Dix-huit morceaux)
Valse in A-flat Major Op.40, No.8 (from Douze morceaux)

Pabst Transcriptions

Fantasy on Themes from "Evgeny Onegin"
Illustrations de l'opera, "La dame de pique"

Rachmaninoff Arrangement

Kolybel'naia pesnia [Lullaby] (song Op.16, No. 1 arranged for piano solo)

Wagner, Richard

Brassin Transcription

Magic Fire Music from Die Walküre

Liszt Transcription

Spinning Song from Der fliegende Holländer

Weber, Carl Maria von

Momento Capriccioso Op.12
Rondo brillante Op.62

Tausig Transcription

Aufforderung zum Tanze [Invitation to the dance]

Rachmaninoff's Repertoire as Conductor

Arenskiĭ, Anton Stepanovich
> Variatsiĭ na temu Chaĭkovskogo dli͡a orkestra
> [*Variations on a Theme of Tchaikovsky for (string) Orchestra*] Op.35a
> Simfonii͡a No.1 [*Symphony No.1*] in B Minor Op.4

Bach, Johann Sebastian
> Prelude from Cantata "Geist und Seel' wird verwirret" BWV 35 (performed in Russia, 1914; possibly an arrangement by Ziloti)

Balakirev, Mily Alekseevich
> *Overture on Three Russian Themes*
> *Tamara* (symphonic poem)

Beethoven, Ludwig van
> *Concerto for Piano and Orchestra No.1 in C Major* Op.15 (with Josef Lhévinne in 1914)
> *Concerto for Violin and Orchestra in D Major* Op.61 (with Eugène Ysaÿe in 1912)
> *Egmont Overture* Op.84
> *Symphony in C Major (Jena)*

Berlioz, Hector
> *Symphonie fantastique* Op.14

Bizet, Georges
> *Carmen* (opera)

Rachmaninoff's Repertoire

Borodin, Aleksandr Porfir'evich
> *Kniaz' Igor'* [*Prince Igor*] (opera)
> *Simfoniia No.2* [*Symphony No.2*] *in B Minor*

Brahms, Johannes
> *Tragic Overture Op.81*
> *Variations on a Theme by Haydn Op.56a*

Dargomyzhskiĭ, Aleksandr Sergeevich
> *Rusalka* (opera)

Davidov, Stepan Ivanovich
> *Kontserty dlia violoncheli s orkestrom*
> [*Concerto for Violoncello and Orchestra*]
> (concerto number not indicated; with Pablo Casals in 1912)

Debussy, Claude
> *Le martyr de St. Sebastian*

Ducasse, Jean Roger
> *Interlude from "Au jardin de Marguerite"*

Dvořák, Antonin
> *Concerto for Violoncello and Orchestra in B Minor Op.104* (with Pablo Casals in 1912)

Elgar, Edward
> *Variations on an Original Theme ("Enigma") Op.36*

Franck, César
> Symphonic Poem, "Le chasseur maudit"

Glazunov, Aleksandr Konstantinovich
> Kontserty dlīa skripki s orkestrom, a moll
> [Concerto for Violin and Orchestra in A Minor]
> Op.82 (with Mischa Elman in 1908)
> Fantaisie finnoise in C Major Op.88
> Lyric Poem in D-flat Major Op.12
> Siuita, A dur [Suite in A Major] (Scènes de
>   ballet) Op.52
> Siuita, E dur "Iz srednikh vekov" [Suite in
>   E Major "From the Middle Ages"] Op.79
> Simfoniīa No.6 [Symphony No.6] in C Minor Op.58
> Vesna [Spring] in D Major Op.34

Glinka, Mikhail Ivanovich
> Kamarinskaīa
> Souvenir d'une nuit d'eté a Madrid [Night in
>   Madrid]
> Zhizn' za tsarīa [A Life for the Tsar] (opera)

Grieg, Edvard
> Concerto for Piano and Orchestra in A Minor
> Op.16 (with Aleksandr Ziloti as soloist in
> 1908 and M. Meichik in 1912)
> Lyric Suite (Op.54)
> "Peer Gynt" Suite No.1 Op.46
> "Peer Gynt" Suite No.2 Op.55

Lalo, Edouard
> Concerto for Violoncello and Orchestra in
> D Minor (with A. Heking in 1912)

Liãdov, Anatol Nikolaevich

Six Miniatures, Russian folk songs (from Op.58)
Iz Apokalipsa [*From the Apocalypse*] Op.66
Skertso, D dur [*Scherzo in D Major*] Op.16

Liszt, Franz

Concerto for Piano and Orchestra No.1 in E-flat Major (with Frieda Kvast-Hozap as soloist in 1905, Josef Hofmann in 1912, and Josef Lhévinne in 1914)
Mazzepa (symphonic poem)
Tasso (symphonic poem)
Totentanz for Piano and Orchestra (with Aleksandr Ziloti in 1902 and 1904)

Mendelssohn, Felix

Scherzo, from the "Midsummer Night's Dream" Op.21
Symphony No.3 (Scottish) in A Minor Op.56

Moskowskiĭ, Moritz

Concerto for Violin and Orchestra in C Major Op.30 (with Karl Karlovich Grigorovich in 1905)

Mozart, Wolfgang Amadeus

Concerto for Violin and Orchestra in G Major [KV 216] (with Eugène Ysaÿe in 1912)
Symphony No.40 in G Minor KV 550

Mussorgsky, Modest Petrovich

Boris Godunov (opera)
Overture to *"Khovanschina"*
Overture to *"Sorochinskaĭa ĭarmarka"* [*Sorochintsy fair*]

Ivanova noch' na Lisoĭ gore [St. John's Night on Bare Mountain]

Rachmaninoff, Sergei Vasil'evich
  Aleko (opera)
  Francheska da Rimini [Francesca da Rimini] (opera)
  Skupoĭ rytsar' [Miserly Knight] (opera)
  Utes [The Rock] Op.7
  Kaprichchio na tsyganskie temy [Capriccio on Gypsy Themes] Op.12
  Vesna [Spring] Op.20
  Die Toteninsel [The Isle of the Dead] Op.29
  Kontserty dlia f-no s orkestrom No.2 [Concerto for Piano and Orchestra No.2] in C Minor Op.18 (with Konstantin Nikolaevich Igumnov as soloist in 1905, and Aleksandr Ziloti in 1902 and 1913)
  Liturgiā Sviātogo Ioanna Zlatousta [Liturgy of Saint John Chrysostom] Op.31
  Simfoniiā No.2, e moll [Symphony No.2 in E Minor] Op.27
  Simfoniiā No.3, a moll [Symphony No.3 in A Minor] Op.44
  Vokaliz [Vocalise] (for orchestra) Op.34

Ravel, Maurice
  Valse nobles et sentimentales

Rimsky-Korsakov, Nikolaĭ Andreevich
  Maiskaiā noch' [May Night] (opera)
  Pan Voyevoda (opera)
  Sadko Op.5
  Sheherazade, Symphonic Suite Op.35
  Svetlyĭ prazdnik [Russian Easter Overture] Op.36
  Simfoniiā No.2 "Antar" [Symphony No.2 "Antar"] Op.9
  "Secha pri Kerzhentse"

Rubinstein, Anton Grigor'evich
    Demon (opera)

Saint-Saëns, Camille
    Concerto for Violoncello and Orchestra No.1 in A Minor Op.33 (with Pablo Casals in 1913)
    Samson et Dalila (opera)

Satz, Ilia
    "Blue Bird Suite" (orchestration by Glière)
    Suite, "Drama of Life" (orchestration by Glière)
    Fanfare and Chorus, "On the Death of Hamlet" (orchestration by Glière)

Schubert, Franz
    Liszt Arrangement for Piano and Orchestra
    Wandererfantasie (with Aleksandr Ziloti as soloist in 1904)

Scriabin, Aleksandr Nikolaevich
    Kontserty fis-moll dlia f-no s orkestrom [*Concerto in F-sharp Minor for Piano and Orchestra*] Op.20 (with Scriabin as soloist in 1911)
    Simfoniia, E dur [*Symphony in E Major*] Op.26

Serov, Aleksandr Nikolaevich
    Rogneda (opera)
    Vrazh'ia sila (opera; excerpts)

Strauss, Richard
> Don Juan Op.20
> Till Eulenspiegel Op.28

Taneev, Sergeĭ Ivanovich
> Oresteia͡ (opera; excerpts)

Tchaikovsky, Peter Ilich
> Fantaziia͡ kontsert dlia͡ f-no s orkestrom [Concert Fantasia for Piano and Orchestra] in G Major Op.56 (with Taneev as soloist in 1905)
> Kontsert dlia͡ f-no s orkestrom No.1 [Concerto for Piano and Orchestra No.1] in B-flat Minor Op.23 (with Aleksandr Ziloti as soloist in 1904 and 1911, and Josef Hofmann in 1912)
> Francheska da Rimini [Francesca da Rimini] Op.32
> Evgeniĭ Onegin [Eugene Onegin] (opera)
> Oprichnik (opera)
> Pikovaia͡ dama [Queen of Spades] (opera)
> Romeo and Juliet Overture
> Iolanta [Yolanthe] (opera)
> Siuita dlia͡ orkestra (No.3) [Suite for Orchestra (No.3)] Op.55 (theme and variations)
> Buria͡ [The Tempest] Op.18
> Simfoniia͡ No.2, c moll [Symphony No.2 in C Minor] Op.17
> Simfoniia͡ No.4, f moll [Symphony No.4 in F Minor] Op.36
> Simfoniia͡ No.5, e moll [Symphony No.5 in E Minor] Op.64
> Simfoniia͡ No.6, b moll [Symphony No.6 in B Minor] Op.74

Verstovskiĭ, Alekseĭ Nikolaevich
> Askol'dova mogila [The Tomb of Askold] (opera)

Vivaldi, Antonio
> *Concerto for Orchestra in D Minor* (arranged by Aleksandr Ziloti)

Wagner, Richard
> *Lohengrin* (introduction to third act)
> *Sigfried Idyll*

Weber, Carl Maria von
> *Overture to "Oberon"*
>
> ### Weingartner Orchestration
> *Aufforderung zum Tanze* [*Invitation to the Dance*]

III

RACHMANINOFF DISCOGRAPHY

Introduction to

Rachmaninoff's Recordings

Rachmaninoff recorded with the Edison Company solely in April 1919 at their New York studio. The recording process used at that time was acoustical, where the performer directed his sound towards a horn chamber, sound being transferred (non-electrically) to a matrix (master). The technicians at Edison preferred the adaptability of the upright piano to their recording apparatus; the use of this size piano limited the fullness of sound, but evidently was necessary for practical purposes. It did not help either that the takes for these eight recordings were generally underrecorded and hence weak. Rachmaninoff also started recording for the Ampico Corporation in 1919. These were sensitively reproduced, high quality piano rolls. Rachmaninoff continued making Ampico piano rolls on and off for ten years. He became a recording artist for the Victor Talking Machine Company (Victor) in 1920 and remained with them throughout his lifetime. Victor records were recorded acoustically until 1925, when the electrical (with microphone) recording process superseded the former method. Rachmaninoff recorded some works in all three modes: acoustic, piano roll, and electric. A dedicated collector might compare interpretations and characteristics of the three versions. Some of the recorded compositions are

truncated. The practice of truncating compositions
was done in order to fit them on a determined number
of sides, and was an accepted custom, although musically disconcerting. The art of presenting a work
in its totality, which is paramount today, was not
a primary concern during the infancy of the recording industry. In 1973, in honor of the centennial
of Rachmaninoff's birth, the Radio Corporation of
America (RCA) issued a five-album, fifteen-record
major collection of Rachmaninoff's recordings, including some discs that were previously unpublished.
"The Complete Rachmaninoff" encompasses the record
numbers ARM 3-0260, 3-0261, 3-0294, 3-0295, 3-0296.
It is sad to note that it is virtually impossible
to obtain this valuable release today. It is to be
hoped that RCA will re-release this recorded legacy
of Rachmaninoff's art at some future time. USSR's
organization, All-Union Firm of Gramophone Records,
under the logos "Melodiya," also has an eight-record
release of the same solo compositions listed in the
RCA ARM 3-0260, 3-0261, and 3-0294 albums. The
"Melodiya" series is entitled, "The Art of Sergei
Vasilevich Rachmaninov" with record numbers
"Melodiya" D-022541/2, D-022563/4, D-031031/2,
D-031033/4, D-131035/6, D-033755/6, D-033757/8,
D-033759/60.

Symbols

Date- date of recording

Company- recording company, followed by the disc
number, album number, the release number
of Victor's British affiliate, His Master's
Voice (HMV), and some past and current
LP releases.

Matrix & Take- (sample matrix disc number: CVE-
34143-3)
This Victor prefix (CVE) is followed by the
matrix number (34143), which in turn is
followed by the take number (-3); the take
number indicates the take agreed upon by
the artist and the technician to be used
for the publishing master. In Edison's

matrix and take numbers (sample: 6736-A,B, C), the takes are designated by the letters A,B,C and indicate that all three takes were used for masters. A person acquiring a version of each take of the Edison recordings will have slightly varying performances.

Recordings Made by Rachmaninoff

Bach, Johann Sebastian

Partita No.4 in D Major (Sarabande) BWV 828

Date- c.1925, Company- Ampico 66483 (piano roll)

Date- 16 December 1925, Company- Victor 6621 (HMV DB-1016), ARM 3-0261 Matrix & Take- CVE-34143-3

Rachmaninoff Transcription

Partita No.3 for Violin in E Major (Prelude) BWV 1006

Date- 8 January 1935, Company- Victor (unpublished), Matrix- CS-87284

Date- 27 February 1942, Company- Victor 11-8607, Matrix & Take- PCS-072127-3

——— *(Gavotte, Rondo, Gigue)*

Date- 26 February 1942, Company- Victor 11-8607, ARM 3-0261, Matrix & Take- PCS-072128-1

Beethoven, Ludwig van

Sonata in F Major Op.10, No.2 (Presto)

Date- 13 May 1920, Company- Victor (unpublished), Matrix- B-23961 (acoustic)

Thirty-two variations in C Minor (variations 1-14,19,22-28,31,32)

    Date- (side 1) 14 May 1925, Company- Victor 6544 & 6819, Matrix & Take- CVE-32506-4; Melodiya D022541/2 (both sides)

    Date- (side 2) 13 April 1925, Company- Victor 6544 & 6818, ARM 3-0261, Matrix & Take- CVE-32507-1

Sonata for Violin and Piano in G Major Op.30, No.3 (with Fritz Kreisler)

    Date- 22 March 1928, Company- Victor 8163-8164 (HMV DB-1463-64), LM 6099, ARM 3-0295; Melodiya D8245/6, Matrix & Take- (four sides) CVE-41759-8, 41760-5, 41761-5, 41762-7

Rubinstein-(Rachmaninoff) Transcription

Turkish March from The Ruins of Athens

    Date- c.1927, Company- Ampico 68771 (piano roll)

    Date- 14 December 1925, Company- Victor 1196 (HMV DA-939), ARM 3-0261, Matrix & Take- BVE-39387-8

Bizet, Georges

    Rachmaninoff Transcription

    Minuet from L'Arlésienne suite No.1 in C Minor

        Date- c.1922, Company- Ampico 61601 (piano roll)

        Date- 24 February 1922, Company- Victor 816 & 66085, ARM 3-0260, Matrix & Take- B-26134-3 (acoustic)

Borodin, Aleksandr Porfir'evich

    Scherzo in A-flat Major

        Date- 23 December 1935, Company- Victor 1762 (HMV DA-1522), ARM 3-0261, Matrix & Take- BS-98394-1

Chopin, Frédéric François

    Ballade in A-flat Major Op.47

        Date- 13 April 1925, Company- Victor (originally unpublished), ARM 3-0294, Matrix- CVE-32510,32511

    Etude in F Minor (op.?)

        Date- 17 May 1920, Company- Victor (unpublished), Matrix- B-24116 (acoustic)

    Etude in G-flat Major Op.10, No.5

        Date- 3 May 1920, Company- Victor (unpublished, Matrix- B-23982 (acoustic)

    Etude in G-flat Major Op.25, No.9

        Date- 13 May 1920, Company- Victor (unpublished), Matrix- B-23964 (acoustic)

    Mazurka in C-sharp Minor Op.63, No.3

        Date- 27 December 1923, Company- Victor 1008 & 66248 (HMV DA-613), VIC-1534, ARM 3-0260, Matrix & Take- B-24644-8 (acoustic)

    Mazurka in A Minor Op.68, No.2

        Date- 23 December 1935, Company- Victor (originally unpublished), ARM 3-0294, Matrix- BS-98395

Nocturne in F-sharp Major Op.15, No.2

> Date- 27 December 1923, Company- Victor
> 6452 & 74885, Vic-1534, ARM 3-0260,
> Matrix & Take- C-27118-8 (acoustic)

Nocturne in F Major Op.15, No.1

> Date- c.1926, Company- Ampico 67673
> (piano roll), Everest SDBR-3377

Nocturne in E-flat Major Op.9, No.2

> Date- 5 April 1927, Company- Victor 6731,
> VIC-1534, LCT-1136, ARM 3-0294,
> Matrix & Take- CVE-37465-3

Scherzo in C-sharp Minor Op.39

> Date- 18 March 1924, Company- Victor
> (originally unpublished), ARM 3-
> 0260, Matrix- C-29671, 29672
> (acoustic)

Scherzo in B-flat Minor Op.31

> Date- c.1928, Company- Ampico 71173
> (piano roll), Everest SDBR-3377

Prelude in E-flat Major Op.28, No.19

> Date- 27 December 1923, Company- Victor
> (unpublished), Matrix- B-29223
> (acoustic)

Sonata in B-flat Minor Op.35

> Date- 18 February 1930, Company- Victor
> 1489-92 & M-95 (HMV DA-1186-89),
> VIC-1534, CAL-396, ARM 3-0294,
> Matrix & Take- (seven sides)
> BVE-59408-2, 59409-2, 59410-2,
> 59411-2, 59412-2, 59413-2, 59414-1

Waltz in E-flat Major Op.18

> Date- c.1921, Company- Ampico 59743
> (piano roll), Everest SDBR-3377

Date- 21 January 1921, Company- Victor 6259 & 74679 (HMV DB-408), VIC-1534, ARM 3-0260, Matrix & Take- C-24903-1 (acoustic)

Waltz in F Major Op.34, No.3

Date- 20 December 1920, Company- Victor (originally unpublished), VIC-1534, ARM 3-0260, Matrix- B-24639 (acoustic)

Date- c.1923, Company- Ampico 63311 (piano roll)

Waltz in A-flat Major Op.42

Date- 18 April 1919, Company- Edison 82197 (released on RCA's ARM 3-0260), Matrix & Take- 6731-A,B,C (three takes used; acoustic)

Waltz in D-flat Major Op.64, No.1

Date- 2 April 1921, Company- Victor 64971 (HMV DA-371), ARM 3-0260, Matrix & Take- B-24192-3 (acoustic)

Date- 5 April 1923, Company- Victor 815, VIC-1534, ARM 3-0260, Matrix & Take- B-24192-5 (acoustic)

Waltz in A-flat Major Op.64, No.3

Date- 19 April 1919, Company- Edison 82202 (released on RCA's ARM 3-0260), Matrix & Take- 6736-A,B,C, (three takes used; acoustic)

Date- 5 April 1927, Company- Victor 1245, 1315 (HMV DA-894), VIC-1534, ARM 3-0294, Matrix & Take- BVE-37455-6

Waltz in C-sharp Minor Op.64, No.2

Date- 5 April 1927, Company- Victor 1245, 1316, VIC-1534, ARM 3-0294, Matrix & Take- BVE-24645-5

Waltz in G-flat Major Op.70, No.1

> Date- 21 January 1921, Company- Victor (originally unpublished), VIC-1534, ARM 3-0260, Matrix- B-24904 (acoustic)

Waltz in B Minor Op.69, No.2

> Date- 3 May 1920, Company- Victor 972 & 66202 (HMV DA-593), VIC-1534, ARM-3-0260, Matrix & Take- B-23962-2 (acoustic)

Waltz in E Minor (Op. Posth.)

> Date- 18 February 1930, Company- Victor 1492 (HMV DA-1189), VIC-1534, ARM-3-0294, Matrix & Take- BVE-59415-3

Liszt Transcriptions

Maiden's Wish (Życzenie from Polish Songs Op.74)

> Date- 1 November 1922, Company- Victor (unpublished), Matrix- C-27108 (acoustic)

> Date- c.1923, Company- Ampico 62803 (piano roll), Everest SDBR-3377

> Date- 27 February 1942, Company- Victor 11-8593, ARM 3-0294, Matrix & Take- PCS-072136-3

Return Home (Narzeczony from Polish Songs Op.74)

> Date- 27 February 1942, Company- Victor 11-8593, ARM 3-0294, Matrix & Take- PCS-072137

Daquin, Louis Claude

> *Le coucou (from Pièces pour le clavecin)*

Date- 21 October 1920, Company- Victor 812 & 64919 (HMV DA-368), ARM 3-0260, Matrix & Take- B-24635-2 (acoustic)

Debussy, Claude

Children's Corner Suite (Dr. Gradus ad Parnassum)

Date- 21 January 1921, Company- Victor 813 & 64935 (HMV DA-369), ARM 3-0260, Matrix & Take- B-24906-1

——————— (Serenade for the Doll)

Date- 21 January 1921, Company- Victor (originally unpublished), ARM 3-0260, Matrix- B-24902 (acoustic)

——————— (Golliwog's Cake-walk)

Date- 2 April 1921, Company- Victor 813 & 64980 (HMV DA-369), ARM 3-0260, Matrix & Take- B-24193-8 (acoustic)

Dohnányi, Ernst von

Etude-caprice in F Minor Op.28

Date- 25 October 1921, Company- Victor 943 & 66059, ARM 3-0260, Matrix & Take- B-25652-6 (acoustic)

Gluck, Christoph Willibald

Sgambati Transcription

Melody in D Minor from the ballet of the blessed spirits, Orfeo ed Euridice

Date- c.1924, Company- Ampico 64921 (piano roll)

Date- 30 December 1924, Company- Victor
(unpublished), Matrix B-31558
(acoustic)

Date- 14 May 1925, Company- Victor 1124
(HMV DA-719), ARM 3-0294, Matrix
& Take- BVE-31558-4

Grieg, Edvard
Lyric Pieces (Valse Op.12, No.2)

Date- 26 April 1920, Company- Victor
(unpublished), Matrix- B-23956
(acoustic)

Date- 12 October 1921, Company- Victor
815 & 66105 (HMV DA-317), ARM 3-
0260, Matrix & Take- B-23963-4

────── *(Elfentanz [Dance of the Elves]
Op.12, No.4)*

Date- 26 April 1920, Company- Victor
(unpublished), Matrix- B-23956
(acoustic)

Date- 12 October 1921, Company- Victor
815 & 66105 (HMV DA-317), ARM 3-
0260, Matrix & Take- B-23963-4

Sonata for Violin and Piano in C Minor Op.45
(with Fritz Kreisler)

Date- 22 March 1928, Company- Victor
8112-14 & M-45 (HMV DB-1259-61),
LM-6099, ARM 3-0295; Matrix & Take-
(six sides) CL-4511-5, 4512-5,
4513-5, 4514-5, 4515-6, 4516-5;
Melodiya D05104/5

Handel, George Frideric
*Air and Variations in E Major (Harmonious
Blacksmith), from Suite No.5 in E Major*

Rachmaninoff Discography

>   Date- 3 January 1936, Company- Victor
>   (HMV DB-3146), ARM 3-0261, Matrix
>   & Take- CVE-98393-3

Henselt, Adolf

>   *Etude, "Si oiseau j'étais"* [Were I a bird]
>   *Op.2, No.6*
>
>   >   Date- c.1923, Company- Ampico 62971
>   >   (piano roll)
>   >
>   >   Date- 27 December 1923, Company- Victor
>   >   1008 & 66249 (HMV DA-613), ARM 3-
>   >   0260, Matrix & Take- B-28691-5
>   >   (acoustic)

Kreisler, Fritz

>   Rachmaninoff Transcriptions
>
>   *Liebesfreud*
>
>   >   Date- c.1925, Company- Ampico 66143
>   >   (piano roll)
>   >
>   >   Date- 29 December 1925, Company- Victor
>   >   1142, 1135, 1136 (HMV DA-786),
>   >   ARM 3-0261, Matrix & Take- (two
>   >   sides) BVE-34154-3, 34155-3
>   >
>   >   Date- 26 December 1942, Company- Victor
>   >   11-8728, LCT-1136, ARM 3-0294,
>   >   Matrix & Take- PCS-072133-1
>
>   *Liebesleid*
>
>   >   Date- c.1923, Company- Ampico 62103
>   >   (piano roll)
>   >
>   >   Date- 25 October 1921, Company- Victor
>   >   6259 & 74723 (HMV DB-408), ARM 3-
>   >   0260, Matrix & Take- C-25653-5
>   >   (acoustic)

Liszt, Franz

Au bord d'une source (from Première années pèlerinage)

> Date- 21 October 1920, Company- Victor (unpublished), Matrix- B-24649 (acoustic)

Hungarian Rhapsody No.2 in C-sharp Minor (with cadenza by Rachmaninoff)

> Date- 22 April 1919, Company- Edison 82169-70 (released on RCA's ARM 3-0260), Matrix & Take- (three sides) 6739-41 A,B,C, (acoustic)

Liebestraum No.3 in A-flat Major

> Date- 18 March 1924, Company- Victor (unpublished), Matrix- C-2967 (acoustic)

Polonaise No.2 in E Major

> Date- 13 April 1925, Company- Victor 6504, 6818, 6819, ARM 3-0294, Matrix & Take- (two sides) CVE-32508-2, 32509-2

Spanish Rhapsody (Rapsodie espagnole)

> Date- 27 December 1923, Company- Victor (unpublished), Matrix- B-29224 (acoustic)

La Campanella (from Grandes études de Paganini)

> Date- 3 May 1920, Company- Victor (unpublished), Matrix- C-23986 (acoustic)

Gnomenreigen

> Date- 16 December 1925, Company- Victor 1184 (HMV DA-827), ARM 3-0294, Matrix & Take- BVE-34146-3

Mendelssohn, Felix

Etude in F Major Op.104, No.2

Date- 5 April 1927, Company- Victor 1266, ARM 3-0294, Matrix & Take- BVE-37453-4

Etude in A Minor Op.104, No.3

Date- 5 April 1927, Company- Victor 1266, ARM 3-0294, Matrix & Take- BVE-37454-4

Rondo Capriccioso Op.14

Date- 17 May 1920, Company- Victor (unpublished), Matrix- B-24117 (acoustic)

Spinning Song (Song Without Words Op.67, No.4)

Date- 4 November 1920, Company- Victor 814 & 64921 (HMV DA-370), ARM 3-0260, Matrix & Take- B-24646-2 (acoustic)

Date- c.1921, Company- Ampico 59661 (piano roll)

Date- 25 April 1928, Company- Victor 1326, LCT-1136, ARM 3-0294, Matrix & Take- BVE-24646-21

Rachmaninoff Transcription

Scherzo from Midsummer Night's Dream

Date- 8 January 1935, Company- Victor (HMV DB-3146), ARM 3-0261, Matrix & Take- CS-87283-4

Moskowskiĭ, Moritz

The Juggler (jongleurin) Op.52, No.4

Date- 6 March 1923, Company- Victor 943 & 66154, ARM 3-0260, Matrix & Take- B-27109-7

Mozart, Wolfgang Amadeus
   Sonata in A Major KV 331 *("Rondo alla Turca")*

   Date- 18 April 1919, Company- Edison 82197, Matrix & Take- 6732-A,B,C, (acoustic)

   Date- 14 May 1925, Company- Victor 1124, ARM 3-0261, Matrix & Take- BVE- 24638-6

   ─────── *("Variations in A Major"; first movement)*

   Date- 25 February 1942, Company- Victor (originally unpublished), ARM 3-0260, Matrix- PCS-072124

Mussorgsky, Modest Petrovich
   Rachmaninoff Transcription
   Hopak (from Sorochinskaĩa ĩarmarka [Sorochintzi Fair])

   Date- c.1922, Company- Ampico 60641 (piano roll)

   Date- 13 April 1925, Company- Victor 1161, ARM 3-0261, Matrix & Take- BVE- 25108-10

Paderewski, Ignace Jan
   Minuet in G Major Op.14, No.1

   Date- c. 1926, Company- Ampico 68283 (piano roll)

Date- 5 April 1927, **Company**- Victor 6731, ARM 3-0294, **Matrix & Take**- CVE-24651-5

Rachmaninoff, Sergei Vasil'evich

Concerto No.2 in C Minor Op.18 (First movement) (with Leopold Stokowski and the Philadelphia Orchestra)

Date- 22 December 1924, **Company**- Victor (originally unpublished), ARM 3-0260, **Matrix**- (three sides) C-31395-97 (acoustic)

———— *(Second and Third movements)*

Date- 3 January 1924, **Company**- Victor 8064-66 (HMV DB-747-49), ARM 3-0260, **Matrix & Take**- (six sides) C-29233-4, 29234-3, 29235-4, 29236-3, 29251-2, 29252-2 (acoustic)

———— *(Complete concerto)*

Date- 10 & 13 April 1929, (five sides recorded at each session), **Company**- Victor 8148-52 & M-58 (HMV DB-1333-37), LCT-1014, LM-6123, ARM 3-0296, **Matrix & Take**- (ten sides) CVE 48963-3, 48964-1 48965-1, 48966-1, 48967-3, 48068-2, 48969-1, 48970-2, 48971-2, 48972-1

Rhapsody on a Theme of Paganini Op.43 (with Leopold Stokowski and the Philadelphia Orchestra)

Date- 24 December 1934, **Company**- Victor 8553-55 & M-250 (HMV DB-2426-28), LM-6123, ARM 3-0296, **Matrix & Take**- (six sides) CS-87066-1, 87067-1, 87068-1, 87069-1, 87070-1, 87071-1

Concerto No.3 in D Minor Op.30 (with Eugene Ormandy and the Philadelphia Orchestra)

> Date- 4 December 1939 (sides 1-5,7,9),
> 24 February 1940 (sides 6,8),
> Company- Victor 17481-85 & M-710
> (HMV DB-5709-13), LM-6123, ARM 3-
> 0296, Matrix & Take- (nine sides)
> CS-045627-1, 045628-1, 045629-1,
> 04630-1, 045631-1, 045632-2,
> 045633-1, 045634-2, 045635-1

Concerto No.1 in F-sharp Minor Op.1 (with Eugene Ormandy and the Philadelphia Orchestra)

> Date- 4 December 1939 (sides 1,3,4),
> 24 February 1940 (sides 2,5,6,),
> Company- Victor 18374-76 & M-865
> (HMV DB-5706-08), LM-6134, ARM 3-
> 0296, Matrix & Take- (six sides)
> CS-045621-2, 045622-3, 045623-2,
> 045624-1, 045625-3, 045636-3

Concerto No.4 in G Minor Op.40 (with Eugene Ormandy and the Philadelphia Orchestra)

> Date- 20 December 1941, Company- Victor
> 11-8611-14 & M-972 (HMV DB-6284-
> 87), LCT-1019, LM-6123, ARM 3-
> 0296, Matrix & Take- (eight sides)
> CS-071277-2, 071278-2, 071279-1,
> 071280-1, 071281-1, 071282-1,
> 071283-1, 071284-1

Barcarolle in G Major Op.10, No.3

> Date- 23 April 1919, Company- Edison
> 82202 (released on RCA's ARM 3-
> 0260), Matrix & Take- 6743-A,B,C
> (acoustic)

> Date- c.1919, Company- Ampico 57604
> (piano roll) Everest SDBR-3377

Daisies (piano arrangement by Rachmaninoff of *Op.38, No.3*)

> Date- 18 March 1940, Company- Victor
> 2127 & M-722 (HMV DA-1789), LCT-
> 1136, ARM 3-0261, Matrix & Take-
> BS-048184-2

Elégie Op.3 No.1

> Date- c.1927, Company- Ampico 69253 (piano roll) Decca DSLO-34, Everest SDBR-3377

Etude-tableau in C Major Op.33, No.2

> Date- 18 March 1940, Company- Victor 2126 & M-722 (HMV DA-1788), LCT-1136, ARM 3-0261, Matrix & Take- BS-048182-2

Etude-tableau in E-flat Major Op.33, No.7

> Date- 18 March 1940, Company- Victor 2126 & M-722 (HMV DA-1788), LCT-1136, ARM 3-0261, Matrix & Take- BS-048183-2

Etude-tableau in G Major Op.33, No.8

> Date- 21 October 1920, Company- Victor (unpublished), Matrix B-24650 (acoustic)

Etude-tableau in A Minor Op.39, No.6

> Date- c.1922, Company- Ampico 60891 (piano roll) Decca DSLO-34

> Date- 16 December 1925, Company- Victor 1184 (HMV DA-827), LCT 1000, ARM 3-0261, Matrix & Take- BVE-34156-1

Humoresque in G Major Op.10, No.5

> Date- c.1920, Company- Ampico 57965 (piano roll) Decca DSLO-34

> ———————— (revised version)

> Date- 9 April 1940, Company- Victor 2123 & M-722 (HMV DA-1771), LCT-1136, ARM 3-0261, Matrix & Take- BS-048175-2

Lilacs (Op.21, No.5, revised and transcribed by Rachmaninoff*)*

    <u>Date</u>- c.1922, <u>Company</u>- Ampico 61761 (piano roll) Decca DSLO-34

    <u>Date</u>- 27 December 1923, <u>Company</u>- Victor 1951 & 64906 (HMV <u>DA-666</u>), ARM 3-0260, <u>Matrix & Take</u>- B-24123-9 (acoustic)

    <u>Date</u>- 26 February 1942, <u>Company</u>- Victor (originally unpublished), ARM 3-0261, <u>Matrix</u>- PCS-072132

Melody in E Major Op.3, No.3

    <u>Date</u>- c.1920, <u>Company</u>- Ampico 57545 (piano roll) Decca DSL0-34; Everest SDBR-3377

    ———— (revised version)

    <u>Date</u>- 9 April 1940, <u>Company</u>- Victor 2123 & M-722 (HMV <u>DA-1787</u>), LCT-1136, ARM 3-0261, <u>Matrix & Take</u>- BS-048174-4

Moment musicale in E-flat Minor Op.16, No.2 (revised version)

    <u>Date</u>- 18 March 1940, <u>Company</u>- Victor 2124 & M-722 (HMV <u>DA-1771</u>), LCT 1136, ARM 3-0261, <u>Matrix & Take</u>- BS-048176-1

Oriental Sketch in B-flat Major

    <u>Date</u>- 18 March 1940, <u>Company</u>- Victor 2127 & M-722 (HMV <u>DA-1789</u>), LCT-1136, ARM 3-0261, <u>Matrix & Take</u>- BS-048185-2

Polichinelle in F-sharp Minor Op.3, No.4

    <u>Date</u>- c.1920, <u>Company</u>- Ampico 57905 (piano roll) Decca DSLO-34; Everest SDBR-3377

Rachmaninoff Discography 111

>Date- 6 March 1923, Company- Victor 6452 & 74807, ARM 3-0260, Matrix & Take- C-24643-2 (acoustic)

Polka de W.R.

>Date- c.1919, Company- Ampico 57275 (piano roll) Everest SDBR-3377

>Date- 23 April 1919, Company- Edison 82187 (released on RCA's ARM 3-0260), Matrix & Take- 6744-A,B,C, (acoustic)

>Date- 12 October 1921, Company- Victor 6260 & 74728 (HMV DB-409), ARM 3-0260, Matrix & Take- C-25651-2

>Date- 4 April 1928, Company- Victor 6857 (HMV DB-1279), LCT-1136, ARM 3-0261, Matrix & Take- CVE-25651-6

Polka italienne (piano duet, with wife Natalia, recorded privately on a home recorder)

>Date- c.1938, (released on RCA's ARM 3-0261)

Prelude in C-sharp Minor Op.3, No.2

>Date- 23 April 1919, Company- Edison 82187 (released on RCA's ARM 3-0260), Matrix & Take-6742-A,B,C (acoustic)

>Date- c.1920, Company- Ampico 57504 (piano roll) Decca DSLO-34; Everest SDBR-3377

>Date- 14 October 1921, Company- Victor 814 & 66016 (HMV DA-370), ARM 3-0260, Matrix & Take- B-25650-3 (acoustic)

>Date- 4 April 1928, Company- Victor 1326 (HMV DA-996), LCT-1136, ARM 3-0261, Matrix & Take- BVE-25650-23

Prelude in G Minor Op.23, No.5

> Date- c.1920, Company- Ampico 57525 (piano roll) Decca DSLO-34; Everest SDBR-3377
>
> Date- 17 May 1920, Company- Victor 6261 & 74628 (HMV DB-410), ARM 3-0260, Matrix & Take- C-23984-4

Prelude in G-flat Major Op.23, No.10

> Date- 18 March 1940, Company- Victor 2124 & M-722 (HMV DA-1772), LCT-1136, ARM 3-0261, Matrix & Take- BS-048177-1

Prelude in E Major Op.32, No.3

> Date- 18 March 1940, Company- Victor 2125 & M-722 (HMV DA-1772), LCT-1136, ARM 3-0261, Matrix & Take- BS-048178-1

Prelude in G Major Op.32, No.5

> Date- 3 May 1920, Company- Victor 6261 & 74695 (HMV DB-410), ARM 3-0260, Matrix & Take- C-23985-1 (acoustic)

Prelude in F Minor Op.32 No.6

> Date- 18 March 1940, Company- Victor 2125 & M-722 (HMV DA-1787), LCT-1136, ARM 3-0261, Matrix & Take- BS-048179-2

Prelude in F Major Op.32, No.7

> Date- 18 March 1940, Company- Victor 2125 & M-722 (HMV DA-1787), LCT-1136, ARM 3-0261, Matrix & Take- BS-047179-2

Prelude in G-sharp Minor Op.32, No.12

> Date- 21 January 1921, Company- Victor 812 & 64963 (HMV DA-368), ARM 3-0260, Matrix & Take B-24642-5

Powder and Paint (Belilitsy rumenitsy vy moĭ, Russian folk-song arranged by Rachmaninoff; with soprano Nadezhda Plevitskaia*)*

Date- 1926, MJA-19662, (released on RCA's ARM 3-0261); Melodiya D031033/4

Serenade in B-flat Major Op.3, No.5

Date- 4 November 1922, Company- Victor 816 & 66129 (HMV DA-372), ARM 3-0260, Matrix & Take- B-27110-5 (acoustic)

Date- c.1923, Company- Ampico 62441 (piano roll) Decca DSLO-34

Date- 2 January 1936, Company- Victor 1762 (HMV DA-1522), ARM 3-0261, Matrix & Take- BS-98396-3

Isle of the Dead Op.29 (Rachmaninoff conducting the Philadelphia Orchestra)

Date- 20 April 1929, Company- Victor 7219-21 & M-75 (HMV D-2011-13), ARM 3-0295, Matrix & Take- (five sides) CVE-48973-5, 48974-4, 48975-4, 48976-5, 48977-4

Symphony No.3 in A Minor Op.44 (Rachmaninoff conducting the Philadelphia Orchestra)

Date- 11 December 1939, Company- Victor 17426-30 & M-712 (HMV DB-5780-84), ARM 3-0295, Matrix & Take- (nine sides) CS-045636-2, 045637-1, 045638-2, 045639-1, 045640-2, 045641-1, 045642-1, 045643-1, 045644-1

Vocalise Op.34, No.14 (Rachmaninoff conducting the Philadelphia Orchestra)

Date- 21 April 1929, Company- Victor 7721, 17430 & M-75, M-712 (HMV D-2013), ARM 3-0295

Rimsky-Korsakov, Nikolaĭ Andreevich
> Rachmaninoff Transcription
>
> *Flight of the Bumble-Bee (from T͡sar Sultan)*
>> Date- c.1928, Company- Ampico 70301 (piano roll)
>>
>> Date- 16 April 1929, Company- Victor (originally unpublished), ARM 3-0261, Matrix- BVE-51805

Rubinstein, Anton Grigor'evich
> *Barcarolle in A Minor Op.45*
>> Date- c.1927, Company- Ampico 69893 (piano roll)

Saint-Saëns, Camille
> Ziloti Arrangement
>
> *Le cygne* [*The Swan*]
>> Date- 30 December 1924, Company- Victor (originally unpublished), ARM 3-0260, Matrix- B-31557 (acoustic)

Scarlatti, Domenico
> Tausig Arrangement
>
> *Sonata in D Minor (Pastorale)* L.413 (K9)
>> Date- 19 April 1919, Company- Edison 82170 (released on RCA's ARM 3-0260), Matrix & Take- 6735-A,B,C (acoustic)

Schubert, Franz
> *Impromptu in A-flat Major Op.90, No.4* D 899

Date- 29 December 1925, Company- Victor
6621 (HMV DB-1016), ARM 3-0294,
Matrix & Take- CVE-341445-5

Date- c.1927, Company- Ampico 69373
(piano roll)

*Sonata for Violin and Piano in A Major
"Duo"* D 574 (with Fritz Kreisler)

Date- 20 December 1928 (sides 2,3,5,),
21 December 1928 (sides 1,4,6),
Company- Victor 8216-18 & M-107
(HMV DB-1465-67), ARM 3-0295;
Matrix & Take- (six sides) CVE-
49280-5, 49281-5, 49282-2, 49283-4,
49284-3, 49285-4; Melodiya D05104/5

Liszt Transcriptions

Serenade (Ständchen D 957*)*

Date- 27 February 1942, Company- Victor
11-8728, LCT-1136, ARM 3-0294,
Matrix & Take- PCS-072138-1

Wandering (Das Wandern D 795*)*

Date- c.1924, Company- Ampico 64561
(piano roll)

Date- 14 April 1925, Company- Victor
1161, ARM 3-0294, Matrix & Take-
BVE-31564-4

Rachmaninoff Transcription

Brooklet (Wohin? from *Die schöne Müllerin*
D 795*)*

Date- c.1925, Company- Ampico 65771
(piano roll)

Date- 29 December 1925, Company- Victor
1196 (HMV DA-939), ARM 3-0261,
Matrix & Take- BVE-34145-7

Schumann, Robert

    Carnival Op.9

        Date- 9 April 1929 (sides 2,4), 10 April 1929 (sides 3,5,6), 12 April 1929 (side 1), Company- Victor 7184-86 & M-75 (HMV DB-1413-15), CAL-396, ARM 3-0294, Matrix & Take- (six sides) CVE-51089-7, 51090-2, 51091-3, 51092-3, 51093-3, 51094-3

    Novelette in F-sharp Minor Op.21, No.8

        Date- 25 February 1942, Company- Victor (unpublished), Matrix- (two sides) PCS-072125, 072126

    Tausig Transcription

    Der Kontrabandiste Op.74, No.9

        Date- 20 November 1922, Company- Victor (unpublished), Matrix- B-27119 (acoustic)

        Date- 27 February 1942, Company- Victor 11-8593, ARM 3-0294, Matrix & Take- PVS-072137-1

Scriabin, Aleksandr Nikolaevich

    Prélude in F-sharp Minor Op.11, No.8

        Date- 16 April 1929, Company- Victor (originally unpublished), ARM 3-0261, Matrix BVE-51806

Smith, John S.

    Rachmaninoff Arrangement

    Star-Spangled Banner

        Date- c.1919, Company- Ampico 57282 (piano roll)

Rachmaninoff Discography 117

Strauss, Johann

    Schulz-Evler Transcription

    Blue Danube Waltz (An der schönen blauen Donau Op.314)

        Date- 5 April 1923, Company- Victor (unpublished), Matrix- C-27732 (acoustic)

    Tausig Transcription

    "Man lebt nur einmal" [*One lives but once*] *(Valse Caprice No.2)*

        Date- 5 April 1927, Company- Victor 6636 (HMV DB-1140), ARM 3-0294, Matrix & Take- (two sides) CVE-37466-1 37467-3

Tchaikovsky, Peter Ilich

    Humoresque in G Major Op.10, No.2

        Date- 27 December 1923, Company- Victor 1951 (HMV DA-666), ARM 3-0260, Matrix & Take- B-28690-4 (acoustic)

    Troika Op.37, No.11 (from Les saisons)

        Date- c.1920, Company- Ampico 57914 (piano roll)

        Date- 3 May 1920, Company- Victor 6260 & 74630 (HMV DB-409), ARM 3-0260, Matrix & Take- C-23983-1 (acoustic)

        Date- 11 April 1928, Company- Victor 6857 (HMV DB-1279), ARM 3-0261, Matrix & Take- CVE-23983-8

    Waltz in A-flat Major Op.40, No.8 (from Douze morceaux)

        Date- c.1923, Company- Ampico 62531 (piano roll)

Date- 20 November 1922, Company- Victor 972 & 66138 (HMV DA-593), ARM 3-0260, Matrix & Take- B-27117-2 (acoustic)

Rachmaninoff Transcription

Lullaby in A-flat Minor Op.16, No.1 (song *Kolibel'naĩa pesnĩa*)

Date- 26 February 1942, Company- Victor (originally unpublished), ARM 3-0261, Matrix- PCS-072131

Weber, Carl Maria von

Momento Capriccioso Op.12

Date- 21 October 1920, Company- Victor (unpublished), Matrix- C-24637 (acoustic)

IV

RACHMANINOFF BIBLIOGRAPHY

1. Abraham, Gerald. "Reviews of Books."
   Music and Letters 15 (July 1934): 273-274.

   A review by Abraham of the disputable pioneer biography of Rachmaninoff by Oskar von Rieseman (1934). A review appeared shortly after the book's publication; it lists passages and details that were prepared carelessly and also points out the book's strengths.

2. Albin, M. "Rakhmaninovski tsykl." [Rachmaninoff's cycle] *Sovetskaia muzyka* 4 (1966): 79-80.

   A review of concerts featuring Rachmaninoff's music, performed by the Gosudarstvennyĭ Simfonicheskyĭ Orkestr SSSR [State Symphony Orchestra of USS], directed by E. Svetlanov, in which the *Simfoniia No.1* [*Symphony No.1*], *Ostrov Mertvykh* [*Isle of the Dead*], *Tri russkie pesni* [Three Russian Songs], as well as other works, were performed. The subject of the difficulty of performing Rachmaninoff's orchestral works is discussed.

3. Aldanov, M. "S.V. Rakhmaninov." *New Review (Novyĭ zhurnal)* 5 (1943): 353-56.

Eulogistic article which describes Rachmaninoff's life as a happy one, both in his private and professional paths. The author met the composer in France and although they were not close friends, Aldanov greatly admired Rachmaninoff. Aldanov describes the composer as humble, sensitive, noble, and having inner warmth.

4. Aldrich, Richard. *Concert Life in New York, 1902-1923.* New York: Putman's Sons, 1941. 795 p. (SR p.584-86); (Reprint-- Freeport N.Y.: Books for Libraries Press, 1971. ML 200.8 N5 A6   OCLC 863225)

A series of concert criticisms written by Richard Aldrich of *The New York Times*. Interesting review of Rachmaninoff's 21 December 1918 recital in Carnegie Hall in which he played the first movement of the Mozart *Sonata in A Major* KV 331, mistakenly mentioned here as Mozart's Variations in D Major. Rachmaninoff frequently programmed the first movement of K 331 under the simple title "Variations by Mozart." Also on the program was the Beethoven *Sonata Op.10, No.3*, a group of Chopin pieces, and the Liszt *Hungarian Rhapsody No.12*. This is one recital where Rachmaninoff did not perform his ubiquitous *Prelude in C-sharp Minor Op.3, No.2*. Aldrich reveals the excitement of the event and comments on the tempi and interpretation of Rachmaninoff's Beethoven. Name index.

5. Alekseev, Aleksandr Dmitrievich. *S.V. Rakhmaninov. Zhizn' i tvorcheskaia deíatel'nost'.* [S.V. Rachmaninoff. His life and creative works] Moskva: Izd-vo Akademii Nauk SSSR, Institut Istorii Iskusstv, Gos. Muzykal'noe, 1954, 240 p. ML 410 R12 A65

A general survey of the composer's life and creative productivity. The author covers Rachmaninoff's conservatory years and compositions written during that time, Rachmaninoff the performer, works written in the years 1906-1917, and the years abroad. In the chapter dealing with the influence of the First Revolution (1905), there is an attempt to interpret Rachmaninoff's works in light of revolutionary activities of that time, remarking that his works reflect the impending national upheaval. All sorts of insurgent interpretations are read into the *Vtoroĭ Kontsert* [Second Concerto]. List of works, bibliography, musical examples, illustrations, no index.

6. ———, ed. Akademiĭa Nauk SSSR. Institut Istoriĭ Iskusstv. *Istoriĭa russkoĭ sovetskoĭ muzyki.* [History of Soviet Russian music] Moskva: Muzgiz, 1956-1963. 4 vols.
ML 300.5 A4   OCLC 5876730

This history of Soviet Russian music is typical of the literature and texts of the time; it is a politically-dictated interpretation of the history of Russian music. The principal intent of this large work is to trace the struggle between realistic (traditional) music and modernistic trends. Attention is concentrated on analyzing those works which preserve the old Russian artistic values. There are many references to Rachmaninoff and his works. Illustrated, musical examples, name index.

7. ———. *Russkaĭa fortepĭannaĭa muzyka. Konets XIX-nachalo XX Veka.* [Russian piano music from the end of the 19th century to the beginning of the 20th century] Moskva: "Nauka," 1969.   391 p. (SR p.106-85)
ML 734 A37   OCLC 3531726

Deals with the development of Russian piano music from the end of the 19th century to 1917. The work is a continuation of a monograph by the author covering early (up to the 19th century) Russian piano music, titled *Russkaia fortepiannaia muzyka ot istokov do vershin tvorchestva*, published by the Akademiia Nauk SSSR [USSR Academy of Science], Moscow 1963. Alekseev places Rachmaninoff, along with Taneev and Arenskiĭ, as a member of the Moscow Composers Circle, in contrast to the St. Petersburg group of composers. Alekseev sets forth a fine survey of Rachmaninoff's piano works, including the later compositions- *Kontsert dlia f-no s orkestrom No.4* [Concerto for Piano and Orchestra No.4] and the *Rapsodiia na temu Paganini* [Rhapsody on a Theme of Paganini]. Illustrated, musical examples, bibliography, no index.

8. Alekseeva, Ekaterina Nikolaevna. "Fond No.18." [Collection No.18] *Sovetskaia muzyka* 4 (1973): 103-05.

   A description of materials in the Rachmaninoff Archive housed in the Gosudarstvennyĭ Tsentral'nyĭ Muzeĭ Muzykal'noĭ Kul'tury Imeni M.I. Glinki [State Central Glinka Museum of Musical Culture] in Moscow. It contains diverse material: scores, drafts, microfilms, programs, reviews, memoirs, photographs, portraits, and related literature. Shortly after the composer's death, Rachmaninoff's wife Natalia sent a number of documents to the museum. Alekseeva reveals that the composer's widow became quite ill after her husband's death and she and her daughters asked Sof'ia Aleksandrovna Satina (Natalia's sister, and Sergei's cousin and sister-in-law) to help put the future archive in order, supposedly to send to Russia; but because of circumstances (the cold war?) the material was instead given to the Library of Congress. Consequently, but fittingly, we have two existing major Rachmaninoff archives: one in his beloved homeland and one in his revered adopted country. See Edward Waters' article "Music" in *U.S. Library of Congress Quarterly Journal of Current Acquistions* 9 (November 1951): 39-42, concerning Mrs. Rachmaninoff's desire to place the material in the Library of Congress on the grounds that it was free of political and commercial interests.

9. Apetiān, Zarui, ed. and comp. *Rakhmaninov: Pis'ma* [Rachmaninoff: letters] Moskva: Muzykal'noe Izd-vo, 1955. 603 p.
ML 410 R12 A42   OCLC 4934984

This collection of Rachmaninoff letters is a result of investigating several archives in a number of state museums, collections, and private holdings. Having first appeared in various USSR journals, the publication of the collected letters initially began in 1944. This volume contains 565 letters, many appearing for the first time. At the conclusion of each letter there is explanatory material on the circumstances for the origin of the letter as well as other pertinent information. Letters cover the span of 1890 to 1943. This volume has been superseded by Apetiān's three volume *S. Rakhmaninov: literaturnoe nasledie* (1978-80), which now is the definitive edition of collected letters. *Rakhmaninov: Pis'ma* (1955) contains musical examples, list of works (through Op.39), list of letters, and name indexes.

10. ———. "Ostorozhno: poshlosti!" [Be careful: Banalities!] *Sovetskaia muzyka* 5 (1964): 138-40.

A critical response by Apetiān to the articles on Rachmaninoff written by Leonid Borisov, member of the Soiuz Pisatelei SSSR [Union of Soviet Writers], appearing in *Zveda* in 1962 and 1963. The articles reported erroneous dates and information about the composer and his works. Apetian fails to understand why the editors of *Zveda* did not notice these obvious errors prior to publication. Unfortunately this publication received wide distribution in the USSR. See Leonid Borisov's *Shchedryĭ rytsar - T͡svety i slezy*. Leningrad: "Det͡skai͡a Kniga," 1964.

11. ———, ed. "Tri interv'i͡u." [Three interviews] *Sovet͡skai͡a muzyka* 4 (1973): 94-103.

Russian translations of three interviews that first appeared in the *Musical Observer* and *Etude*. Interviews are published here in abbreviated form. "Govorit Sergeĭ Rakhmaninov" is an interview by Frederick Martens appearing in the *Musical Observer* 20 (April 1921), titled "Sergei Rachmaninoff Talks of Russia and America." The second interview presented here, "Interpretat͡sii͡a zavisit ot talanta i individualnosti" is an interview by Florence Leonard originally appearing in the *Etude* (April 1932), titled "Interpretation Depends on Talent and Personality." "Muzyka dolzhna idti ot serdt͡sa" is an interview originally appearing in the *Etude* (December 1941), titled "Music Should Speak From the Heart." There is an interesting introduction to these articles, which includes a remark from Medtner concerning Rachmaninoff's piano performance and an explanation of Rachmaninoff's aversion to interviews.

12. ———, ed. and comp. *Vospominanii͡a o Rakhmaninove*. [Reminiscences of Rachmaninoff] 4th ed. Moskva: Muzyka, 1974. 2 vols. 480 p., 575 p. ML 410 R12 M6 OCLC 4722054

The two volumes of reminiscences of Rachmaninoff depict the life and creative activities of the musician, composer, pianist, and conductor. They also reveal his relations with outstanding representatives of Russian culture from the end of the 19th century to the first half of the 20th century. This is the fourth edition of *Vospominaniia o Rakhmaninove;* it was first published in 1957 by Muzyka and through several subsequent editions has grown by inclusion of new material not published in the USSR before; articles by Sergei L. Bertensson, Mstislav Valerianovich Dobuzhinskiĭ, Mikhail Aleksandrovich Chekov, and the composer's wife Nataliā Aleksandrovna Rakhmaninova. There are many other reminiscences written by diverse friends and colleagues such as Boris Vladimirovich Asaf'ev, Aleksandr Borisovich Gol'denveizer, Antonina Vasil'evna Nezhdanova, Matvei Leont'evich Presman, Sof'iā Aleksandrovna Satina, Marietta Sergeevna Shaginian, Vera Dmitrievna Skalon, Alfred Swan, and Anna Andreevna Trubnikova. Authors of articles include detailed explanatory information. General comments by the editor are presented at the conclusion of each volume. A valuable collection of recollections. Musical examples, illustrations, list of works (through Op.39), and name index.

13.   ———, ed. and comp. *S. Rakhmaninov: literaturnoe nasledie.* [S. Rachmaninoff: literary heritage] 3 vols., Vol.1 *Vospominaniiā, stat'i, interv'iū, pis'ma.* [Reminiscences, articles, interviews, letters] 647 p.; Vol.2 *Pis'ma* 583 p.; Vol.3 *Pis'ma* 573 p. Moskva: Sovetskii Kompozitor, vol.1 1978, vol.2 1980, vol.3 1980.   ML 410 R12 R33   OCLC 5344768

This new edition of the Rachmaninoff letters supersedes the previous edition of 1955 (*Rakhmaninov: Pis'ma*) also edited by Zarui Apetian. Apetian spent some time culling letters and diverse materials housed in the Rachmaninoff Archive in the Library of

Congress. This new edition brings together
the collections of letters contained in
several museums, archives, and libraries in
the USSR, with the letters found in the
Rachmaninoff Archive of the Library of
Congress. Apetīan also includes segments
of several articles from British and USA
magazines and journals; there are seven
articles from *Etude* magazine alone. A total
of 1296 letters are represented in three
volumes; first letter dated 1 September 1890,
to Natalīa Dmitrievna Skalon, and the last
letter dated in February 1943. The three
volumes contain many recollections, articles,
illustrations, lists of Rachmaninoff's
recordings and concert seasons, several
indexes, as well as extensive notes on the
articles and the letters. A valuable collection of Rachmaninoff material.

14.   Aranovskiĭ, Mark Genrikhovich. *Etīudy-
Kartiny Rakhmaninova*. [Rachmaninoff's
Etudes-tableaux] Moskva: Muzgiz, 1963.
40 p.

An essay on the *Etīudy-Kartiny* [Etudes-
tableaux], in two parts. In the first part
Aranovskiĭ comments on the universal popularity of Rachmaninoff's music and views
the influential factors in his artistic
career in Russia. Part two is concerned
with the *Etudes-tableaux Opp. 33* and *39*.
Some of Aranovskiĭ's comments on the Etudes:
they demonstrate Rachmaninoff's best characteristics of piano style, such as virtuosity,
richness of associations, simplicity, melo-
diousness, and variety. Rachmaninoff continued the miniature style of Chopin, Liszt,
Glinka, and Tchaikovsky, though the étude
genre is given a different treatment by
Rachmaninoff. Aranovskiĭ gives a description of each Etude-tableau.

15.   Arnold, Elliot. "The Maestro Announces ... Puts Last Touch on New Opus." *New York World-Telegram* 17 October 1940.

An interview held in the composer's Manhattan apartment. Rachmaninoff announces that he has just completed the *Symphonic Dances* and expects the Philadelphia Orchestra to perform the work for the first time in January. He comments on his daily composing schedule, his pleasure in composing and performing, American orchestras, George Gershwin, and "Senar," his summer home in Switzerland.

16.   Asaf'ev, Boris Vladimirovich [pseud. Igor Glebov]. *Russkai͡a muzyka ot nachala XIX stoletii͡a*. Moskva: Izd-vo Akademiĭ Nauk SSSR, 1930. 322 p. Also in English: *Russian Music from the Beginning of the Nineteenth Century*: translated from the Russian by Alfred J. Swan. Ann Arbor, Mich.: Published for the American Council of Learned Societies by J.W. Edwards, 1953. 329 p. ML 300 A844 OCLC 933640

Historical and critical commentary on Russian composers and their works. Excellent description of Rachmaninoff's style and emotions. Asaf'ev compares Rachmaninoff, Medtner, and Scriabin; finds a common direction in their music.

17.   ———. "Rachmaninoff." *VOKS Bulletin* 5-6 (1943): 55-59.

VOKS is an anagram for Vsesoi͡uznoye Obshchestvo Kul'turnoĭ Svyazi s Zagranit͡seĭ [USSR Society for cultural relations with foreign countries]; bulletins were published in English. This obituary by Asaf'ev vividly summarizes Rachmaninoff's artistic contributions. The author floridly expresses his view of the beauty, nature, and

Russianism in Rachmaninoff's compositions.
He stresses the importance of the influence
of Russia's church bells, streams, poetry,
and landscapes in his works. Asaf'ev affirms
that the *Simfoniiā No.3* [Third Symphony] is
a valuable contribution to the evolution of
Russian national symphonism. He proudly
concludes by stating that Rachmaninoff, during the war years, was concerned and cared
dearly for his motherland. This was made
evident by the concert proceeds and dona-
tions (to the medical fund for the Red Army)
that he often forwarded to the USSR.

18.   ———. *Isbrannye trudy*. [Selected works]
        Moskva: Izd-vo Akademii Nauk SSSR, 1952-
        1957. 5 vols. (SR Vol.2 p.289-302)
        ML 300 A842   OCLC 270419

        Asaf'ev was an important Russian musicolo-
        gist (graduate of the St. Petersburg Conser-
        vatory) and also a composer and pedagogue;
        he received many honors during his lifetime,
        including two Lenin and two Stalin awards.
        This substantial work by Asaf'ev is a series
        of critical essays on the history of Russian
        music. The second volume contains essays on
        Rachmaninoff. The longest and most impor-
        tant essay deals with Rachmaninoff's creative
        life beginning with the *Vtoroĭ Kontsert*
        [Second Concerto] (for which the composer
        received acclaim) up to his departure from
        Russia. Included in the essay is a letter
        by the composer dated 1917, which incorpor-
        ates a list of his works (to Op.39, 1916),
        and gives details such as circumstances of
        composition, dates of first performances,
        date written, etc.. The second essay exam-
        ines the *Tret'iā simfoniiā* [Third Symphony].
        Name index.

19.   ———. "S.V. Rakhmaninov." (k desiātiletiiū
        so dniā smerti kompozitora) [S.V. Rachmani-
        noff: (on the 10th anniversary of his
        death)] *Sovetskaiā muzyka* 3 (1953): 55-65.

Musicologist Asaf'ev offers a recollection
of the composer on the 10th anniversary of
his death. He writes about Rachmaninoff's
mature years, from the *Vtoroĭ Kont͡sert*
[Second Concerto] until his departure from
Russia. Asaf'ev relates his first impressions: the stern figure on stage, sensitive
performances, etc.. He includes a revealing response from Rachmaninoff to a letter
he wrote requesting some information regarding his works. In the letter to Asaf'ev
dated 13 April 1917, Rachmaninoff states
that he performs the *Variat͡siĭ na temu
Shopena* [Variations on a Theme of Chopin]
in abbreviated form, and comments on the
Pervai͡a simfonii͡a [First Symphony] Op.13,
remarking that many good works end in
disaster and very often poor works are admired; the symphony had some good music and some
weak music; it was poorly orchestrated and
poorly directed by Aleksandr Konstantinovich
Glazunov. The composer remarks that after
this tragic performance, the effect it had
on him was similar to a person afflicted
with a stroke, unable to control head and
hands. Asaf'ev valued this letter. The
article goes on to describe Rachmaninoff's
works and style. Asaf'ev hears a strong
Russian influence in the *Tret'i͡a simfonii͡a*
[Third Symphony], which Rachmaninoff wrote
at his Swiss villa, "Senar" in 1935-36.
For other comments on the Russianism of the
Tret'i͡a simfonii͡a see Georgiĭ Khubob's
Muzykal'nai͡a publit͡sistika raznykh let,
Moskva: Sovet͡skiĭ Kompozitor, 1976, and
Konstantin Kuznet͡sov's "Nove o Rakhmaninove,"
in *Literatura i Iskusstvo* 13 (25 March 1944).

20. ———. "Rakhmaninov." *Muzykal'nai͡a zhizn'*
6 (March 1973): 2-3 (edition in honor of
the 100th anniversary of Rachmaninoff's
birth)

This article was originally written in
1943 and is included in vol.2 of Asaf'ev's
Izbrannye trudy (1954). The author highly

praises Rachmaninoff the pianist, composer, and conductor and observes his Russian heritage, his training as a "Moscow School" composer, and his gift of melody.

21. Baca, Richard. "A Style Analysis of the Thirteen Preludes, Op.32, of Sergei Rachmaninoff." Ph.D. diss., Peabody Conservatory of Music, 1975. 133 p.
MT 4 B2 P42

An interesting analysis of the pianistic and compositional style of the *Preludes Op.32*. Broad subjects: Sound (with subdivisions of chordal textures, crossed-hand work, cadenzas, pedal points, etc.), Harmony (contrapuntal writing, chromaticism, etc.), Melody and Form (melodic lines, growth, etc.), and Rhythm (tempi, meters, etc.) are used as the basis of the analysis. The preludes are not analyzed individually, rather they are examined in the context of the above-mentioned catagories; stylistic similarities are noted and a general overview or recurrent styles and techniques is presented. Contains a biographical sketch, musical examples, and a bibliography.

22. Bachauer, Gina. "My Study With Rachmaninoff." *Clavier* 12 (October 1973): 12-14.

Pianist Bachauer tells of her first encounter with Rachmaninoff in 1933, her lessons (or "discussions," as she calls them) with him, his inevitable point (climax) in performing and composing, as well as his interpretive conviction in performance.

23. Baker, Harry Jay. *Biographical Sagas of Will Power*. New York: Vantage Press. 1970. 320 p. (SR p. 138-42)   CT 105 B28
OCLC 1386286

Baker, a psychologist, sets out to prove that many great celebrities had handicaps that were eventually overcome because of sheer will power. These handicaps, or unfavorable conditions, could be: parental rejection, family disorganization, social deprivation, business failures, or physical and sensory problems. The author presents 54 biographical sagas of people in diverse fields from poets to engineers. Rachmaninoff's handicaps, as Baker sees them, are parental indifference and mental depression. Name and subject index.

24. Bakst, James. *A History of Russian-Soviet Music*. New York: Dodd, Mead, and Co., 1966. 406 p. (SR p.251-60) ML 300 B28 OCLC 712036

The author's chapter on Rachmaninoff is divided into sections dealing with heritage and influences, biographical material, compositional style; includes a description of the Second Concerto, the operas, and *The Rock Op.7*. Important for the view of the composer's heritage and his use of imagery as a stimulus for composition. Illustrations, bibliography, and index.

25. Bazhanov, Nikolaĭ Danilovich. *Rakhmaninov*. Moskva: Moldaia͡ Gvardiia͡, 1962. 448 p. ML 410 R12 B44 OCLC 3896794 Also in French: Bajanov, N. *Rachmaninov*. translated from the Russian by Antoinette Mazzi. Moscou: Editions du Progres, 1974. 463 p. ML 410 R12 B44 OCLC 1864098

Biography in narrative style. A dramatic account of the composer's life and artistic development, utilizing portions of letters from friends, family, and colleagues. Biographical calendar, illustrations, bibliography, no index.

26.   Beckett, Henry. "Rachmaninoff as Seen by
        His Own Piano Tuner." *New York Evening
        Post*, 26 December 1933, p.9

    Tuner William Hupfer's remarks are interesting but in this case incidental, because the important part of this piece is Rachmaninoff's comments on missing his homeland and regretting that the USA now recognized the new government in the USSR, for he could see no good in the Soviet system. After the USA recognized the Soviet government, Rachmaninoff feared the U.S. government might deport Russian refugees. He was very relieved that no such order was decreed.

27.   Belaiev, Victor. "Sergei Rakhmaninov."
        Translated from the Russian by S.W. Pring.
        Musical Quarterly 13 (July 1927): 359-76.

    Descriptive commentary on the works of Rachmaninoff. A view of the influencing factors in the First Concerto, an analysis of the Rachmaninoff style, and the critical attitude of musicians and critics towards his work, are subjects examined by Belaiev.

28.   Belousov, V. "Ivanovka." *Muzykal'naiā
        zhizn'* 18 (September 1968): 18-19.

    Description of the "Ivanovka" estate located in the Tambov district. The Satin estate, which was turned over to Rachmaninoff in 1910, was an idylic setting where the composer rested and worked in the summer months. Evidently this type of environment was necessary for inspiration and concentration. There is an interesting account of Rachmaninoff shipping his piano to "Ivanovka"- the estate was eight miles from the train station; the piano was loaded on a carriage and pulled by eight horses to the summer home. Many of the locals in the neighborhood of "Ivanovka" remember Rachmaninoff practicing until midnight on occasion. Spring of 1917 was the last time Rachmaninoff visited his beloved "Ivanovka."

29. Belza, Igor Fedorovich. "Sergei Rachmaninov." *Soviet Literature* 1 (1946): 63-67.

A biographical overview, stressing Rachmaninoff's compositional productivity in Russia. Belza demonstrates that Rachmaninoff was a gifted conductor and important to the development of Russian opera. He contends that the composer wrote little after leaving Russia because of his sadness at being separated from his beloved homeland.

30. ———, ed. *S.V. Rakhmaninov i russkaia opera*. sbornik statei. [S.V. Rachmaninoff and Russian opera. collection of articles] Moskva: Vserossiiskoe Teatral'noe Obshchestvo, 1947. 200 p.

A series of monographs read by the authors (whose texts are included here) at a symposium dedicated to Rachmaninoff. The symposium was held in Moscow 29-30 October 1945. The opening address was given by Antonina Vasil'evna Nezhdanova (dedicatee of the *Vokaliz* [Vocalise]). The following authors participated in the symposium (name followed by topic presented): I.F. Belza- "Opernoe tvorchestvo Rakhmaninova" [Rachmaninoff's operatic creativity], T.N. Livanova- "Tri opery Rakhmaninova" [the three operas of Rachmaninoff], V.V. Iakovlev- "Rakhmaninov i opernyi teatr" [Rachmaninoff and the operatic theater], E.V. Varvatsi- "Opery Rakhmaninova na sovetskoi stsene" [Rachmaninoff's operas in the Soviet scene], and B.S. Iagolim- "Rakhmaninov i teatr (bibliografiia i notografiia)" [notes and bibliography on the subject of Rachmaninoff's operatic career]. A USSR renewal of interest in Rachmaninoff's operas. The bibliography is extensive. Name index.

31.   Berkov, V. "Rakhmaninovskaia͡ garmonii͡a."
      [Rachmaninoff's harmony] *Sovetska͡ia muzyka*
      8 (1960): 104-09.

      A music theory monograph on the subject
      of the composer's characteristic harmonies.
      With musical examples, Berkov demonstrates
      Rachmaninoff's particular harmonic progress-
      ions and also his utilization of altered
      chords. The author notes similar harmonic
      passages in the music of Schubert, Wagner,
      Tchaikovsky, and Mussorgsky.

32.   Bertensson, Sergei. "Rachmaninoff as I
      Knew Him." *Etude* 66 (March 1948): 138.
      Also in Russian, "Iz memuarov." [from the
      memoirs] in *Sovetska͡ia muzyka* 3 (1968):
      82-84.

      Bertensson and Rachmaninoff first met in
      1923 when Bertensson visited New York City
      with the Moskovskiĭ Khudozhestvenniĭ Teatr
      [Moscow Art Theater] group which was on tour
      in this country. The author enjoyed watch-
      ing the composer socialize with his Russian
      friends and colleagues at Rachmaninoff's
      residence on Riverside Drive. After Berten-
      sson left the Moscow Art Theater he settled
      in Hollywood and in 1942 helped Rachmaninoff
      find a house to rent in Beverly Hills.
      Bertensson vividly describes the musicales
      at the Rachmaninoff home, where Horowitz
      and Rachmaninoff collaborated in playing
      two-piano works.

33.   Bertensson, Sergei, and Jay Leyda, with the
      assistance of Sophia Satina. *Sergei
      Rachmaninoff: A Lifetime in Music*. New
      York: New York University Press, 1956.
      464 p.   ML 410 R12 B47   OCLC 344823
      Also- London: Allen and Unwin, 1965.
      446 p.   ML 410 R12 B47   OCLC 3711604

So many years after publication this remains the definitive English language biography of the composer. The authors have made good use of materials available, primarily the letters published in Soviet publications and the collected letters (*Rakhmaninov: Pis'ma*, 1955). The authors were fortunate to have the helpful assistance of Sof'i͡a Aleksandrovna Satina (Rachmaninoff's cousin and sister-in-law), who was the principal family collator of information on the composer. Satina probably acted as a clearing agent on much of the data. The work is essentially a biography, devoid of the usual descriptive commentary on the compositions (except where described in the letters). The volume is nicely laid-out, chronologically paced by year, with a non-abstruse text in narrative fashion. Illustrated, musical examples, list of works, discography (compiled by Philip L. Miller), index.

34. Blumenberg, Marc. "Rachmaninoff." *Musical Courier* 59 (17 November 1909): 22-23.

A review of Rachmaninoff's performance of the Second Concerto with the Boston Symphony Orchestra in Carnegie Hall on 13 November 1909. Blumenberg (editor of *Musical Courier*) remarks on the simple and direct performance of the concerto- "he played with total disregard for any effect outside the pure delivery of the message." This was Rachmaninoff's first tour in the USA.

35. Bobykina, Irina. "Pervye sochinenii͡a Rakhmaninova." [First works by Rachmaninoff] *Muzykal'nai͡a zhizn'* 6 (March 1973): 20-21. (edition in honor of the 100th anniversary of Rachmaninoff's birth)

Recollections of the composer's conservatory years. Some early works and sketches are commented upon: *Esmeralda, Boris Godunov* (opera fragments), *Romans* [Romance], *Skertso* [Scherzo] (chamber ensemble sketches), *Russkaĭ rapsodiia* [Russian Rhapsody] for two pianos, and *Kontsert No.1 dlia f-no s orkestrom* [Concerto No.1 for Piano and Orchestra].

36. Bogdanov-Berezovskiĭ, Valer'ian Mikhailovich, ed. *Molodye gody Sergeia Vasil'evicha Rakhmaninova: Pis'ma, vospominaniia.* [S.V. Rachmaninoff's youthful years: letters, reminiscences] Leningrad-Moskva: Muzykal'noe Izd-vo, 1949. 192 p.

    Valuable collection of reminiscences and letters containing Liudmila Rostovtsova's (Skalon) reminiscences of the composer, and over 70 letters written by Rachmaninoff to the three Skalon sisters during the period of fall 1890 to summer 1906. The collection offers a detailed descriptive account of Rachmaninoff in his formative years: summers at the Satin's estate "Ivanovka" in the Tambov region, his friendship with the Skalons, the works written during the summers at "Ivanovka," and his happiness at visiting his relatives at this summer home. Rostovtsova describes the "Ivanovka" estate vividly- an idylic place for the young composer to work and play. An essay *Tvorchesky oblik S.V. Rakhmaninov* [creative make-up of Rachmaninoff] p.111-59 written by the editor V.M. Bogdanov-Berezovskiĭ is also included in the volume. It comments on the composer's diversification of works, stressing that he was not limited in his choice of genres. Illustrations, no index.

37. ———. *Stat'i o muzyke.* [Articles on music] Leningrad: Sovetskiĭ Kompozitor, 1960. 237 p. (SR p.45-86) ML 300 B66 OCLC 7759187

Largely biographical; the chapter on Rachmaninoff titled "Tvorcheskiĭ oblik Rakhmaninova" [Rachmaninoff as composer] is partly based on material from Sof'ia͡ Satina, Tamara Erastovna T͡sytovich, Oskar von Riesemann, and various Rachmaninoff letters. The author contends that both the Riesemann material (which he states is suspect) and the Satina information offer subjective enlightenment of facts, not always correct, which cannot be compared with material revealed by the composer himself in his letters. Bogdanov-Berezovskiĭ finds the Mikhail Akimovich Slonov letters important for details of Rachmaninoff's opera plans; letters of Nikita Semenovich Morozov describe his creative process; Marietta Sergeevna Shaginia͡n letters assist Rachmaninoff in selecting song texts and the Vladimir Robertovich Vil'shau [Wilshaw] letters reveal his pianistic activities. The author also describes influences on Rachmaninoff and terms him the last traditional classic Russian composer. Name index and bibliography; title and table of contents are printed in English and in Russian.

38. Bokshchanina, Evgenii͡a A. *Istorii͡a muzyki narodov SSSR do velikoĭ okti͡abr'skoĭ sot͡sialisticheskoĭ revoli͡ut͡sii.* [Music history of the peoples of the USSR up to the October Revolution] 2 izd. Moskva: Muzyka, 1978. 429 p. ML 3680 B62
OCLC 5895104

Textbook for music conservatories; traces the history of music of the peoples of the USSR up to the 1917 Revolution. First edition was published in 1968. This volume deals with the history of musical culture of Ukrain, Georgia, Armenia, Estonia, Lithuania, and Azerbaijan. It also explains the process of establishing professional national music schools. References to Rachmaninoff relate to his concert tours of Georgia, the influence of Rachmaninoff on the Georgian composer Arakshvile, and several performances of *Aleko* in a Latvian opera house. Illustrations, musical examples, bibliography, name index.

39. Boldt, Kenwyn Guy. "The Solo Piano Variations of Rachmaninoff." D.M.A. diss., Indiana University, 1967. 72 p.
ML 410 B3 B60   OCLC 2097720

   An analysis of the *Variations of a Theme of Chopin Op.22*, and the *Variations on a Theme of Corelli Op.42*. Each set is separately examined as to variations in (and thematic comparison of) melody, phrase structure, harmony, tonality, rhythm, texture, dynamics, tempi, and touch. Boldt ascribes two variation techniques to Rachmaninoff- parallel construction (and modifications) and free development. The composer often develops and varies a motive borrowed from a previous variation. Musical examples, bibliography.

40. Borisov, Leonid. *Shchedryĭ rytsar - Tsvety i slezy*. [Generous knight - Flowers and tears] Leningrad: "Detskaia Kniga," 1964. 206 p.   ML 410 R12 B78

   The second part of this narrative tale (in this case, fiction based on facts) about Rachmaninoff, *Tsvety i slezy* first appeared in the literary journal *Zveda* 8 (1963): 49-83 and 9 (1963): 105-22 under the title *V toske i slave* [in anguish and glory]. A review and justification of this novelette is presented in the volume by E. Brandis. Borisov based his stories on facts he derived from letters and memoirs of the composer, then added a liberal amount of fantasy. See Zarui Apetian's reaction to Borisov's inaccuracies of dates and information in "Ostorozhno: Poshlosti!" *Sovetskaia muzyka* 5 (1964): 138-40. In Borisov's story, protagonist Rachmaninoff

opens his inner personality, revealing his
joys and sorrows. Shchedryĭ rytsar is
concerned with Rachmaninoff's early years
as a novice composer- the productive and
happy years of his career. T͡svety i slezy
is based on the last years of his life- the
period during which he was away from his
homeland. Here Rachmaninoff is portrayed
as a dried-out composer, left without the
inspiration he derived from Russia.
Borisov dramatically depicts these scenes:
Rachmaninoff's emotional reaction to
Chaliapin's death, his last concert in
Europe, lilacs from Feka I͡akovlevna Russo,
Kolokola [The Bells] and the Philadelphia
Orchestra, helping fellow emigrants, meeting Hemingway, beginning of illness, Beverly
Hills, aid to Soviet war relief, and weakness, pain and death. In his historical-
fiction novel, Borisov attempts to penetrate
the inner world of the artist, his thoughts
and emotions, through conjecture. The theme
of lost motherland increases in importance
with each chapter. In reality, the psychological profile of this very complex person
will never be fully revealed or understood.

41. Bortnikova, Evgenii͡a, ed. and comp. "Pis'ma
S.V. Rakhmaninova k M.A. Slonovu i A.V.
Zataevichu." [Rachmaninoff's letters to
M.A. Slonov and A.V. Zataevich] Sovetskai͡a
muzyka: sbornik chetvertyĭ, (1945): 133-51.

The Rachmaninoff letters to Mikhail
Akimovich Slonov and Aleksandr Viktorovich
Zataevich are preserved in the Gosudarstvennyĭ T͡sentral'nyĭ Muzeĭ Muzykal'noĭ
Kul'tury [State Central Museum of Musical
Culture] in Moscow. Sixteen letters, eight
of which were written in 1906, five in 1907,
and one each in 1895 and 1897, are reproduced here. Zataevich is the dedicatee of
Shest' muzykal'nukh momentov [Moments
musicaux] Op.16. Slonov and Rachmaninoff
were students together at the Moskovskai͡a
Konservatorii͡a [Moscow Conservatory] and

they later collaborated on a draft of *Monna Vanna*, Slonov blocking out a libretto from the Maeterlinck play for the never-completed opera. Slonov also selected texts for several Rachmaninoff songs. The letters reveal aspects of the composer's creative process. See Joseph Yasser's article concerning the Zataevich 1897 letter, "Symphony Post-Mortem," in the *New York Times* (28 March 1948): x7.

42. ———, ed. *Avtografy S.V. Rakhmaninova: v Fondakh Gosudarstvennogo T͡sentral'nogo Muzei͡a Muzykal'noĭ Kul'tury Imeni M.I. Glinki: katalog-spravochnik*. [Rachmaninoff's autographs in the State Central Glinka Museum of Musical Culture: reference catalog] Moskva: Ministerstvo kul'tury SSSR, 1955. 35 p.

    Catalog of 170 items from 1887-1917, mostly manuscripts of compositions written in Russia, arranged by genre, then listed in chronological order. Some works have comments pertaining to specific data. This catalog of items housed in the Fondakh Rakhmaninova [Rachmaninoff Archive] in the Gosudarstvennom T͡sentral'nom Muzee Muzykal'noĭ Kul'tury Imeni M.I. Glinki [State Central Glinka Museum of Musical Culture] in Moscow has been superseded by the new (1980) edition of the catalog, edited by M.G. Ryt͡sareva.

43. Bowers, Faubion. *Scriabin: A Biography of the Russian Composer, 1871-1915.* Tokyo; Palo Alto, Cal.: Kodansha International, 1969. 2 vols. 646 p. ML 410 S5988 B7 ISBN 0-870-11081-7 OCLC 23205

    It is of interest to view segments of Rachmaninoff's life from a different perspective. Scriabin and Rachmaninoff's lives crossed many times; their education came from a common source; and they were

friends and respected colleagues. Bowers'
biography of Scriabin is candidly written;
therefore observations of Rachmaninoff are
equally frank. Similar circumstances that
existed for Scriabin and Rachmaninoff, such
as studying with Zverov, Taneev, and Arenskiĭ,
performing together as conductor and pianist
(with Scriabin playing and Rachmaninoff
conducting), etc. are examined with Rachmaninoff in the background. Rachmaninoff, who
was not the protagonist in this case, is
observed obliquely. Bowers offers an interesting account of Rachmaninoff in relation
to Scriabin.

44.   Boyd, Malcom. "'Dies irae': Some Recent
      Manifestations." *Music and Letters* 49
      (October 1968): 347-56.

      The author investigates works quoting the
      Dies irae theme, including works by
      Mīaskovskiĭ, Khachaturīān, Respighi, Dalla-
      piccola, Ronald Stevenson, Rachmaninoff,
      and Mahler. Boyd cites the *Isle of the Dead,
      The Bells, Rhapsody on a Theme of Paganini,*
      and the *Symphonic Dances.* Musical examples.

45.   Braggiotti, Mary. "A Life Full of Beautiful
      Music." *New York Post,* 18 August 1944.

      An interview with Rachmaninoff's widow
      Natalīā. Part of the interview is concerned
      with the Rachmaninoff Foundation Piano
      Competition that was to be inaugurated in
      the spring, but the major portion of the
      interview consists of Natalīā reflecting on
      her husband's career and the part she played
      in it. Natalīā tells of her father's 2,000-
      acre estate in Tambov, her first meeting
      with her talented cousin and future husband
      when she was 11 and he 15 years of age, her
      ambition to become a concert pianist (she
      graduated from the Moscow Conservatory),
      and her travels with her husband. She always

accompanied Sergei on his tours and supported him with devoted care. Nataliâ affirms that she was not sorry to sacrifice her career; she lived her husband's career. Illustrated.

46. Brewerton, Eric. "Rachmaninoff's Songs." *Music and Letters* 15 (January 1934): 32-36.

A monologue on Rachmaninoff's song-writing style. The author is critical of the composer's climaxes in the songs and of the difficulty and texture of accompaniments. Brewerton contends that Rachmaninoff's dreamy and meditative songs, e.g., *How Fair This Spot* and *Lilacs* are more successful than the highly emotional ones.

47. Briân&seva, V.N. "Tvorcheskoe svoeobrazie khudozhnika." [Creative originality of the artist] *Sovetskaiâ muzyka* 1 (1965): 35-40.

Basically a study of Rachmaninoff's style, noting similarities and differences between his style and those of his contemporaries. Briân&seva contends that Rachmaninoff is musically closer to Scriabin than to his other immediate contemporaries Taneev, Medtner, and Glazunov. She presents the concept of the struggle or contrast between light and dark, commenting on how Tchaikovsky, Scriabin, Glazunov, and Rachmaninoff solve the traditional practice of contrasts in music. Briân&seva maintains that Rachmaninoff rejected sharp contrasts in the *Simfoniiâ No.1* [Symphony No.1].

48. ———. "Gde rodilsiâ S.V. Rakhmaninov?" [Where was Rachmaninoff born?] *Muzykal'naiâ zhizn'* 19 (1969): 20.

Letter to the editor of *Muzykal'naia zhizn'* from V.N. Briantseva disclosing new information on the composer's birthplace. Rachmaninoff remembers foremost the estate in Oneg where he was raised, but information gathered from his father's estate ownership documents shows that the family was living on the estate in Semonovo at the time of Sergei's birth. The composer believed he was born in Oneg district but his birth registration implies he was born in the district of Semonovo. The documentation proof is inconclusive and Briantseva does not claim that this information proves without a doubt his proper birthplace.

49. ―――. *Detsvo i iunost' Sergeia Rakhmaninova.* [Rachmaninoff's childhood and youth] Moskva: Sovetskiĭ Kompozitor, 1970. 136 p. ML 410 R12 B7 OCLC 9179349

    A view of Rachmaninoff's youthful years through the year 1893. Events described are recollections made by his contemporaries through letters, newspaper articles, and material gathered from archives. Includes many early photographs of the composer and his family.

50. ―――. *S.V. Rakhmaninov.* Moskva: Sovetskiĭ Kompozitor, 1976. 644 p.

    A biographical work with emphasis on the composer's early life and attention to his musical style. Unlike former Russian biographies of Rachmaninoff that ignore or slight his years abroad, this does examine this period in his life, drawing upon USA periodicals as well as reminiscences, letters, and material from Sof'ia Satina. Briantseva's work specifically concentrates on describing Rachmaninoff's characteristic musical style, utilizing numerous musical examples. Illustrated, musical examples, name index and index of works.

51.   Brower, Harriette. "'Beware of the Indifferent Piano Teacher' Warns Rachmaninoff." *Musician* 30 (February 1925): 11-12. Also in- Harriette Brower's *Modern Masters of the Keyboard*. New York: Frederick Stokes, 1926. 303 p. (SR p.1-11) ML 397 B6 OCLC 686506

   An interview with the composer at his New York residence on Riverside Drive. Rachmaninoff stresses the importance of studying with a good teacher and the practice of pure technique. He reiterates his feeling for modern music, compliments works of MacDowell and Deems Taylor, and affirms that America has great artistic possibilities.

52.   Bukinik, Michael. "Reminiscences of Young Rachmaninoff." *American Federation of Musicians, Local 802 Official Journal*, 17 (May 1943): 6-10. Also in Russian- in *Novoye russkoye slovo*, 18 December 1932. p.4.

   Interesting and colorful article written by student colleague and friend of Rachmaninoff. Bukinik gives a detailed description of the Moscow Conservatory faculty (through the eyes of a student), as well as notable students such as Zverev, Busoni, Ziloti, Pabst, Taneev, Arenskiĭ, Lhévinne, Scriabin, Rachmaninoff, etc.. The author vividly describes Rachmaninoff as a student- his temperament and character- and also mentions his performance of the Anton Rubinstein *Concerto in D Minor* (mistakenly referred to as Concerto in A Minor) at the Electric Exposition in Moscow (1892).

53.   Bunimovich, Vladimir [pseud. Muzalevskiĭ, V.]. *Russkoe fortepiannoe iskusstvo XVIII pervoĭ poloviny XIX Veka*. [The art of Russian piano music from 1800-1850]

Leningrad: Muzykal'noe Izd-vo, 1961.
(Reprint--Ann Arbor, Mich.: University
Microfilms International, 1979. 316 p.
ML 734 B78 OCLC 6843647)

An historical survey of Russian piano
music from 1800 to 1850. Rachmaninoff is
referred to in the chapter on John Field.
The *Preliŭdiia* [Prelude] *Op.32, No.12* is
examined for its harmonic figuration which
presumably was influenced by Field's
accompaniment style. Field lived in Russia
for over 30 years, teaching piano in Moscow
and St. Petersburg. Field was the teacher
of Sergei's grandfather, Arkady Aleksandrovich Rakhmaninov. Bunimovich contends that
the *Detskaia pol'ka* [Children's polka] by
Glinka initiates the tradition of polkas
that was carried on by Rubinstein, Tchaikovsky, and finally Rachmaninoff and his
Polka de W.R.. There are other references
to Rachmaninoff concerning influencing
factors. Illustrations, portraits, musical
examples.

54. Burke, Harry R. "Overflow Audience Cheers
     Mastery of Rachmaninoff." *St Louis Daily
     Globe-Democrat*, 10 December 1941, p.5C.

     A review of a Rachmaninoff concert given
     in the St. Louis Municipal Auditorium on
     9 December 1941. Rachmaninoff performed
     Mozart's Variations in A Major (from *Sonata
     in A Major* KV 331). Beethoven's *Sonata in
     C Minor Op.111*, the Schumann *Novellette in
     F-sharp Minor Op.21, No.8*, and nine tran-
     scriptions: four of his own and five of
     Liszt's. There were radios set up in the
     refectory so that those interested could
     hear President Roosevelt's statement on the
     Japanese war situation.

55. Butzbach, Fritz. *Studien zum Klavierkonzert
     Nr.1, Fis-moll, Op.1 von S.V. Rachmaninov.*

Kölner Beiträge zur Musikforschung, herausgegeben von Heinrich Huschen, Band 109. [Studies on the Piano Concerto No.1, F-sharp Minor, Op.1 by S.V. Rachmaninoff. Cologne's Contribution to Music Research, edited by Heinrich Huschen, Vol. 109.] Regensburg: Gustave Bosse, 1979. 321 p. MT 130 R2 B9 ISBN 3-7649-2207-9 OCLC 6357681

Butzbach utilized resources at the Library of Congress and the Gosudarstvennom Tsentral'nom Muzee Muzykal'noĭ Kul'tury Imeni M.I. Glinki [State Central Glinka Museum of Musical Culture] in Moscow for his detailed analysis of the First Concerto. The author observes influences of the early concerto (1899, sketches only) and the Grieg *Piano Concerto in A Minor Op.16* in Rachmaninoff's First Concerto. Butzbach offers an in-depth comparison of the 1890-91 version of the First Concerto with the revised 1917 version, illustrating the comparisons effectively by placing segments of the differing scores side by side. A valuable study of the First Concerto and Rachmaninoff's creative process; recommended. Musical examples, life-calendar, bibliography, discography (First Concerto only). See also- Geoffrey Norris' "Rakhmaninov's Second Thoughts" in *Musical Times* 114 (April 1973): 364-68., which examines the revisions of several works, including the First Concerto.

56.   Calvocoressi, Michel D. "The Bells." *Listener* 17 (3 February 1937): 244.

Calvocoressi points out the influences of German romanticisim on Rachmaninoff and the typical Russian melancholic and introspective aspects in his music, and discusses *The Bells*. He contends that Balmont's Russian translation of *The Bells* differs from the original by Poe, mainly in attitude; Balmont prefers to evoke only the gloomy elements of the last stanza, whereas Poe stresses the joyous aspects.

57.   ———. *A Survey of Russian Music.* Middlesex, Eng.: Penguin Books, 1944. (Reprint-- Westport, Conn.; Greenwood Press, 1975. ML 300 C3 S8   ISBN 0-8371-6888-0 OCLC 799518

Book based on lectures delivered by Calvocoressi at Glasgow University as Cramb lecturer for 1935. It offers an historical placement of Rachmaninoff, i.e., successor to Tchaikovsky, conservative, non-national, etc.. The author generally compares Rachmaninoff with Tchaikovsky.

58.   Carples, Esther. "Unchanging Aristocrat of Artists." *Boston Transcript,* 22 January 1927.

Article originally printed in the *New Yorker,* is about Rachmaninoff's austere, aristocratic personality and how it has not changed despite his huge success as pianist and composer. Carples relates that the *Prelude in C-sharp Minor Op.3, No.2* started it all and that Rachmaninoff accepts the success calmly, as if it were a natural predetermined actuality. She tells how secretive Rachmaninoff is in revealing his philosophy and musical tendencies. Carples then describes the Rachmaninoff residence in New York City on Riverside Drive- elegant, quiet, and old-fashioned are a few characteristics observed.

59.   *Chaliapin, An Autobiography as told to Maxim Gorky;* With supplementary correspondence and notes, translated from the Russian, compiled and edited by Nina Froud and James Hanley. New York: Stein and Day, 1967. 320 p.   ML 420 S53 A2533 1967 OCLC 2825498

The story of Chaliapin's life as related to Gorky in Capri, summer 1916 is colorfully written and absorbing to read. There are several references to Rachmaninoff; one specific incident, when Chaliapin and Rachmaninoff visited Lev Nikolaevich Tolstoĭ (9 January 1900) and were duly asked to perform for him, is vividly depicted. Both young artists were in awe of the great man. This was Rachmaninoff's second visit with Tolstoĭ, Chaliapin's first. It is also of interest to read Rachmaninoff's observation of the visit, as related in Alfred and Katherine Swan's "Rachmaninoff, Personal Reminiscences" in the *Musical Quarterly* 30 (April 1944): 185. Chaliapin's autobiography contains illustrations, bibliography, personalia, index.

60. Charton, Jean Marie. *Les années françaises de Serge Rachmaninoff*. Paris: Editions de la Revue Moderne, 1969. 163 p.
ML 410 R12 C5   OCLC 1477537

A retrospective of Rachmaninoff's concerts and visits in France. Partly biographical, the work also comments on several of Rachmaninoff's compositions and describes the composer's first concert in Paris (1907) at L'opera, when he participated in the *Saison russe* (series of concerts featuring Russian music of the 19th century). Charton offers a French view of the composer at rest during the summers when he resided at Chateau de Corbeville (1925) and in Clairfontaine (1929). Charton recalls Rachmaninoff's many concerts in France, from 1928 until his last concert in Paris at Palais de Chaillot in 1939. Illustrations, bibliography, index.

61. Chasins, Abram. "The Rachmaninoff Legacy-I." *Saturday Review* (29 October 1955): 37-39, 64 and "The Rachmaninoff Legacy-II." (26 November 1955): 46,70-72.

An announcement of the release of the Rachmaninoff recordings of the four concerti and the *Rhapsody on a Theme of Paganini* on RCA Victor (LM-6123), followed by a discourse on the role of the interpreter in bringing a score to life. The second part (Legacy-II) views Rachmaninoff's own interpretations of his concerti and how he occasionally departs from indications in the score. Chasin describes interpretations of other pianists' recordings of the concerti. Illustrations; discography (concerti only).

62.   ———. *Speaking of Pianists*. New York: Alfred Knopf, 1957. 291 p. (SR p.40-47, 254-58) ML 397 C5 OCLC 335692

This notable book on pianists describes the attributes and personality of Rachmaninoff and comments on his interpretation of his concerti. Index.

63.   Chekov, Mikhail Aleksandrovich. "Iz memuarov." [from the memoirs] *Sovetskaiā muzyka* 3 (1968): 78-82.

Reminiscences of summer 1931 when Chaliapin was visiting Rachmaninoff at Clairefontaine, by actor-designer Mikhail Aleksandrovich Chekov, nephew of Anton Pavlovich Chekov. On the occasion, Rachmaninoff was moved to tears listening to Chaliapin sing. Upon Chekov's request, Rachmaninoff gave his advice on music in the theater and in opera production. The author reflects on other occasions when he was with the composer.

64.   Chernukhin, Jacob. "With the Enemy at the Gates: Moscow Holds Rachmaninoff Exhibition." *Musician* 47 (October 1942): 47.

An account of the Rachmaninoff exhibition held in the State Conservatory (Tchaikovsky) in Moscow in 1942. The article title reflects the times of war. Exhibited were photographs, paintings, scores, new publications of several works, posters, reviews, and articles. Rachmaninoff, in this country, did receive word of this tribute to him.

65.   Citkowitz, Israel. "Orpheus With His Lute." *Tempo* 22 (Winter 1951-52): 8-11.

Short monograph compares characteristics of piano-playing with the creative styles of the composers who wrote for the instrument. For example, Beethoven used the piano in his own individual manner just as Rachmaninoff did his. Citkowitz implies that the capabilities of the instrument are defined by the individuality of the pianist. Citkowitz sees impressive growth in Rachmaninoff's music since the Second Concerto, i.e., greater integration of line, texture and form, and less ornamental and rhetorical superfluities. An examination of Rachmaninoff's pianistic style follows.

66.   Conus, Olga [Olga Nikolaevna Koniûs]. "Memories of a Personal Friend." *Clavier* 12 (October 1973): 17-18.

Author's husband Leo Conus (Lev Eduardovich Koniûs) was a classmate of Rachmaninoff during the conservatory years. The families were always very close. Rachmaninoff's younger daughter Tatiana married Boris Iùl'evich Koniûs, son of violinist Iuliĭ Eduardovich Koniûs in 1932. Olga Koniûs taught piano to Rachmaninoff's granddaughter Sophie. The author reflects on the composer's warmth, humor, and love of friends.

67.   Cooke, Deryck. *Vindications: Essays on Romantic Music.* Cambridge: Cambridge University Press, 1982. 226 p. ML 196 C66 ISBN 0-521-24765-9 OCLC 8429931

Also- London: Faber and Faber, 1982.
226 p.   ML 196 C66   ISBN 0-571-11795-3
OCLC 8776453

A posthumous collection of articles previously published by the author. Article titled "The Futility of Music Criticism," first published in *The Musical Newsletter* (January 1972) deserves reading. On Beethoven, Cooke points out, "nobody can prove he [Beethoven] is great; nobody has ever proved it. He remains great because everyone believes he is great- everybody knows he is great, one might say- and no music critic is needed to confirm the fact." Cooke goes on to note that because of continued enthusiasm by both performers and listeners, both Puccini and Rachmaninoff remain within our musical experience "despite the most concentrated barrage of negative criticism." Cooke gives his reasons as to why we should give up criticism of the dead masters. Musical examples, name index.

68.   Coolidge, Richard. "Architectonic Technique and Innovations in the Rakhmaninov Piano Concertos." *Music Review* 40 (August 1979): 170-216.

A two-part monograph, first part dealing with fashions in music and how tastes change through the years; the chic fashion in 1979 was anti-romanticism and pro-classicism, Coolidge effectively reveals why Rachmaninoff is the "prime target of all the fashionable scoffers." He goes on to show evidence that Rachmaninoff is undeniably a master craftsman. In the second section of the monograph, Coolidge presents a detailed analysis of the form and structure of the four piano concerti and *Rhapsody on a Theme of Paganini*. Along with the analysis of the Rhapsody, the author includes the composer's programatic scheme that formed the basis of Rachmaninoff-Fokine's ballet "Paganini." Coolidge's valuable study concludes with a summary. Bibliography.

69.   Culshaw, John. "Rachmaninov, Two Years
     After." *Gramophone* 22 (March 1945): 116.

   Written while S/Lieut. (A.) John R.
   Culshaw, R.N.V.R. was in the British military
   and before he wrote his book on Rachmaninoff
   (1950). Culshaw comments on the continued
   popularity of the composer's music two years
   after his death and briefly reviews his
   recordings.

70.   ———. *Rachmaninov: The Man and His Music*.
     New York: Oxford University Press, 1950.
     174 p.   ML 410 R12 C82   OCLC 1205254

   Culshaw states that this work is not primarily a biography and that material not
   bearing on Rachmaninoff the composer has
   been omitted. The bulk of the book is comprised of critical studies of the composer's
   compositions. Culshaw chooses to be
   impartial in discussing strengths and weak-
   nesses in Rachmaninoff's works, a stance
   that Mrs. Rachmaninoff, after reading the
   proofs, was not happy with. Culshaw in a
   later article, "Rachmaninov Revisited"
   (1973), reflects that he was influenced to
   some extent by the prevailing climate of
   opinion at the time of writing the work.
   In *Rachmaninov: The Man and His Music*,
   Culshaw is inclined to be too removed and
   objective in his presentation. Illustrations, musical examples, list of works,
   bibliography, discography.

71.   ———. "Rachmaninov: The Legacy." *Listener*
     75 (3 March 1966): 328.

   Essay on the lasting popularity of Rachmaninoff's music twenty-four years after
   his death. In this reflective and probing
   article Culshaw offers his rationale as to
   why certain works- even superior ones- have
   been rarely heard or have disappeared from
   the concert repertoire.

72.   ———. "Rachmaninov Revisited." *Soundings* 3 (1973): 2-6.

Interesting article finds the author questioning his critical opinions expressed in his earlier book on Rachmaninoff (1950). Culshaw recalls the icy response he received when Mrs. Rachmaninoff read the galley proofs of the work. The author, in the year of Rachmaninoff's centenary, is gladdened to note how wrong the adverse critical pundits have been.

73.   ———. "Rachmaninoff: The Proper Place." *High Fidelity* 28 (June 1978): 22.

Culshaw recalls events such as missing Rachmaninoff's last concert at Carnegie Hall in 1942, and his visit to "Senar" with the galley proofs of his book on the composer (1950). Mrs. Rachmaninoff's reaction to reading the book was very cool, if not icy. The author comments on the re-evaluation of the composer in recent years. Illustration.

74.   ———. *Putting the Record Straight: The Autobiography of John Culshaw*. London: Secker and Warburg, 1981. Also- New York: Viking Press, 1982. 362 p. ML 429 C8 A3 ISBN 0-670-58326-X OCLC 7796886

Culshaw had almost completed the draft of this arresting autobiography when he contacted hepatitis in Australia and died in 1980. Rachmaninoff and his music were important factors in Culshaw's life. He again relates the episode of leaving the manuscript of his book (1950) with Natalĩa Rachmaninoff for her approval, and describes the critical attitude towards the composer prevalent at the time he was writing the work, and the effect this had on him and his book. Epilogue by Erik Smith, name index.

75. Daniel, Oliver. *Stokowski: A Counterpoint of View.* New York: Dodd and Mead, 1982. 1090 p. ML 422 S76 D3 ISBN 0-396-07936-9 OCLC 8281551

   Daniel makes several references to Rachmaninoff in his book on Stokowski. Stokowski and Rachmaninoff frequently collaborated in concert and recording. A letter from Stokowski to Rachmaninoff (18 March 1933) is cited, informing the composer that he was soon to direct an uncut performance of the *Isle of the Dead.* Illustrations, discography, appendixes, name index.

76. Davidson, Gladys. *The Barnes Book of the Opera.* New York: A.S. Barnes, 1962. 890 p. MT 95 D2 B4 OCLC 926625

   This edition is a compilation of opera plot synopses previously published by Gladys Davidson. Rachmaninoff's operas *Aleko* and *Francesca da Rimini* are outlined in short-story fashion. These two Rachmaninoff opera synopses by Davidson first appeared in *Stories From Russian Operas* published by J.B. Lippincott (Philadelphia) in c.1922. This first edition contained synopses for 16 Russian operas, including works by Cui, Rimsky-Korsakov, and Tchaikovsky. This present 1962 edition contains all of the Russian operas in the 1922 edition plus three additional operas each for Rimsky-Korsakov and Stravinsky. Illustrated, short biographies, no index.

77. Davies, Laurence. *Paths to Modern Music: Aspects of Music from Wagner to the Present Day.* London: Barrie and Jenkins, 1971. 330 p. (SR p. 195-209) ML 196 D4 ISBN 0-214-65249-1 OCLC 194003 Also- New York: Scribner's Sons, 1971. ML 196 D4 ISBN 0-684-12440-9 OCLC 157334

A collection of critical essays on the history of modern music. Some of the essays have been previously published, some have been emended and enlarged for this edition. Davies presents material on Rachmaninoff that is largely biographical, while interpolating bits of reflective analysis endeavoring to bring attention to, and better understand, the elusive Rachmaninoff. Davies delves into the composer's influences, comparison with other pianists, Russian musical training, historians' attitude, and examines several works. Bibliography, name index.

78. "Devilish Discords." *Time* 51 (29 March 1948): 76.

   Title based on Cui's remarks (1897) upon hearing Rachmaninoff's First Symphony (fateful premier on 15 March 1897). The brief article relates the discovery of the four-hand piano version of the score in Moscow and the orchestral parts in Leningrad, and reviews the first American performance of the First Symphony with the Philadelphia Orchestra under Ormandy, just performed during the week previous to the publication of this article.

79. "A Distinguished Russian Composer." *Outlook* 120 (25 December 1918): 652.

   An announcement of the arrival of the Rachmaninoffs in New York City, stating that they will remain in this country until conditions are more settled in Russia. The article describes the composer, his Russian lineage, his tonal color, and gives a brief account of his works.

80. Dobuzhinskiĭ, Mstislav Valarianovich., ed. *Pamiati Rakhmaninova*. sbornik [Recollections of Rachmaninoff, collection]

New York: Izd. S.A. Satinoĭ, 1946. (copyrighted and published by Sof'i͡a Satina, printed by Grenich Printing Corp., New York) 184 p.   ML 410 R12 D7   OCLC 697-7137

This collection of reminiscences, articles, and letters by various friends and colleagues of Rachmaninoff was gathered by Sof'i͡a Aleksandrovna Satina (Rachmaninoff's cousin and sister-in-law), who invited their contributions to be included in this volume. Most of the material was written in May-June 1945. Some of the material is translated from English (written by Americans who knew him) so that the entire collection is in Russian. Satina's primary purpose for this volume is to preserve the image of Rachmaninoff as a person remembered by his contemporaries. She feared that with the death of more and more of his contemporaries, Rachmaninoff might be forgotten by future generations. The promulgation of Rachmaninoff and his artistic legacy was a lifelong preoccupation of Sof'i͡a Satina. Some of the contributors for this volume are- J. Steinway, C. Spalding, Somov, I.I. Sikorskiĭ, S. Bertensson, and J. Hofmann. Illustrated, index of authors.

81.   ———. "Iz memuarov." [from the memoirs] *Sovet͡skai͡a muzyka* 3 (1968): 85-86.

Dobuzhinskiĭ and Rachmaninoff first met in 1916 at the Moskovskyĭ Khudozhestvennyĭ Teatr [Moscow Art Theater] with subsequent meetings in 1927 and 1937 in Paris, and in 1940 in New York, when the author arrived in the USA. Rachmaninoff was instrumental in assisting Dobuzhinskiĭ acquire a position with the Metropolitan Opera Company, staging an opera. The author reflects on the composer's kindness and humility.

82.   Dolinskiĭ, M. and S. Chertok. "Znamenitye." [famous one] *Muzykal'nai͡a zhizn'* 6 (March 1963): 10.

A first-time-published photograph, originally presented to the Gosudarstvennoĭ Biblioteke SSSR Imeni V.I. Lenina [Lenin State Library] by I͡uriĭ Slonov, son of Mikhail Akimovich Slonov, in 1916, and subsequently lost there until recently rediscovered. The photo shows Chaliapin, Marii͡a Rakhmanova, Nina Koshits [Koshetz], S. Rachmaninoff, Koussevitzky, Marii͡a Gorshanova, and Petr Figurov seated at an out-door banquet in the garden of Figurov's summer house in Essentukakh. Chaliapin often rented a section of the house for summer respites.

83. Downes, Olin. "Own Works Given by Rachmaninoff." *New York Times*, 27 November 1939, p.L12.

    Review of the first concert of the series, "Rachmaninoff Cycle" which was comprised of three concerts featuring Rachmaninoff as composer, pianist, and conductor. The reviewed concert was given in Carnegie Hall on 26 November 1939; Ormandy directing the Philadelphia Orchestra in the Second Symphony, First Concerto, and the *Rhapsody on a Theme of Paganini* with Rachmaninoff as soloist. Downes wrote off the First Concerto as old-fashioned, although he praised the execution of the work. "The Second Symphony is a strong work, masterfully treated, coherent in structure, full of invention, and definitely carries the stamp of Rachmaninoff," states Downes. He was equally impressed with the *Rhapsody on a Theme of Paganini*. This was an important event in Rachmaninoff's career, a culmination of his artistry- the audience stood in his honor when he came out to perform the concerto.

84. ————. "A Romantic Passes: Sergei Rachmaninoff, who pursued his own path as a composer." *New York Times*, 4 April 1943. p.X7.

Downes dwells on the composer's training, Russian heritage, and the position he holds as composer. In summation of his tribute to the composer Downes states that Rachmaninoff's sincerity and greatness of spirit is reflected in the genuineness and greatness of his music.

85. ──────. "In Composer's Name." *New York Times*, 26 March 1944, P.X4.

An announcement of the founding of the Rachmaninoff Memorial Fund, Inc. with Vladimir Horowitz as president and Serge Koussevitzky as artists' advisory board chairman. Plans included contests which awarded young pianists concert tours in this country and hopefully in the USSR as well. The committee members were contemplating having a similar contest in the USSR, with the result being that the winners would play in each other's country. Downes comments on Rachmaninoff's talent as pianist and conductor, regretting that the composer did not pursue the latter talent in this country. The author includes the contents of the 70th birthday greetings from the Soiuz Sovetskikh Kompozitorov SSSR [Union of Soviet Composers] to Rachmaninoff wishing him courage, strength and health for many more years, also telling him how the Soviet public follows his career and how proud they are of his triumphs. The letter reached him on his death bed. For information on the demise of the Rachmaninoff Fund see "Rachmaninoff Fund Forced to Discontinue," in *Musical America* 69 (June 1949): 4.

86. ──────. *Olin Downes on Music:* A Selection from His Writings During the Half-Century 1906-1955. New York: Greenwood Press, 1968. 473 p.   ML 60 D78   OCLC 218588

Excellent first-hand vivid descriptions of Rachmaninoff the pianist and conductor (in concert of 18 December 1909); a performance of the *Isle of the Dead* (concert of 23 April 1910); and Downes' sensitive article (4 April 1943) on Rachmaninoff's death. The reviews and articles originally appeared in the *New York Times*.

87. Eberle, Merab. "Noted Teacher Pays Tribute to Rachmaninoff." *Journal Herald* (Dayton, Ohio), 31 March 1954.

    Olga Conus (Olga Nikolaevna Konius) née Olga Kovalskii, studied piano with Leon Conus (Lev Eduardovich Konius) at the Imperial Russia's Moscow School for daughters of generals and high officials; they fell in love and married. It is through her husband, Lev Konius that she met Rachmaninoff, for at this time Rachmaninoff had the post of vice-president of the Imperial Russian Musical Society, in which his duty was to inspect the quality of the music schools. He visited the school where Lev Konius was teaching and there Olga met the composer for the first time. Lev Konius and Rachmaninoff graduated together from the Moscow Conservatory and were life-long friends. Rachmaninoff's daughter Tatiana married a Konius (Boris) in 1932. Madam Olga Konius taught piano in Dayton and Cincinnati, Ohio. She recalls the happy times she and her husband had with the Rachmaninoff family, how warm and loving the composer was, and how three years after the Revolution the Konius family fled for France.

88. Eberlein, Dorothee. *Russische Musikanschauung um 1900*, von 9 russischen Komponisten: dargestellt aus Briefen, Sebstzeugnissen, Erinnerungen und Kritiken. [Russian Musical View in 1900, by 9 Russian composers: described in letters, personal testimonies, reminiscences, and interviews] Regensburg: Gustav Bosse, 1978. 207 p.   ML 300 E24   ISBN 3-7649-2136-6   OCLC 5354150

A study of the St. Petersburg-Belaiev Circle composers Rimsky-Korsakov, Glazunov, Li︠a︡dov; and the Moscow composers Scriabin, Medtner, and Rachmaninoff. Stravinsky, Prokofiev, and Miaskovskiĭ are considered in a separate chapter titled "St. Petersburg-Modern." Eberlein asserts that Rachmaninoff demonstrates his skill of sound and rhythm of speech in the solo songs and in his excellent choral settings, utilizing old Russian song traditions, and for this he should be acknowledged and commended. Eberlein offers a rationale for Rachmaninoff's lack of interest in writing for the voice after his exile from Russia in 1917. Illustrations, musical examples, bibliography, name index.

89.   Emeli︠a︡nova, N.N. ed. *S.V. Rakhmaninov v Ivanovke:* sbornik materi︠a︡lov i dokumentov. [S.V. Rachmaninoff in Ivanovka: collection of materials and documents] Voronezh: Knizhnoe Izd-vo, 1971. 295 p.   780.923 R11
OCLC 4768547

Detailed description of the Satin's estate (later Rachmaninoff's) in the Tambov district, where Rachmaninoff found beauty, peace and relaxation. "Ivanovka" was an important source of inspiration to the composer. His work flourished in this idyllic setting. The volume is well illustrated, containing house and grounds diagrams (by Sof'i︠a︡ Satina), photographs of Rachmaninoff and friends, as well as photographs of the house and countryside. Emeli︠a︡nova includes a chronology of the composer's creative activity at "Ivanovka," a chronology of events in the life of Rachmaninoff, and many Rachmaninoff letters.

90.   Engel, I︠U︡liĭ Dmitrievich. "'Skupoĭ ryt︠s︡ar' i 'Francheska,' opery Rakhmaninova." [Miserly Knight and Francesca, operas by Rachmaninoff] *Russkie vedomosti,* 2 October 1912.

Performance of *Skupoĭ ryt͡sar'* [the Miserly Knight] and *Francheska da Rimini* [Francesca da Rimini] at the Bol'shoĭ is reviewed by I͡uliĭ Engel. Critic Engel writes that it was daring of Rachmaninoff to employ the same thematic subject of *Francheska da Rimini* that Tchaikovsky previously used. Engel points out that Rachmaninoff uses interesting innovations in his setting of Francheska, such as using an unseen choir, utilizing wordless singing (bouche fermée) creating the impression of moans, etc.. In contrast *Skupoĭ ryt͡sar'* is entirely different, employing a Wagnerian-style orchestra, more recitatives, etc. Engel enjoyed the operas.

91. ―――. "Simfonicheskiĭ kont͡sert, 22 okti͡abri͡a [Symphonic concert of 22 October] *Russkie vedomosti*, 24 October 1912.

Review of a concert dedicated to the memory of Edvard Grieg on the fifth anniversary of his death. Engel was very impressed by Rachmaninoff's performance, conducting *Anitra's Dance*, and remarked on his ability as conductor, "Rachmaninoff by the grace of God is truly a conductor; he is the only Russian conductor whom we can compare with such names in the West as Nikisch, Colonne, and Mahler. He is not totally successful in everything, but after all we do not measure the mountains by their peaks." The full house demanded that *Anitra's Dance* be repeated as an encore.

92. ―――. "Skri͡abinsky zikl; fortepi͡anny kont͡sert Skri͡abina v ispolneniĭ Rakhmaninova." [Scriabin's cycle; piano concerto by Scriabin played by Rachmaninoff] *Russkie vedomosti*, 13 October 1915, p.4.

A review of a symphonic concert dedicated to the memory of Scriabin. The first concert

of the 1915-16 season in Moscow, 12 October
1915 consisted of Scriabin's *Simfoniiā No.1
i No.3* [Symphony No.1 and No.3] and the
Kontsert fis-moll dliā f-no s orkestrom
[Concerto in F-sharp Minor for Piano and
Orchestra]. The complete orchestral works
of Scriabin were to be performed in a series
of four concerts. Rachmaninoff was the soloist in the concerto with Koussevitzky conducting the Russkogo Muzykal'nogo Obshchestva
[Russian Musical Society Orchestra] and is
reported as playing sensitively, bringing
out the beauty of the work especially in the
theme and variation section. The audience
responded enthusiastically and demanded more;
Rachmaninoff returned with Scriabin's D-sharp
Minor (Op.8) and C-sharp Minor (Op.42)
Etiūdy [Etudes] as encores. Only once does
Engel reflect on Scriabin's own interpretations, stating that only he could bring
out the soul of his music. Scriabin had
just died in April of that year (1915).

93.   ———. Edited and compiled by I. Kunin.
Glazami sovremennika, isbrannye stat'i o
russkoĭ muzyke, 1898-1918. [Through the
eyes of a contemporary, selected articles
about Russian music. 1898-1918] Moskva:
Sovetskiĭ Kompozitor, 1971.   524 p.
ML 300.1 E54   OCLC 8004110

In honor of the 100th anniversary of
Engel's birth held in 1968, this volume of
reviews (from 1898 to 1917) was compiled
and edited by I. Kunin. It is but a small
portion of reviews written by important
music critic Iuliĭ Engel (1868-1927), who
also wrote under pseudonyms- Giusto, G-o,
and his initials Iu E. All the reviews
selected for this compilation are solely
concerned with Russian music; reviews dealing
with foreign musical art are not considered
in this volume. There are nine articles
(reviews) on Rachmaninoff in the collection:
"Prem'era opery *'Zhizn' za Tsariā'*" [Premiere
of the "Life of the Tsar"], a review of the

performance of Glinka's opera at the Bol'shoĭ
with Rachmaninoff conducting, originally
published in *Russkie vedomosti* (22 September
1904). "*Zhizn' za T͡sari͡a,*" again Rachmaninoff conducting at the Bol'shoĭ, review published in *Russkie vedomosti* (25 September
1904). "S. Rakhmaninov (kont͡sert 3 i 4
i͡anvari͡a)," concerts of 3-4 January in which
Rachmaninoff performed his *Kont͡sert dli͡a f-no
s orkestrom No.2* [Concerto for Piano and
Orchestra No.2], *Sonata dli͡a f-no No.2*
[Sonata for Piano No.2], and conducted his
Simfonii͡a No.2 [Symphony No.2] and Strauss'
"*Don Zhuana*" [Don Juan], review appeared 6
April 1909. "Pervai͡a simfonii͡a Skri͡abina
pod upravleniem S. Rakhmaninova" [Scriabin's
First Symphony conducted by S. Rachmaninoff],
fifth Moscow Philharmonic concert performed
on 15 April 1909, review appeared 17 April
1909. "Rakhmaninov i Skri͡abin" [Rachmaninoff
and Scriabin], sixth Philharmonic Society
concert of the 1909 season, featuring Rachmaninoff conducting his *Simfonii͡a No.2*
[Second Symphony], *Ostrov mertvykh* [Isle of
the Dead] (first performance), and Mussorgsky's *Noch' na Lysoĭ gore* [Night on Bare
Mountain], review appeared 21 April 1909.
"Rakhmaninovskiĭ kont͡sert" Rachmaninoff performing his own works- *Variat͡sii na temu
Shopena* [Variations on a Theme of Chopin],
Preli͡udii [Preludes] Opp.23 and 32 (selec-
tions), etc., recital performed on 13 Decem-
ber 1911, review appeared 15 December 1911.
"Rakhmaninovskiĭ kont͡sert" Rachmaninoff per-
forming his own works- *Sonata dli͡a f-no No.2*
[Sonata No.2], *Eti͡udy-Kartiny soch.33*
[Etudes-tableaux Op.33] (selections), *Siren'*
[Lilacs], *Barkarola* [Barcarolle], *Pol'ka de
W.R.*, etc., performed on 3 December 1913,
review appearing in *Russkie vedomosti* 5
December 1913. "Kont͡sert S. Rakhmaninova i
N. Koshits" [Rachmaninoff and Nina Koshetz
concert], concert featuring Nina Koshetz
with Rachmaninoff as accompanist in songs
by the composer, including the first per-
formance of *Shest' stikhotvoreniĭ* [Six
Poems], the Six Songs Op.38 (dedicated to
Nina Koshits), concert on 24 October 1916,

review appearing 25 October 1916. *"Utes i 'Kolokola'* S. Rakhmaninova" [The Rock and The Bells by Rachmaninoff], concert of 7 January 1917, Rachmaninoff conducting the Bol'shoĭ Orchestra and Chorus, review appeared 10 January 1917. Illustrated, name index.

94.   Espina, Noni. *Repertoire for the Solo Voice:* A fully annotated guide to works for the voice published in modern editions and covering material from the 13th century to the present. Metuchen, N.J.: Scarecrow Press, 1977. 2 vols. 1290 p. (SR p.849-51)   ML 128 S3 E8   ISBN 0-8108-0943-5   OCLC 2645164

A listing of 10,000 vocal works by 930 composers. There are 15 songs by Rachmaninoff entered in the second volume; all are properly categorized as to: title, type of voice, source of poetry, range, tessitura, available publisher, difficulty of accompaniment, and all have a brief comment on the musical requirements needed to perform the work. This is more information than offered in the Kagen work (1968).

95.   Estrin, Morton. "Playing the Preludes, Opus 32." *Clavier* 12 (October 1973): 19-20.

Estrin describes Rachmaninoff's pianistic style and gives interpretive suggestions for *Preludes Op.32, Nos.5 and 13.*

96.   Evans, May Garrettson. *Music and Edgar Allen Poe: A Bibliographic Study.* Baltimore, Md.: Johns Hopkins Press, 1939. 97 p. ML 80 E62 M9   OCLC 598220   (Reprint--New York: Greenwood Press, 1968. 97 p. ML 80 P65 E9   OCLC 2260)

A study of the influence of Poe's works on composers and musicians. Evans examines Rachmaninoff's setting of *The Bells*, relating the unusual translation process that occured—an English translation of a German translation of a Russian translation, and comments on the 1931 USSR performance of *The Bells* when the composer was denounced and Poe insulted by the press. This incident eventually led to the ban of Rachmaninoff's works in the USSR. Evans' study includes a bibliography of musical settings of Poe's texts. Those interested in an extension of Evans' survey of Poe and music, see Burton Pollin's article "More Music to Poe" in *Music and Letters* 54 (October 1973): 391-404.

97.   Ewen, David, ed. *The New Book of Modern Composers*. 3d ed. New York: Knopf, 1961. 491 p. (SR p.311-21)   ML 390 E83 OCLC 599747

This collection of essays on 32 composers has undergone several revisions since the first edition in 1943 as *The Book of Modern Composers*. It was revised and enlarged in 1950 and 1956. The current edition includes some new material. Each composer is represented by a short biographical sketch, a personal note, a short essay by the composer, and an essay by an authority on the subject. The Rachmaninoff material included in the 1943 edition and the revised 1961 edition is the same with the exception of the essay on the composer. The 1943 essay, excerpted from Riesemann's *Rachmaninoff's Recollections* (1934), is replaced in the current edition with an essay by Richard Anthony Leonard, taken from his work *A History of Russian Music* (1957). Riesemann's work is also dropped in the new bibliographical list. List of principal works, bibliography, list of contributors, index.

98.   Fagan, Keith. "Rachmaninoff's Major Works."
        Musical Opinion 91 (May 1968): 431-33.

        Fagan quotes Rachmaninoff on the subject
        of modern music and concurs with his
        position. He briefly examines the composer's
        personality and describes several works,
        including the First Symphony, *Isle of the
        Dead, Symphonic Dances,* and *The Bells.*

99.   Farwell, Arthur. "Keeping in Touch With
        World's Musical Growth Through the Piano:
        Sergei Rachmaninoff, the Leader Among
        Russian Composers of the Younger Genera-
        tion- He Prefigures the Brooding, Somberly
        Reflective State of Soul." *Musical America*
        13 (1 April 1911): 13.

        One of a series of articles by American
        composer Arthur Farwell describing composers
        and music of various countries. Farwell
        shows unusual insight in understanding
        Rachmaninoff. He reflects on hearing the
        composer on tour in this country in 1909,
        stating that Rachmaninoff at that time
        cleared the doubts about his slight achieve-
        ment (*Prelude in C-sharp Minor Op.3, No.2*),
        by proving his ability as a great composer
        in performances of the Third Concerto and
        the *Isle of the Dead.* Farwell effectively
        describes Rachmaninoff's work in terms of
        colors and hues. He briefly examines selec-
        tions from *Morceaux de salon* Op.10, *Moments
        musicaux* Op.16, *Preludes* Op.23, *Variations
        on a Theme of Chopin,* and *Sonata in D Minor*
        Op.28.

100.   Faurot, Albert. *Concert Piano Repertoire,*
        A Manual of Solo Literature for Artists
        and Performers. Metuchen, N.J.: Scarecrow
        Press, 1974. 338 p. (SR p.234-41)
        ML 128 P3 F39   ISBN 0-8108-0685-1
        OCLC 703192

This is a more thorough listing of Rachmaninoff's piano works than shown in Friskin and Freundlich's volume of 1954. Faurot's work includes informative annotations but lacks publisher data. There is no mention of the composer's revision of several of the solo pieces, such as *Humoresque, Melodie in E Major* (Op.3, No.3), and the second *Moment musicale* (Op.16 No.2). Performers should be aware of these revised pieces and use them. Unfortunately only two of the transcriptions are mentioned. Bibliography, chronology of composers, no index.

101. Flanagan, William. "Sergei Rachmaninoff: a Twentieth-Century Composer." *Tempo* 22 (Winter 1951-52): 4-8.

    After a long period of not composing, Rachmaninoff returned to writing music in 1926, which happened to be when musical trends were inclined towards neo-classic styles. The author discusses the surrounding changes taking place, remarking that Rachmaninoff was undergoing a definite stylistic re-evaluation and that his compositions demonstrate modification made evident through comparative examination of early and late works. Flanagan points out stylistic changes in the works written after 1926.

102. Frank, Jonathan. "Rachmaninov and Medtner- a Comparison." *Musical Opinion* 81 (March 1958): 387.

    The author compares the compositional styles of Rachmaninoff and Medtner. Frank asserts that Medtner's piano solos contain more melody and less technically motivated figuration than exhibited in Rachmaninoff's solo piano works. He contends that Rachmaninoff's solo piano pieces are virtuoso-based in content. Medtner generally comes out ahead in the article.

103. Frankenstein, Alfred. "S.F. Symphony Concerts Given." *San Francisco Chronicle* 6 February 1937, p.4.

A review of a Friday evening Rachmaninoff recital presented at the War Memorial Opera House on 5 February 1937. Program consisted of the Bach-Liszt *Organ Fantasy and Fugue in G Minor*, Beethoven *Sonata in C Minor Op.111; Sonetto 123 di Petrarca in A-flat Major* and a Paganini Etude by Liszt, and also a group of Rachmaninoff's *Etudes-tableaux*. Frankenstein gave the performance a rave review, stating that the piano splashed great floods of color.

104. Friskin, James, and Irwin Freundlich. *Music for Piano*. A Handbook of Concert and Teaching Material from 1580 to 1952. New York: Holt, Rinehart and Winston, 1954. 432 p. ML 128 P3 F7 OCLC 526075 (Republication-- New York: Dover Publications, 1973. 434 p. ML 128 P3 F7 1973 ISBN 0-486-22918-1 OCLC 763470)

The Dover edition is an unabridged, slightly corrected republication of the work originally published in 1954. A new preface by Freundlich and a new biographical appendix have been added to the Dover edition. The book was innovative in its time and filled a void which then existed. Not all of Rachmaninoff's piano works are listed. Out of the 24 Preludes only 10 are described and the *Etudes-tableaux* are not enumerated at all. The four concerti and the *Rhapsody on a Theme of Paganini* are described in more detail. Bibliography, list of publishers, composer index.

105. Gaisberg, Frederick W. *The Music Goes Round*. New York: Macmillan Co., 1942. 273 p. ML 1055 G15 M8 OCLC 582301 (Reprint-- New York: Arno Press, 1977. ML 1055 G15 1977 ISBN 0-405-09678-X OCLC 2465083)

Also- (different title) *Music on Record.*
London: R. Hale, 1947. 269 p. ML 1055
G15 1947   OCLC 8167312

A history of the first fifty years of the
recording industry, with glimpses of many
great artists of the time; related in reminiscent, anecdotal style. Rachmaninoff's
recording career proved to be very successful
and lucrative. The author recalls the composer's dour personality and relates several
social encounters with him. Illustrations,
name index.

106.   ———. "The Last of the Three Giants of
the Volga Has Departed." *Gramophone*
(August 1943): 37-38.

Descriptive article relates the friendship
of three artistic giants: Rachmaninoff,
Gorky, and Chaliapin. Gaisberg states that
they were all born in 1873 (Maksim Gorky was
born in 1868), within a radius of 100 miles
of each other. Gaisberg reveals Rachmaninoff's humor, shrewd business sense, admiration and love for his family, and his
Russian pride.

107.   Gakkel', L. "Besedy o muzyke: Tretiĭ
fortepiannyĭ kont͡sert Rakhmaninova."
[Conversations about music: Rachmaninoff's
Third Piano Concerto] *Muzykal'nai͡a zhizn'*
6 (March 1963): 9-10.

The author investigates why the Third
Concerto is so well liked; lyricism, virtuosity, sadness, pathos are a few of the
elements mentioned. Gakkel' asserts that
the true Rachmaninoff is best represented
in the Third Concerto. The author continues
with a dramatic description of the concerto.

108. Gitel'makher, V. "Rakhmaninov v Lebedine."
      [Rachmaninoff in Lebedine] *Muzykal'naiā zhizn'* 18 (September 1968): 18.

      Reminiscences of the summer of 1893, when Rachmaninoff visited the Lysikov family estate in Lebedine, a small town in the Kharkov district. It was through Mikhail Akimovich Slonov that Rachmaninoff met this kind and generous family. The Lysikovs invited him to stay in their summer house to work on his music. It proved to be a fruitful summer, partly due to the Lysikov family, which took special care that Rachmaninoff was comfortable and that working conditions were optimal. The composer was occupied with *Fantaziiā* [Fantasy] Op.5, *Dve p'esy* [Morceaux de salon] Op.6, *Shest' romansov* [Six Songs] Op.4, and *Utes* [The Rock] Op.7 during that summer. Evdokīā Lysikova pampered the young composer. Rachmaninoff dedicated the song *Uzh ty, niva moiā* [Oh thou, my field] Op.4, No.5 to her. Illustrated.

109. Glinsky, M. "Kontserty v Petrograde."
      [Concerts in Petrograd] *Russkaiā muzykal'-naiā gazeta* (6 December 1915): 795-96.

      A review of Rachmaninoff performing his own piano works and those of Scriabin. This includes the controversial (in interpretation) Scriabin program that Rachmaninoff was then performing in Scriabin's memory (Scriabin had died in April of that year). Glinsky remarks on Rachmaninoff's conservative style, obliviousness to modern trends, and his use of neo-classic formulas. He feels that Rachmaninoff is most convincing and at his best when he performs his own works. All his performing characteristics were apparent in his appearances in Petrograd: purity, noble pathos, sincerity, and directness. Glinsky declares that Rachmaninoff, the pianist, is in full maturity and possesses the gift of keen musical perception.

The Scriabin works were played in the Rachmaninoff manner, with his definite stamp of interpretation. The author heard more Rachmaninoff than Scriabin in his performance. An interesting and informative review.

110. Goddard, Scott. "Rachmaninov the Composer." *Listener* 26 (11 September 1941): 385.

Goddard examines the popularity of Rachmaninoff the pianist, in contrast to Rachmaninoff the composer. Are people expecting too much of the composer? The author offers an appreciation of the songs, in particular, *Vesennie vody* [Spring Waters] Op.14, No.11.

111. Gol'dshtein, Mikhail. "Rakhmaninovskiĭ konkurs v Moskve." [Rachmaninoff competition in Moscow] *Novoye russkoye slovo*, 72 1 November 1983, p.4.

A description of the newly-formed Vsesoiûznyĭ Konkurs Imeni Rakhmaninova [All union Rachmaninoff competition], held in honor of the 110th anniversary of the composer's birth. The competition to be held in Moscow in November 1983 is open only to USSR pianists. There are several stages to the competition: the first stage consists of solo compositions, the second stage demands skill in accompanying (chamber music), and the final stage requires the performance of the *Rapsodiâ na temu Paganini* [Rhapsody on a Theme of Paganini]. Gol'dshtein recalls the unfair treatment that Rachmaninoff received from the Soviet press in 1931, when a ban was placed on the performance of his music. Gol'dshtein also reports on the naming of a concert hall, in a section of the Moskovskaiâ Konservatoriiâ [Moscow Conservatory] in memory of Rachmaninoff. It occupies the old building (since refurbished) that originally housed the Moskovskiĭ Sinodal'nyĭ Institut [Moscow Synodical Institute]. The

The famed Synodical Choir performed the premieres of Rachmaninoff's *Vsenoshchnoe bdenie* [All Night Vigil (Vespers)] and the *Liturgiĩa Ioanna Zlatousta* [Liturgy of Saint John Chrysostom]. Gol'dshtein wonders if these religious works will ever be performed in the new Rachmaninoff Hall. Curiously, there is no reference to the very first Rachmaninoff piano competition that was inaugurated in the USA in Spring 1945. ̆The winners of the first Soviet Vsesoĭuznyĭ Konkurs Imeni Rakhmaninova are mentioned in a review of the event in *Novoye russkoye slovo* 73 5 January 1984, p.5.

112.   Goldsmith, Harris. "'The Complete Rachmaninoff'- Homage Well Paid." *High Fidelity* 24 (January 1974): 58-60.

A review of the first three albums (volumes) of RCA's five-volume, fifteen-record release called, "The Complete Rachmaninoff." The author laments that RCA did not capture more of Rachmaninoff's repertoire on disc. He reports that Rachmaninoff proposed that his 1942 recital tour be recorded for possible future release, but unfortunately RCA rejected his suggestion. Goldsmith compares different recorded versions of several pieces. Contents of Vols. 1-3 of "The Complete Rachmaninoff" are listed. Note- unfortunately this important collection of Rachmaninoff recordings is unavailable; hopefully RCA will consider a re-release.

113.   Gozunpud, Abram Akimovich. *Opernyĭ slovar'*. Moskva: Muzyka, 1965. 479 p. ML 102 06 G68   OCLC 5898491.

Opera dictionary describes Rachmaninoff's *Aleko*, *Francheska da Rimini* [Francesca da Rimini], and *Skupoĭ rytŝar'* [Miserly Knight], along with first performance dates and other pertinent information. Illustrated, name index.

114.   ———. *Russkiĭ opernyĭ teatr na rubezhe XIX-XX vekov i F.I. Shaliapin 1890-1904.* [Russian opera theater at the turn of the XIX-XX century and F.I. Chaliapin 1890-1904] Leningrad: Muzyka, 1974. 263 p. (SR p.74-76)   ML 420 S53 G695   OCLC 4055751

A history of criticism of Russian opera at the turn of the century, with attention to the roles acted and sung by Fedor Ivanovich Chaliapin from 1890-1904. Gozunpud examines an opulent period in the history of Russian opera. Tchaikovsky, Rimsky-Korsakov, Taneev, and Borodin are the principal composers discussed in this work. Gozunpud gives the history of Rachmaninoff's *Aleko*, from its conception to its first staged performance at the Bol'shoĭ Teatr on 27 April 1893. There is also an investigation of the personalities of the principal characters, as well as an examination of the musical development of *Aleko*. Illustrated, no index.

115.   Gray-Fisk, Clinton. "Rachmaninoff's Seventieth Birthday." *Musical Opinion* (April 1943): 221-22.

Gray-Fisk calls to attention the critical abuse that Rachmaninoff received from the press, quoting many of the critics' remarks. He recommends that critics and historians judge the composer on his total output and not summarize his role in music based on one or two compositions. He also ventures to prophesy, "It is probable that he will be assigned a position, if below the very greatest, at least alongside such figures as Dvořák, Tchaikovsky, and Elgar." The article concludes with reports of Rachmaninoff's continued activity as composer and that at seventy he is anything but "played out." Unfortunately, as noted in the article, Rachmaninoff died shortly before his seventieth birthday, while the article was in press.

116.   Greenawalt, Terrence Lee. "A Study of the
         Symphony in Russia from Glinka to the
         Early Twentieth Century." Ph.D. diss.,
         University of Rochester, Eastman School
         of Music, 1972. Ann Arbor, Mich.: Univer-
         sity Microfilms, 1974. 214 p. ML 1255
         G65M   OCLC 1061829

         Forty symphonies by fifteen Russian com-
         posers are used as a basis for this study
         on the symphony in Russia. Rachmaninoff's
         First Symphony is structurally analyzed and
         examined. Greenawalt points out that themes
         from this symphony are based on themes from
         the *Okteodos* (Russian book of chants) and
         observes the use of the *Dies irae* in the
         work. Author vita, biographies, musical
         examples, bibliography, no index.

117.   Gronowicz, Antoni. *Sergei Rachmaninoff*.
         Translated from the Polish by Samuel
         Sorgenstein and Edna Ruth Johnson. New
         York: E.P. Dutton and Co., 1946. 153 p.
         ML 410 R12 G72   OCLC 1703854

         A dramatic narrative biography for
         juvenile readers. A young people's intro-
         duction to Rachmaninoff. Illustrations,
         list of works, bibliography, index.

118.   Grove, Sir George. *Dictionary of Music and
         Musicians* 5th ed., ed. by Eric Blom.
         London: Macmillan; New York: St. Martin's
         Press, 1954. 9 vols. 8,923 p. ML 100
         G885 1954   OCLC 6085892

         A meager representation of Rachmaninoff
         and his productivity written by Rosa New-
         march, with later additions by Eric Blom.
         This adverse summation of the composer's
         work reflects the prevalent critical and
         scholarly consensus of Rachmaninoff, based
         largely on the premise that because his
         music was so readily accessible to the

masses it would not survive long after the composer was not around to propagate it. For a contrast in coverage of the composer see Geoffrey Norris' survey of Rachmaninoff in the *New Grove Dictionary* (1980).

119. Hanson, Lawrence, and Elisabeth Hanson. *Prokofiev - A Biography in Three Movements.* New York: Random House, 1964. 368 p. ML 410 P865 H3   OCLC 986827   Also- London: Cassell, 1964. 243 p.   ML 410 P865 H3 OCLC 2468067

   There are several references to Rachmaninoff in this biography of Prokofiev. The adverse encounter of the two composers after Rachmaninoff's performance of works of Scriabin in 1915 is presented here. The authors point out the influence Rachmaninoff had on Prokofiev and his music. There is a stylistic comparison of the two pianists, as well as remarks from both of them about each other's music. Illustrations, catalogue of works (Prokofiev), bibliography, name index.

120. Harris, Jr., George. "Rachmaninoff as a Writer of Songs." *Musical Monitor* 9 (October 1918): 61-63.

   A descriptive survey of Rachmaninoff's song literature. The author touches on about half the songs, selecting from the entire output (through Op.34). Commenting on the two schools of vocal writing, opera and song, he states that Rachmaninoff's vocal expression has "welded together the broad style of operatic vocalism and the delicacies of lyric thought."

121. Hazen, David W. "Famous Russian Musician Frowns on Cold Weather." *The Daily Oregonian*, 23 January 1937, p.6.

Rachmaninoff sharply repudiates a tactless comment made by the interviewer, who understood that this was to be his farewell tour. Reflecting on *The Bells* Rachmaninoff regrets that he did not have the original text of Poe's poem to work with; instead he used a Russian version translated by Konstantin Dmitrievich Bal'mont, which was then translated into German by Berthold Feivel, and finally from the German translated into English by Fanny Copeland. The composer sarcastically remarks on the numerous translations- "...so there was nothing of Poe left."

122.   Henderson, A.M. "Personal Memories of Rachmaninoff." *Musical Opinion* (May 1943): 257-58.

Henderson and his wife first met Rachmaninoff in 1933 at his villa "Senar" on Lake Lucerne. They became good friends and visited each other often; Rachmaninoff reciprocated by spending some time with the Hendersons in Glasgow when he toured the UK. The last time they heard him play was in 1939 at the International Musical Festival in Lucerne. The author freely reminisces about the warm, friendly visits with the composer's family, his generosity, simplicity, etc.. Henderson also describes "Senar." This article must have made good copy, for basically the same article, under different titles, appeared in *Etude* 72 (April 1954): 9, as "Rachmaninoff as I Knew Him;" in *Music and Musicians* 5 (November 1956): 15, as "Rachmaninoff at Home"; and an early version by Mrs. A.M. Henderson also titled, "Rachmaninoff at home" in *Musical Opinion* (April 1938): 593-94.

123.   Hill, Edward Burlingame. "Sergei Rachmaninoff, A Retrospect." *New Music Review* 9 (1910): 573-75.

Hill views Rachmaninoff's conservative compositional style as a healthy balance with the "ultramodernity" that seemed prevalent at the time. He contends that the *Isle of the Dead* is Rachmaninoff's most vital and significant achievement. Note- manuscript score of the *Isle of the Dead* was just completed the year before this article was published. Rachmaninoff conducted the work on his first USA tour (Chicago and New York), the winter of 1909-10. Evidently the author attended one of these performances.

124. Hill, Ralph, ed. *The Concerto*. London, Baltimore, Md.: Penguin Books, 1952. (Reprint-- Westport, Conn.: Greenwood Press, 1978. 448 p. [SR p.298-300] MT 125 H498 ISBN 0-837-19083-5 OCLC 3541540)

A chapter on Rachmaninoff, written by John Culshaw, offers a stylistic comparison of Rachmaninoff and Medtner, as well as presenting a basic summary of Rachmaninoff's First, Second, and Third Concerti and Medtner's Second and Third Concerti. No index.

125. Hinson, Maurice. *Guide to the Pianist's Repertoire*. Bloomington, Ind.: Indiana University Press, 1973. 831 p. (SR p.504-06) ML 128 P3 H5 ISBN 0-253-32700-8 OCLC 599530

126. ─────. *Guide to the Pianist's Repertoire-Supplement*. Bloomington, Ind.: Indiana University Press, 1979. 413 p. (SR p.266-67) ML 128 P3 H5 ISBN 0-253-32701-6 OCLC 4835408

127. ———. *Music for Piano and Orchestra*. An annotated guide. Bloomington, Ind.: Indiana University Press, 1981. 327 p. (SR p.237-38)   ML 128 P3 H5   ISBN 0-253-12435-2   OCLC 6863119

The *Guide to the Pianist's Repertoire* supersedes the 1954 pioneer work of Friskin and Freundlich in this genre. Hinson's comprehensive volume lists and grades the solo piano works of Rachmaninoff; it also lists publishers of same. The transcriptions are not listed. The appendix to this volume contains a valuable inclusion of Anton Grigor'evich Rubinstein's historical recital programs that he presented in Moscow in 1885-86. Young Rachmaninoff was there to hear the series and was much impressed and greatly influenced by the grand pianist-composer. The *Guide to the Pianist's Repertoire-Supplement* volume of 1979 adds some new publishers to the list, including the USSR edition of the complete piano works (not fully identified here, but presumedly the Moskva: Mugiz, P.A. Lamm edition), and includes an edition containing most of the transcriptions, minus two: the Kreisler *Liebesfreud* and *Liebesleid*. Hinson's *Music for Piano and Orchestra* (1981) includes the four piano concerti and the *Rhapsody on a Theme of Paganini* and is fully annotated. All three of Hinson's books include biographical material, bibliographies, indexes and appendixes.

128. Hodgson, Leslie. "Rachmaninoff, the Pianist." *Musical America* 63 (10 April 1943): 6,26, 33.

A qualitative summation of Rachmaninoff's career as pianist. Hodgson sheds some light on Rachmaninoff's maturation as concert pianist. Rachmaninoff's performances as pianist were not always conceived and played on an equally high level. Hodgson cites performances when Rachmaninoff played with hard tone and austere expression and was considered a purely cerebral performer. The concert season of 1940-41 marked the highest interpretive level of his career, informs Hodgson, when his performance was, "suffused with glowing emotion and rare graciousness of delivery." The author sees a mellowing development in Rachmaninoff's piano performance. Illustrated.

129.   Hofmann, Michel-Rostislav. *La vie des grands musiciens russes*. [The life of the great Russian musicians] Paris: Editions du Sud, 1965. 288 p. (SR p.183-90 and 275-76)   ML 390 H71   OCLC 6328347

Biographical sketches of Russian musicians from Glinka to Shostakovich and Khachaturĩan. The chapter on Rachmaninoff titled, "Rachmaninov, masque de cire et coeur vibrant" [Rachmaninoff, mask of wax and vibrant heart] concentrates on his musical upbringing, study with Zverov, failure of the First Symphony, N. Dahl's cure, and his pursuit of three musical paths. Includes an illustration of a portion of the song *Fragment from de Musset* Op.21, No.6, autographed by Rachmaninoff. Hofmann also highlights several common quotes made by the composer- why he wrote the *Prelude in C-sharp Minor Op.3, No.2*, importance of melody, and his anti-futurism statement. Illustrated, musical examples, list of works (selections), no index.

130.   ———. *Histoire de la musique russe* - des origines à nos jours. [History of Russian music - up to the present] Paris: Buchet/ Chastel, 1968. 278 p. (SR p.177-79) ML 300 H59

131.   ———. *Petite histoire de la musique russe* - des origines à Stravinski. [Short

history of Russian music - up to Stravinsky] Paris, Montreal: Bordas, 1972. 159 p. (SR p.141-45) ML 300 H62

Both of Hofmann's volumes on the history of Russian music are basically similar in content. Hofmann (native Russian who lived in Paris) offers a survey of Rachmaninoff's education, failure (First Symphony), success (Second Concerto), style, Russianism and influences. Hofmann claims that Rachmaninoff is little appreciated in France because Russian lyricism is not felt properly by the French, just as Fauré is felt by the French and not understood by others. Hofmann criticizes the symphonies for their lack of innovation and the First Concerto for sounding like Tchaikovsky and Liszt. List of major works.

132.   Holcman, Jan. "Hidden Treasures of Rachmaninoff." *Saturday Review* 41 (30 August 1958): 31-33.

Holcman aptly describes Rachmaninoff's technical skill and offers interesting commentary on several of his recordings. Illustrated.

133.   Holt, Richard. "The Genius of Rachmaninov." *Gramophone* 6 (January 1929): 352-54.

Descriptions of several works, including the Second Concerto, *Isle of the Dead*, *Variations on a Theme of Chopin*, and the *Etudes-tableaux*. Holt bemoans the fact that out of Rachmaninoff's vast output only a half-dozen piano pieces and a few songs have been recorded. He asks why the Second Concerto was not recorded in a complete edition. Note- The second and third movements, of the <u>first</u> recording of the Second Concerto, were recorded in January 1924, and the first movement was later recorded in

December 1924 and issued separately. A new recording of the Second Concerto was made in April 1929 and issued as a complete work.

134. Hopkins, Antony. *Talking About Concertos.* An analytical study of a number of well-known concertos from Mozart to the present day. London: Heinemann Educational, 1970. 148 p. (SR p. 123-34) MT 125 H667 ISBN 0-435-81420-6 OCLC 151452

   Critical descriptions of eleven concerti, including Rachmaninoff's Third Concerto. Hopkins examines the composer's use of thematic variation, motivic recurrences, and other stylistic peculiarities of the concerto. Musical examples, index.

135. Howes, Frank. "Musical Imagination: The Case of Rachmaninov." *Listener* 23 (22 February 1940): 391.

   Elements that make a composer great are examined by the author. Howes, in regard to Rachmaninoff's creative productivity, assesses the composer's imagination, thought process, weakness, and musical genius. He emphasizes Rachmaninoff's strength of musical imagery.

136. ―――. "Rachmaninov." *Monthly Musical Record* (May 1943): 81-85.

   A critical summation of Rachmaninoff's pianistic temperament and compositional style. Howes dwells on the composer's slavic fatalism, melancholic expression, and innate musical talents. He compares Rachmaninoff's gift of melody with that of Schubert's.

137.   Hughes, Rupert, ed. and comp., revised and
       edited by Deems Taylor and Russell Kerr.
       Music Lovers' Encyclopedia. New York:
       Garden City Books, 1954. 885 p. ML 100
       H892 ISBN 0-385-00124-X OCLC 4739860

       Collection of biographical and critical
       essays written by noted authorities. The
       material on Rachmaninoff is written by
       Richard Anthony Leonard, who views the com-
       poser as the historical link between the
       Nationalists (mainly the "Five") and the
       Eclectics (Tchaikovsky and Rubinstein) who
       lean towards music of the West. Charts,
       dictionary of terms, pronunciation guide,
       opera stories, etc.

138.   Hull, Robin. "The Problem of Rachmaninoff."
       Musical Opinion (April 1942): 229-31.

       Differences of opinion about Rachmaninoff's
       music. Hull reveals what the pro-Rachmani-
       noff people maintain and the sentiments of
       those who are anti-Rachmaninoff. The author
       stresses that in evaluating Rachmaninoff's
       music one must consider his entire output.
       Another article based on differing opinions
       about Rachmaninoff is Eric Salzman's,
       "Rachmaninoff, Da-Nyet" in *Stereo Review*
       (May 1943).

139.   Isaev, N., ed. "Nove e Rakhmaninove." [New
       information about Rachmaninoff] *Sovetskaia
       muzyka* 6 (1961): 72-76.

       Thirteen letters relating to Rachmaninoff
       are published here for the first time. The
       first letter, dated 27 June 1942, is from
       soldiers of the Red Army congratulating the
       composer on his impending 70th birthday and
       thanking him for his support in the war
       effort. The last letter, dated 28 August
       1943, is addressed to Vladimir Robertovich
       Vil'shau [Wilshaw]. The letters are housed

in the Tsentral'nom Gosudarstvennom Arkhive Oktiabr'skoĭ Revoliutsii [Central State Archive of the October Revolution].

140.   Jacobson, Robert. "The Vocal Rachmaninoff." *Opera News* 38 (22 December 1973): 24-27.

A centennial anniversary article that surveys Rachmaninoff's opera activity both as writer and conductor. Jacobson observes the three Rachmaninoff operas, as well as the opera sketches that were left unfinished. He comments on Rachmaninoff's experience as opera conductor with the Mamontov Private Opera Company and during his tenure at the Bol'shoĭ. The solo songs are briefly discussed. There are interesting remarks on interpreting the songs made by Maria Kurenko and Jennie Tourel. Illustrated.

141.   Johnson, Harrison W. "Musical Musings." *International Musician* (December 1942): 5.

A recital review. Program included-Beethoven *Sonata in D Minor Op.31, No.2,* Chopin *Scherzo in C-sharp Minor Op.39, Ballade in F Minor Op.52,* and the Liszt *Tarantella* (from *Années de pèlerinage,* "Venezia e Napoli"). The review regards Rachmaninoff's style and interpretation and offers a comparison with Busoni.

142.   Jong, W.C. De. "Rachmaninoff's persoonlijkheid: Tien jaar na zijn dood (28 maart 1943)." [Rachmaninoff's personality: Ten years after his death (28 March 1943)] *Mens en melodie* 8 (March 1953): 69-72.

An interesting psychological study of the composer. De Jong looks at Rachmaninoff's complex personality and notes the effect this had on his life and artistic creativity.

The author, Rev. W.C. De Jong, points out
that Rachmaninoff never made a religious
statement or ever referred to his religious
affiliation. De Jong contends that the composer's music lacks development, with the
Second Concerto initiating the style, and
subsequent works never surpassing this
style. He goes on to assert that Rachmaninoff suffered from psychic instability,
melancholia, and hypochondria and, being an
introverted person, was unable to adapt
himself to life situations. De Jong compares
him to his literary counterpart, Stefan
Zweig, who left his country and in his vision
saw no future. Note- Austrian writer Zweig
was forced into exile because of his Jewish
origin and longed for his Salzburg; he
eventually took his own life in Brazil.
Circumstances for comparison with Rachman-
noff are not quite applicable.

143.   Kagen, Sergius. *Music for the Voice*. A
       Descriptive List of Concert and Teaching
       Material. New York: Rinehart and Co.,
       1949. 507 p. (SR p.368,382-85) Also-
       Second and revised ed.--Bloomington, Ind.:
       Indiana University Press, 1968. 780 p.
       (SR p.595-98) ML 128 V7 K3 ISBS 0-253-
       33955-3 OCLC 1722

       A listing of 19 Rachmaninoff songs with
       information on compass, tessitura, suitabil-
       ity of voice type, translations, and
       editions. Included are descriptive remarks
       on each song. Only songs with English trans-
       lations have been considered. Kagen comments
       on the difficulty of translating Russian
       into English, two of the problems being the
       rhythmical (metric patterns) differences of
       the language and the use of obscure folk
       metaphors.

144.   Kalashnikov, Dmitriĭ. *Shkol'nikam o S.V.
       Rakhmaninove*. [For students - about Rach-

maninoff] Voronezh: T͡sentral'no - Chernozemnoe, Knizhnoe Izdatel'stvo, 1969. 67 p.

Written under the direction of the Tambovskiĭ Oblastnoĭ Institut Usovershenstvovaniĭa Uchiteleĭ [Tambov Regional Institute for Teacher Enrichment]. This work is directed towards high school teachers, as an aid in teaching aesthetics by means of study and understanding the life of a great composer. Tambov's greatest musical representative is Rachmaninoff. The Tambov district and specifically "Ivanovka" is where he loved to be, both at play and at work. Kalashnikov based his material on documents, letters, and reminiscences from available archives. A map of the Tambov area, showing where Rachmaninoff resided, and a diagram of the "Ivanovka" estate are included in the volume. The Tambov district has been prepared for tourism since 1968, when improvements and restorations were made to the "Ivanovka" property. The author delves in depth into the Rachmaninoff family lineage, going back as far as the 13th century. He includes a short biography, stressing the stays at "Ivanovka" and some 60 letters, first dated 18 February 1892 and the last dated 19 November 1941. The letters help reveal the nature and personality of the composer. The Tambov district was of great inspiration to Rachmaninoff, who spent many of his youthful days here ("Ivanovka") visiting and playing with the Satins and the Skalons. Later in life he often returned there to spend time composing. Illustrated, bibliography, no index.

145.   Kammerer, Rafael. "Golden Age of Pianists Preserved on Old Records." *Musical America* 77 (February 1957): 28-29.

A sampling of artists and their recordings made in the early years of recording. Kammerer comments on early recordings of Busoni, De Pachmann, Backhaus, Paderewski, Godowsky,

Hofmann, Grainger, Sauer, Rosenthal, and Rachmaninoff. He examines several of Rachmaninoff's recordings of his transcriptions-*Liebesleid, Liebesfreud, Scherzo from a Midsummer Night's Dream* and recordings of his *Polichinelle*, as well as Tchaikovsky's *Troika* (Op.37, No.11), and Handel's *Harmonious Blacksmith Variations* (from *Suite No.5 in E Major*). Kammerer makes some biased remarks in comparing the styles of the old masters to the contemporary styles of the pianists of this generation.

146. ―――. "The Golden Art of Sergei Rachmaninoff." *American Record Guide* (October 1966): 156-65.

    Kammerer believes Rachmaninoff was the most "phonogenic" of all pianists, stating that his command of the keyboard comes through on every recording he made, even better on discs than it did in recital. The author surveys Rachmaninoff's recordings. Included is a listing of all the records, with date of recording, matrix number, and record number. Rachmaninoff recorded for RCA Victor and HMV (RCA's British affiliate) from 1920 to 1943.

147. Kandinskiĭ, Alekseĭ. *Opery S.V. Rakhmaninova.* [Operas of S.V. Rachmaninoff] Moskva: Muzykal'noe Izd-vo, 1960. 47 p. ML 410 R12 K2

    Published as part of a series of opera guides. A survey of Rachmaninoff's operatic creativity, chiefly examining *Aleko, Skupoĭ rytsar'* [Miserly Knight], and *Francheska da Rimini* [Francesca da Rimini] with some comments on the unfinished projects- *Monna Vanna, Salummbo,* etc.. An introductory chapter describes the composer's skill in writing for voice, his operatic style, and influences. Kandinskiĭ contends that one reason *Francheska da Rimini* and *Skupoĭ rytsar'* are rarely heard is because they are both vocally and orchestrally difficult to perform.

148. ———. "O simfonizme Rakhmaninova." ocherk pervyĭ [Rachmaninoff's symphonism, first essay] *Sovetskaia muzyka* 4 (1973): 83-93.

This is the first essay of two essays by Kandinskiĭ on Rachmaninoff's symphonism; second essay is in *Sovetskaia muzyka* 7 (1973). The subject is covered broadly in this essay, with more specific detail in the second essay. The author points out that Rachmaninoff considered the *Kontsert No.2* i *Kontsert No.3* [Second and Third Concerti], the *Rapsodiia na temu Paganini* [Rhapsody on a Theme of Paganini], *Simfonicheskie tantsy* [Symphonic Dances], and *Kolokola* [The Bells] as his most important works. Kandinskiĭ states that lyric and epic-dramatic idioms are the composer's primary symphonic styles and that he reaches his highest point of lyric conception in the *Kontsert No.3*.

149. ———. "Simfonizm Rakhmaninova i yevo poema 'Kolokola'." ocherk vtoroĭ [Rachmaninoff's symphonism and his poem *The Bells*; second essay] *Sovetskaia muzyka* 7 (1973): 88-98.

This is the second essay by Kandinskiĭ on the subject of Rachmaninoff's symphonism; first essay appeared in *Sovetskaia muzyka* 4 (1973). The author presents a detailed analysis of *Kolokola* [The Bells]. He stresses that, contrary to opinion (see *Modern Russian Composers* by L. Sabaneyeff) he finds no pessimism in *Kolokola*. The epic style prevails; the first movement has a picturesque character, the second movement is lyric, and the last two movements exhibit the dramatic-epic form. Kandinskiĭ finds *Kolokola* the most complex of Rachmaninoff's creations.

150.　　Kardinar, N. "Neizvestnaiā stranitsa biografiĭ S.V. Rakhmaninova." [Unknown pages from the biography of S.V. Rachmaninoff] *Sovetskaiā muzyka* 2 (1979): 102-07.

Kardinar investigates Rachmaninoff's friendship with German painter Robert Sterl (1867-1932). The friendship began in Dresden in 1900 through Nikolaĭ Georgievich Struve. Sterl visited Rachmaninoff in Moscow in 1914 and painted the composer at the piano. The illustrations of paintings by Sterl accompanying the article show- a self-portrait by Sterl, portraits of Rachmaninoff (1909), view from Rachmaninoff's Dresden apartment (1914), Rachmaninoff at the piano in concert (1910), and an autographed letter (photographed) from Rachmaninoff to Sterl dated 23 February 1909. There is reference to several letters to the artist.

151.　　Kashkin, Nikolaĭ. "S.V. Rakhmaninov." *Moskovskie vedomosti,* 245, 5 September 1904, p.5.

Review of Rachmaninoff's first appearance as conductor at the Bol'shoĭ with Dargomyzhski's opera *Rusalka,* performed on 3 September 1904. The review gives attention to Rachmaninoff's innovation (but already in use in Europe) in the placement of the conductor's podium. For the first time in Russia, he faced both the orchestra and the stage instead of using the customary opera conducting position of facing the stage only, with back to the orchestra (similar to the prompter's position). Kashkin comments on the elegance of performance, subtle shading in the orchestra, and freshness of approach. Note- Rachmaninoff as conductor of the Bol'shoĭ gave that staid institution a new and fresh source of talent- the future looked promising.

152.   ———. "Novaĩa opera." [New opera]
           Moskovskie vedomosti, 247, 7 September
           1904.

   An announcement of Rachmaninoff's new
   opera, *Francheska da Rimini* [Francesca da
   Rimini]. Kashkin comments on the composer's
   setting of a subject that was previously
   used by other composers. A positive
   appraisal.

153.   ———. "Bol'shoĭ teatr." *Moskovskie
           vedomosti*, 260, 20 September 1904.

   Review of the Bol'shoĭ performance of
   Kniaz' Igor' [Prince Igor] by Borodin,
   directed by Rachmaninoff on 17 September
   1904. The very favorable review takes note
   of Rachmaninoff's polish as a conductor,
   subtle shadings in the overture, the use of
   choice tempi, fine accompaniment for the
   singers, etc. Kashkin remarks that the old
   established clichés were absent; freshness
   has appeared in the Bol'shoĭ Teatr.

154.   ———. *Ocherk istoriĭ russkoĭ muzyki*.
           [Outline of the history of Russian music]
           Kiev: D. Jurgenson, 1908. 223 p.
           (SR p.185-86)   ML 300 K17

   A condensed review of phases of the development of Russian music, partly based on
   personal impressions of Russian musical life;
   offers a wide-based overview of the history
   of Russian music. A brief biographical
   sketch is followed by general commentary on
   Rachmaninoff's compositions. Kashkin points
   out Rachmaninoff's success (at this early
   date) as a composer and pianist, and contends
   that his conducting prowess also qualifies
   him to become a professional conductor.

155.   Kehler, George, comp. *The Piano in Concert*.
        Metuchen, N.J.: Scarecrow Press, 1982.
        2 vols.   1431 p.   (SR vol.2, p.1013-24)
        ML 105 K43   ISBN 0-8108-1469-2   OCLC
        7653481

        A listing of over 10,000 programs of some
        2,000 pianists. A sampling of programs by
        diverse pianists, chronologically arranged
        and preceded by a short biographical sketch.
        There are 121 programs of Rachmaninoff listed
        in this massive work, starting with a student recital at the Moscow Conservatory, in
        1891 and concluding with the program of his
        last recital given in Knoxville on 17 February 1943. Some programs lack the location information and titles are not always
        listed uniformly (the latter not necessarily
        the author's fault). Preface, history of
        piano concert-recital, list of pianists.

156.   Keldysh, I͡uri. "Opernyĭ debut Rakhmaninov."
        [Rachmaninoff's opera debut] *Sovet͡skai͡a
        muzyka* 8 (1970): 66-78.

        Based on material in Keldysh's *Rakhmaninov
        i ego vremi͡a*. There is a detailed examination of *Aleko*, tracing the work from its
        conception to its first complete staged performance at the Bol'shoĭ, in 1893. Keldysh
        quotes reviewer Kruglikov's reaction to the
        performance. The opera performance was
        quite successful, an outcome that Rachmaninoff was not counting on. Keldysh observes
        compositional similarities to Tchaikovsky's
        Pikovai͡a dama [Queen of Spades] and influences of Rimsky-Korsakov, Ki͡ui [Cui], and
        Borodin. The article is important for its
        detailed observations surrounding the composer's first work to receive acclaimed
        success.

157.   ―――. *Rakhmaninov i ego vremi͡a*. [Rachmaninoff and his time] Moskva: Muzyka, 1973.
        450 p.   ML 410 R12 K4   OCLC 6693911

A biography, with emphasis on the artistic
activity of Rachmaninoff in close relationship to the cultural development in Russia,
from the end of the 19th century through the
first half of the 20th century. Important
events of the time, in the musical and
theatrical arts of Russia, are observed. A
large part of the volume is concerned with
descriptive analyses of the composer's works.
Keldysh's concluding remarks are sentimental
but sincere, "Rachmaninoff's creations have
not lost their freshness and attraction with
the passing of time. His music is dear to
the hearts of the Soviet people with the
depths of its truth, simplicity, feeling,
and undying faith in man...." Illustrations,
list of works, name index. A German translation of the introductory chapter of *Rakhmaninov i ego vremià* is in *Kunst und Literatur*
24 (April 1976): 426-35, titled "Rachmaninov
und seine Zeit."

158.   ———. "Tvorcheskiĭ put' velikogo muzykanta." [Artistic biography of a great
musician] *Sovetskaià muzyka* 4 (1973): 74-83.

A 100th anniversary (birth) commemorative
article. Keldysh presents biographical
material that focuses on the composer's
musical education. He claims that Rachmaninoff's most important works, in quality and
quantity, are the piano compositions and
that he was their best performer. Keldysh
regrets that even though Rachmaninoff
greeted the overthrow of Russian tsarism in
February 1917, he did not understand the
significance of the October Revolution and
soon afterward fled the country. The author
declares in eulogistic tones that Rachmaninoff's music is loved because of its truth-
fulness, simplicity, and direct feeling. A
German translation of "Tvorcheskiĭ put'
velikogo muzykanta" is in *Kunst und Literatur*
21 (October 1973): 1028-39, titled, "Der
Schaffensweg von Sergej Rachmaninow" translated by Christof Rüger.

159. Khentova, Sof'i͡a. "Mladshai͡a doch' Rakhmaninova." [Rachmaninoff's youngest daughter] *Muzykal'nai͡a zhizn'* 18 (September 1968): 19-20.

   Khentova relates her engaging visit with Tati͡ana Conus [Koni͡us], née Rakhmaninova, in her Paris apartment. Tati͡ana was much like her father, shy and retiring. Irina, Rachmaninoff's older daughter (who lived in New York) loved the USA and had an outgoing personality. Tati͡ana purportedly did not enjoy the USA and was apt to be gloomy. These descriptive remarks about Irina and Tati͡ana were made by their father, in 1922 when they were 19 and 15 years old respectively. Khentova describes the Paris apartment in vivid detail. Tati͡ana, her husband Boris Koni͡us, and son Alexander were in Paris during the Nazi occupation, which greatly disturbed her father. He was afraid that the Nazi officials might recognize that she was the daughter of a Russian artist, who at the time (1941) was aiding the Russian war relief program (concert proceeds, etc.), and retaliate against her. Khentova divulges that Rachmaninoff asked his daughters to destroy all his personal letters to them after his death. Irina complied; Tati͡ana did not. An interesting article that reveals Rachmaninoff's strong family bond. Illustrations.

160. Khubov, Georgiĭ Nikitich. *Muzykal'nai͡a publit͡sistika raznykh let.* stat'i, ocherkĭ, ret͡senziĭ [Musical publicism-various years. articles, stories, reviews] Moskva: Sovet͡skiĭ Kompozitor, 1976. 431 p. (SR p.234-37 and 286-87) ML 300.1 K5 OCLC 3969552

   Rachmaninoff is represented by two reviews in this collection of articles, stories, and reviews taken from diverse publications. "Tret'i͡a simfonii͡a Rakhmaninova" appeared in *Pravda* 26 July 1943. It comments on Rach-

maninoff's allegiance to his homeland, views
the early years, moral support from Tchaikovsky, and reviews a performance of the
Simfoniiā No.3 [Symphony No.3] performed by
the Gosudarstvennyĭ Simfonicheskiĭ Orkestr
Soiūza SSR [USSR State Symphony Orchestra]
under N. Golovanov. The symphony was performed with "Strong interpretation" and
was well received by the public. The review
states that the work is permeated with the
composer's deep love of his homeland and
stands as a reflection of Russian national
character. *Pravda* goes on to judge *Simfoniiā
No.3* as one of the deepest creations of
Russian symphonic music of the 20th century.
"Kont͡sert iz proĭzvedeniĭ Rakhmaninova"
is also from *Pravda*, appearing 13 October
1945. The first concert in a series of
concerts dedicated to the music of Rachmaninoff, it included *Simfoniiā No.2* [Symphony
No.2], *Utes* [The Rock] Op.7, and *Kont͡sert
No.2* [Concerto No.2] performed by the Simfonicheskiĭ Orkestr Vsesoiūznovo Radiokomiteta [Radio Committee Symphony Orchestra]
under N. Golovanov. Soloist in the concerto
was Sviātoslav Richter, who was noted as
appearing among the most talented of Soviet
youth. Generally, the review stresses
Rachmaninoff's mastery of Russian lyricism.

161. King, William G. "Music and Musicians:
Rachmaninoff Returns- A Talk With the
Russian Composer-Pianist." *New York Sun*,
13 October 1937, p.34.

An interview with the 64-year-old composer
at his Manhattan apartment. The interview
touches on- present composing inactivity,
Third Symphony's lack of success, the radio
(he had an aversion towards playing for that
medium), some latest Toscanini recordings,
and his daughters and grandchildren.

162.   Kogan, Grigori. "Rakhmaninov - Pianist."
        Sovetskaia muzyka sbornik chetvertyĭ,
        (1945): 58-80.

        Descriptive commentary on Rachmaninoff the
        pianist. Kogan describes Rachmaninoff's
        performances of Tchaikovsky's *Troika* (Op.37,
        No.11), several *Etiudy-Kartiny* [Etudes-
        tableaux], *Liebesfreud*, etc. Beautiful
        tone, marked rhythm, and sincere interpre-
        tation are characteristic in his performances.
        Kogan declares that Rachmaninoff was and
        remains a national pride of Russia and
        laments that he departed from his homeland.

163.   ———. "Iz perepiski S.V. Rakhmaninova."
        [Correspondence from Rachmaninoff] *Sovets-
        kaia muzyka* (March-April 1948): 117-22.

        Collection of 14 letters (some abbreviated),
        written by Rachmaninoff to Moscow teacher
        and friend, Vladimir Robertovich Vil'shau
        [Wilshaw]; first letter dated 9 September
        1922 and last letter dated 26 July 1939.
        Letters reveal the composer's mood, person-
        ality, views on art, condition of his life,
        and artistic work abroad.

164.   ———. "Zametki ob "Etiudakh-Kartinakh."
        [Notes about "Etude-Pictures"] *Sovetskaia
        Muzyka* 6 (1961): 77-78.

        Kogan differs with the use of the French
        title, *Etudes-tableaux* for Rachmaninoff's
        studies of Opp.33 and 39. He believes that
        the French title is misleading; tableau
        does not always mean picture in French and
        that the set would be better titled as
        "Kartinka"--small picture. Kogan also com-
        ments on the confusion in numbering of the
        Etudes because of the fact that Rachmaninoff
        originally withdrew three *Etudes* from Op.33.
        One was reworked and placed in Op.39 (No.6)
        by the composer; the other two (Op.33, Nos.3
        and 5) were published posthumously by Pavel
        Lamm (Muzgiz). Musical examples.

165. ———. "Vidennoe i slyshannoe." [The seen and heard] Sovetskaia muzyka 8 (1980): 95-101.

Recollections of Rachmaninoff by composer and critic Grigori Kogan. Kogan first heard Rachmaninoff perform in Kiev in 1913, performing his own works, and was very impressed by his pianism. The author, having heard Rachmaninoff many times subsequently, especially remembers his playing having an individual natural style, authoritative technique, beautiful tone, dramatic crescendi, and a smashing virtuosity. Kogan was firmly convinced of Rachmaninoff's greatness and placed him as number one pianist and he often made this opinion known. He also reflects on Chaliapin in the article.

166. Kolodin, Irving. "Sergei Rachmaninoff." In *Great Modern Composers*, edited by Oscar Thompson. New York: Dodd, Mead and Co., 1943. 383 p. (SR p.230-43) ML 390 T39 G7 OCLC 381639

Great Modern Composers is a compilation of concise biographies of 33 composers, written by various authors. Chapters appear as first printed in *The International Cyclopedia of Music and Musicians*, with some emendations and additions. Kolodin's biography is largely based on Oskar von Riesemann's, *Rachmaninoff's Recollections* (1934). There is descriptive commentary on Rachmaninoff's works and attention to his pianistic style, noting his "detail, lyric sensitivity, and manly tenderness." A list of works is included.

167. Koltypina, G.B., ed. and comp. *Bibliografiia muzykal'noi bibliografii*: annotirovannyi perechen' ukazatelei literatury, izdannoi na russkom iazyke. Moskva: Publichnaia biblioteka, 1963. 226 p. ML 120 R8 M65 OCLC 7904975

A bibliography of music bibliographies
and an annotated list of literature on
music published in the Russian language.
Qver 1200 bibliographical titles are listed.
There are 16 entries for Rachmaninoff. Name
index.

168.   Konen, Valentina. "Amerikanskaĩa kniga o
       Rakhmaninove." [An American book about
       Rachmaninoff] *Sovetskaĩa muzyka* 5 (1958):
       142-44.

       A review of Bertensson and Leyda's book on
       Rachmaninoff (1956). Konen commends the
       work, stating that sections dealing with
       the composer's years in the USA are of
       special interest to the Soviet reader.
       Aside from the review, she makes some acrid
       remarks, stressing the composer's lack of
       productivity in the USA compared to his
       creativity in Russia. Konen blames this
       degeneration on the "damaging influences
       of the atmosphere where he was transported"
       and also on the fact that Rachmaninoff lost
       important contact with live creative
       surroundings (perhaps meaning that he did
       not readily mix with creative American
       musicians). Konen makes interesting
       comments and offers a curious Soviet view
       of American music and its history. She
       labors too much on the fact that Rachmani-
       noff did not write as much in the USA as he
       did in Russia and does not reflect on Rach-
       maninoff's great success as pianist, which
       was in effect an alternate creative outlet.

169.   Kozhin, Nikolaĭ. "Sad poyot." [the garden
       sings] Otchuzna- "Golos Rodiny" i zhurnal
       Rodina 3 (1973): 2-5.

       100th anniversary (birth) article printed
       in a literary supplement to the newspaper
       Rodina, Izdanie Sovetskogo Komiteta po
       Kul'turnym Sviaziam s Sootechestvennikami

za Rubezhom [published by the Soviet committee for cultural relations for compatriots abroad]; this is written by a close friend and neighbor who lived near the Rachmaninoff estate in Russia. Reminiscent in content, the article recalls visits to the Rachmaninoffs and their good times together. Kozhin relates that Chaliapin tried to relieve the animosity between Rachmaninoff and Rimsky-Korsakov by offering a peace toast at a party where they were present, but instead made matters worse by doing so.

170. Kramer, Walter A. "Rachmaninoff, the Composer." *Musical America* 63 (10 April 1943): 6,29.

A qualitative summation of Rachmaninoff's career as a composer. Kramer professes that the quality which makes Rachmaninoff's music different from contemporary works of that time is its "breath of life." His music sounds like no one else's, and is readily recognizable because of its unique melody, harmony, and personal expression. Kramer notes that critics were eager to revel in composers' novel approaches to music, and deemed Rachmaninoff unworthy of serious consideration because he was unaffected by trends. "Where are the works of the composers then held up as significant," asks Kramer, who notes that Rachmaninoff's music is still heard, whereas the music of many of those who followed trends has disappeared. The author examines several works, including concerti and vocal works. Illustrated.

171. Kupferberg, Herbert. *Those Fabulous Philadelphians:* The Life and Times of a Great Orchestra. New York: Scribner's Sons, 1969. 257 p. ML 200.8 P52 074 OCLC 28276 Also- London: W.H. Allen, 1970. ML 200.8 P52 0744 OCLC 112412

A history of the Philadelphia Orchestra. There are several references to Rachmaninoff, who claimed this orchestra as his favorite. Stokowski remarks how the composer, upon hearing his new work rehearsed for the first time, would alter many things, because it did not sound the way he wanted it to sound. There are recollections of Rachmaninoff and Ormandy in a rehearsal of the Third Symphony in 1938 and the "Rachmaninoff Cycle Concerts" in 1939. Illustrations, discography, appendixes, name index.

172.   Kurenko, María. "The Songs: An Appreciation." *Tempo* 22 (Winter 1951-52): 25-26.

Kurenko explains that it is unfortunate that Rachmaninoff's songs are not performed often because of the language difficulty; they reflect his heritage and are perhaps his finest work. Kurenko notes stylistic changes in viewing the total output of songs.

173.   ———. "The Musical Forum - The Songs of Rachmaninoff." *Musical Courier* 147 (1 April 1953): 4.

Article published in observance of the 10th anniversary of the composer's death. Kurenko points out that it was Rachmaninoff's love of poetry that inspired him to compose songs; he drew upon Pushkin, Lermontov, Bunin, Balmont, Tolstoĭ and others. She divides the songs into several groups- dramatic songs, those based on Russian folklore, songs in the oriental style and lyric songs. Kurenko sees a change in the songs of Op.38, which were written to poetry of authors considered extreme and decadent at the time; in these songs, she maintains, Rachmaninoff was more intricate in the harmonic development and the accompaniment; a sign of growth in the composer's development.

174. Kuznetsov, Konstantin. "Rakhmaninov i russkaia muzyka." [Rachmaninoff and Russian music] *Literatura i Iskusstvo*, 8 August 1942.

A laudatory article on the composer in which Kuznetsov declares that Rachmaninoff is the principal preserver of all that comprises the traditions of Russian music. He quotes a Tchaikovsky letter (1893) praising *Aleko* after its first performance in the Bol'shoi Teatr. Upon hearing *Simfoniia No.2* [Symphony No.2], Kuznetsov realized the spiritual connection with Tchaikovsky.

175. ———. "Novoe o Rakhmaninove." [New material on Rachmaninoff] *Literatura i Iskusstvo*, 13, 25 March 1944.

Written the year after the composer's death, Kuznetsov reflects on material from the letters to "Re" (Marietta Sergeevna Shaginian), dated 1912-17, then recently published in *Novy mir* 4 (1943). He comments on Rachmaninoff's dislike of Riesemann's book *Rachmaninoff's Recollections Told to Oskar von Riesemann* (1934) and notes Sof'ia Satina's more precise material on the composer. Recollections by Kuznetsov are largely biographical in concept, referring often to Satina's material and the Shaginian [Shaginyan] letters. Kuznetsov remarks (as have other authors) that Rachmaninoff's *Simfoniia No.3* [Symphony No.3] reflects Russian thematic principles and is a recollection of the composer's native land.

176. ———. "Tvorcheskaia zhizn' S.V. Rakhmaninova." [Creative life of S.V. Rachmaninoff] *Sovetskaia muzyka* sbornik chetvertyi (1945): 25-52.

Biographical material up to 1917, with subsequent information based on material from

Sof'ia Satina (Rachmaninoff's cousin and sister-in-law). Kuznetsov describes several works and holds that Rachmaninoff's life abroad was not as fruitful as expected, due to his separation from Russia.

177. ———. "Sergei Rachmaninoff's Musical Life." *VOKS Bulletin* 6 (1945): 40-51.

VOKS is an anagram for Vsesoiuznoye Obshchestvo Kul'turnoĭ Sviazi s Zagranitsei [USSR Society for cultural relations with foreign countries]. Bulletins were published in English. The article is based on a report made by the author at a meeting of the Scientific Research Section of the Moscow Conservatory, and also at the Composer's Union, on the occasion of the first anniversary of the death of Rachmaninoff. The author had access to the memoirs of Sof'ia Satina, whose manuscript was sent from the USA to VOKS. The article is partly biographical, especially pointing out Rachmaninoff's teachers and commenting on what role they played in his artistic development. Kuznetsov observes violin technique derived from Rachmaninoff's association with colleague Fritz Kreisler (they collaborated in concert and recording) in the *Variations on a Theme of Corelli*. There is much stress made of the influence of Taneev's teaching on the composer. Satina's perspective of the First Symphony and its premiere is evident in the text. The article is important for the vivid overview of Rachmaninoff's career, and the inclusion of material from Sof'ia Satina's memoirs.

178. L.,E. "Kolokola zvoniat'..Ob' odnom kontserte v konservatorii." [The Bells are tolling, a concert in the Conservatory] *Verchernaia Moskve* (9 March 1931); also reprinted in *Rossiia i slavianstvo* (21 March 1931) as, "*Kolokola*- S.V. Rakhmaninov v Moskve." [Rachmaninoff's *The Bells* in Moscow]

Ostensibly a review of a performance of *Kolokola* [The Bells] directed by Al'bert Kouts [Albert Coates] who travelled from England to conduct the work in Moscow. It was performed in the Moskovskaĭa Konservatoriĭa [Moscow Conservatory]. The review is scathing.... "this music belongs to an emigrant, a raging enemy of Soviet Russia; Rakhmaninov,...words belong to E.A. Poe and another emigrant Bal'mont...they invited the former conductor of the Marinskogo Opernogo Teatra [Marinsky Opera Theater], A. Kouts, who in 1917 left Russia and now returns with a foreign passport.... the concert was of strange character, tolling of bells, liturgy, devil...it is all that which the October Revolution swept away...for whom is this concert.... who arranged this event?" This political assailment is in repercussion to the frank open letter, published in the *New York Times* on 15 January 1931 titled, "Tagore on Russia-," protesting the Soviet government and the Communist oppression, etc. which Rachmaninoff, I. Ostromislensky, and Ilĭa Tolstoy signed. As a result Rachmaninoff's music was banned in Russia. The ban was lifted in 1934.

179. La Magra, Anthony James. "A Source Book for the Study of Rachmaninoff's Preludes." Ed.D. diss., Columbia University, 1966. Ann Arbor, Mich.: University Microfilms International, 1977. 254 p. MT 145 R32 L3 OCLC 1210403

A comprehensive study of the complete Preludes. La Magra presents biographical material on the composer, a history of the prelude, structural analysis of the Preludes (with attention to form, harmonic vocabulary, rhythmic devices, texture, melody, and performing problems), bibliography, and a discography of Rachmaninoff Preludes. An informative work; recommended.

180. Lang, Christoph. "Der Pianist Sergej
      Wassiljewitsch Rachmaninoff." *Oester-
      reichische Muzikzeitschrift* 28 (September
      1973): 425-32.

   A centenary anniversary article dedicated
to Rachmaninoff's recorded legacy. Lang
laments that Rachmaninoff did not record
more works of his own and of others. He
remarks that it was unfortunate that Rachmaninoff's performance of the Third Concerto,
with young Furtwängler in Berlin (1928) was
not captured on discs. Lang offers an excellent description of Rachmaninoff's highly
individual piano style, via-à-vis his recordings, that is very perceptive. Article
includes biographical material, descriptions
of several works and recordings, and a discography of Rachmaninoff's recordings.

181. Larson, Richard. "The Four Rachmaninoff
      Piano Concerti." Master's thesis, Catholic
      University of America, 1967. 72 p. M4 C3
      L334

   Larson examines the concerto from early
concerto forms up to the modern concerto;
offers a short biographical sketch of the
composer; describes the history and character
of each concerto; provides a formal analysis
of the concerti, concentrating on the form
of each movement. The analyses are rather
succinct and there are no observations as to
similarities in the concerti.

182. "Lectures by Mr. Nathan." *Musical Standard*
      5 (26 June 1915): 492.

   A review of Montagu Montagu-Nathan's lecture on Rachmaninoff's *Aleko* presented at
the Boudoir Theatre in Kensington, on 9 June
1915. Nathan discusses the term "nihilist,"
which first appeared in Ivan Turgenev's
novel *Fathers and Sons* (1862), which centers

on the conflict of traditionalism and
radicalism (the proverbial generation gap).
Pushkin's poem "Tsygany" [Gypsies] enters
into Turgenev's novel, and there we see
the connection to Rachmaninoff. Nathan
states that the term "nihilist" has been
applied, in the musical sense, to Borodin
by contemporary critics; Rachmaninoff had
not yet earned that curious distinction.

183.   Legge, Robin. "Rachmaninoff's Opera
         'Aleko'." *Musical Leader* 30-7 (1915): 194.

   This piece by Legge previously appeared
in the London *Daily Telegraph* (n.d.). It
is a plot outline of *Aleko*. Legge notes
that the story of *Aleko* strongly resembles
the plot of Leoncavallo's *Pagliacci*. The
author encourages the performance of *Aleko*,
asserting that its production should not be
difficult; there are but 13 numbers in the
opera, five principal characters, and a
comparatively simple score to read.

184.   Leonard, Richard A. *A History of Russian
         Music*. New York: Macmillan, 1957.   395 p.
         (SR p.227-50)   ML 300 L45   OCLC 223748

   The chapter on Rachmaninoff is largely
biographical in which Leonard points out
elements such as stylistic features, influences, Soviet boycott, Rachmaninoff's personality; he also includes descriptive comments
on a few works, with *The Bells* and *Vespers*
given extended attention. Leonard interjects
comparisons between Rachmaninoff and Scriabin
in style and productivity. Illustrations,
bibliography, index.

185.   Levasheva, Olga E. *Istoriia russkoĭ muzykĭ*.
         Moskva: Muzyka, 1972. Moskovskaia Gosudar-
         stvennaia Konservatoriia Imeni P.I. Chaĭ-

kovskogo. Institut Istoriĭ Iskusstva
Ministerstva Kul'tury SSSR. 595 p.
ML 300 L462 I8 OCLC 4713590

A conservatory textbook written by the
staff of the Moskovskai͡a Konservatorii͡a Imeni
P.I. Chaĭkovskogo [Moscow Tchaikovsky Conservatory]. The Moscow Conservatory was
designated as the Tchaikovsky Conservatory
in 1940. The volume covers the history of
Russian music from early times to the middle
of the 19th century. The text traces the
basic regularity of the formation and development of Russian musical culture, emphasizing its close connection with social,
historical, and spiritual experiences of
the Russian people. References to Rachmaninoff include remarks on his lyric song
style (inspired by nature), a description
of his use of unaccompanied choral passages
(which show influence of Dargomyzhskiĭ),
and the influence of Glinka's polyphonic
style on his music. Levasheva declares that
Rachmaninoff is heir apparent to Glinka and
Dargomyzhskiĭ. Illustrations, musical
examples, bibliography, name index.

186. Liebling, Leonard. "Variations." [editorial page] *Musical Courier* 127 (5 April 1943): 17.

Liebling reveals the contents of a letter
(c.1939) that Rachmaninoff wrote to him on
the subject of modern music (the composer's
opinion had been solicited by Liebling).
Rachmaninoff made a request to Liebling that
his discourse on the subject not be made
public, "at least, not while I am alive..."
In the letter, the composer reiterates his
impressions of modern music and how it disturbs him that this music does not seem to
come from the heart, but from the head.
Rachmaninoff was outspokenly biased on the
subject.

187. Lipaev, Ivan. *S.V. Rakhmaninov*. Saratov: M.F. Tideman, Izdanie Muzykal'nogo Magazina, 1913. 39 p.

   A provincial publication by music critic Ivan Lipaev, who presents a biographical sketch and a summary of the composer's compositions. Lipaev offers an interesting view of Rachmaninoff's accomplishments as a conductor, commenting on his style, his precise adherence to the score, appropriate tempi, effect on orchestral members, clarity of rhythm, and projection of line. Lipaev notes that Rachmaninoff's conducting was similar to his piano performance in its simplicity and honesty, lack of tension, purity, and classic interpretation. List of works (through Op.34), bibliography, no index.

188. Lipman, Samuel. "In Praise of Rachmaninoff." *Commentary* 65 (May 1978): 67-71.

   Lipman reviews Rachmaninoff's popularity and the critical indifference he endured. Biographical material is followed by a critical evaluation of selected works and an interesting examination of the composer's historical status, as interpreted in several notable music history works. Lipman himself also offers an objective appraisal of Rachmaninoff.

189. ———. *Music After Modernism*. New York: Basic Books, 1979. 256 p. (SR p.92-103) ML 197 L53   ISBN 0-465-04740-8   OCLC 4859130

   Critical commentary on music history, composers and performers, beginning with Wagner. Material originally appeared in the *Times Literary Supplement, Music Journal,* and in *Commentary*. Lipman laments on the lack of audience and the lack of enthusiasm

for the music written during the last 60
years. He comments on the critical reaction Rachmaninoff's popularity has had on
music historians. While the chapter on
Rachmaninoff is primarily biographical,
there are interesting remarks on the negative
appraisals the composer received from
historians.

190. Lissa, Zofia, ed. *Polsko-rosyjskie miscel-
lanea muzyczne*. [Polish-Russian musical
miscellany] Krak'ow: Polskie Wydawn.
Muzyczne, 1967. 469 p. (SR p.156-76)
ML 300 L495 P6 OCLC 9156946

A collection of over twenty essays on
various musical subjects. The study on
Rachmaninoff is written by Wiera Briancewa
(Russian scholar V.N. Briantseva) titled,
"Wplywy Chopinowskie w tworczosci forte-
pianowej S. Rachmaninowa" [Chopin's influence
on the piano compositions of S. Rachmani-
noff]. The author points out Rachmaninoff's
admiration of Chopin's music and the fre-
quency with which he performed it. Similarities to Chopin's works are noted- Chopin's
Etude in E Major Op.10, No.3 and Rachmaninoff's *Melodie in E Major Op.3, No.3; Etude-
tableau in G Minor Op.33, No.8* and Chopin's
Ballade in G Minor Op.23, etc.. There is
a detailed examination of the *Variations on
a Theme of Chopin Op.22*. Briantseva concludes that Chopin's influence on Rachmaninoff was of wide scope- dramatic concepts,
motives, sadness, etc. Illustrations,
musical examples, bibliographies, name index.

191. Lochner, Louis Paul. *Fritz Kreisler*. New
York: Macmillan, 1950. 455 p. ML 418 K7
L16 OCLC 909784; second printing, revised
ed. 1951. 459 p. OCLC 6207855 Also--
London: Rockliff, 1951. ML 418 K9 L6
OCLC 3714900 (reprint of 1950 ed. pub. by
Macmillan, St. Clair Shores, Mich.:

Scholarly Press, 1977. OCLC 3444599)
Also- (reprint of expanded 1950 ed. pub.
by Macmillan, Neptune, N.J.: Paganiniana
Publications, 1981. OCLC 8753078)

There are many references to Rachmaninoff in Lochner's book on Fritz Kreisler. Lochner observes the collaborations of the two artists and notes how opposite they were, both in personality and attitude; Rachmaninoff was apt to be somber, whereas Kreisler was ebullient. Their recording sessions together are described in anecdotal fashion, and the sad occasion is related when Kreisler stood as concertmaster *pro tem* of the New York Philharmonic during the performance of the *Vocalise* in memory of his friend who had just passed away. Illustrations, list of works (Kreisler), discography, bibliography, name index.

192. Loftis, Eric Kenneth. "An Investigation of the Textural Contrasts in Sergei Rachmaninov's 'Night Vigil,' Opus 37." Ph.D. diss., University of Southern Mississippi, 1980. 292 p. Ann Arbor Mich.: University Microfilms International, 1980. OCLC 7755100

An examination of the 15 choral compositions comprising the *Night Vigil (Vespers)*, in regard to textural contrasts in setting the liturgical melodies; those contrasts relating to melody, harmony, dynamics, rhythm, text, special coloristic effects, and choral texture (number and types of voices used at a given point, along with register, spacing, and linear doubling) are observed. The work contains a brief biographical sketch and a substantial amount of historical background on Russian liturgical music; material on the latter drawn from Alfred Swan, Richard Leonard, and Rey Longyear. Loftis points out that the apparent liturgical style in Rachmaninoff's *Night Vigil* leans towards nationalistic, eclectic, traditional, late 19th century and early 20th century elements. Musical examples, vita, appendix, bibliography.

193.   Lvov, L. "Rakhmaninov, ko dniu evo shestidesiatiletiia." [Rachmaninoff, on his 60th birthday] *Rossiia i slavianstvo*, 1 April 1933, p.3.

Examination of Rachmaninoff's achievements. Lvov considers *Vsenoshchnoe bdenie* [All-Night Vigil (Vespers)] Op.37 the composer's greatest work and elaborates on this premise. A view of Rachmaninoff's conducting career is offered, as well as discussion of several of his major works. Contrary to the usual Soviet opinion, Lvov asserts that Rachmaninoff's art reached its peak in the USA.

194.   Lyle, Watson. "Rachmaninoff: A Personal Sketch." *Musical News and Herald* 62 (17 June 1922): 740.

Lyle comes to the defense of Rachmaninoff. London critics remarked at the time that Rachmaninoff seemed tired and appeared to have a careless attitude in his approach to the keyboard, to which Lyle counters that critics should discuss the art, not the behavior of the artist as an individual. Lyle goes on to relate a conversation with Rachmaninoff and endeavors to dismiss the belief that the composer is not interested in contemporary music.

195.   ———. "Rachmaninoff and Music Today." *Apollo* 8 (July-December 1928): 81-83.

An interview with the composer, given during his 1928 tour of the UK. Interesting discussion on booking artists in the USA (who buys the tickets and how the Americans attract the best talent because of financial backing). Lyle contends that the best orchestras in the USA owe their existence to this financial security.

196.   ―――. *Rachmaninoff*. London: W. Reeves, 1939. 247 p. ML 410 R12 L9 OCLC 2801711 (Reprint-- New York: AMS Press, 1976).

Lyle's biography of Rachmaninoff followed shortly after Riesemann's biography of 1934 and is partly based on that material. Rachmaninoff, in a letter to Vladimir Vil'shau [Wilshaw] in 1936, expressed some dissatisfaction with the Lyle book as well as Riesemann's work. Lyle does present some interesting reminiscences of the composer. He recalls meeting Rachmaninoff in 1922, when he was reviewing two of the composer's concerts, given in London at Queen's Hall. Lyle also wrote the program notes for Rachmaninoff's 1924 and 1928 concerts. He presents an interesting observation of the pianist at ease between concerts. Illustrated, list of works, critical survey of Rachmaninoff's recordings by Wilson G. Lyle.

197.   ―――. "Rachmaninov's Last Phase." *Gramophone* 25 (August 1947): 35-36.

Lyle perceives a subtle change in Rachmaninoff's performance style, noted in the recordings of the First and Third Concerti, as well as in recordings of several short piano pieces. The author senses a preoccupation with technique; fingers becoming steely and an apparent impatience, strife and disregard for good tone enter into his normally well-thought-out, well-balanced interpretations.

210   *Rachmaninoff Bibliography*

198.   Mach, Elyse. *Great Pianists Speak for Them-
          selves.* New York: Dodd, Mead, 1980.
          204 p.   ML 397 M28   ISBN 0-396-07824-9
          OCLC 5942753

          Interviews with 13 pianists. In the inter-
          view with Horowitz, the pianist discusses
          his friendship with Rachmaninoff and his
          own revision (which would be a revision of
          Rachmaninoff's own revision of 1931) of the
          Second Sonata. Illustrations. index.

199.   Machavariliĭ, M. "Rakhmaninov v Gruziĭ."
          [Rachmaninoff in Georgia] *Sovetskai͡a
          muzyka* 6 (1961): 76-77.

          An account of Rachmaninoff's concert tours
          of Georgia. He appeared in Tiflis, the
          capital city of Georgia, on 14 November 1911,
          when *Aleko* was produced and the *Sonata dli͡a
          violoncheli i f-no* [Sonata for Cello and
          Piano], and *Elegicheskoe trio* [Trio élé-
          giaque] Op.9 were performed. Another concert
          on 18 November included the *Kont͡sert dli͡a
          f-no s orkestrom No.3* [Piano Concerto No.3]
          and Tchaikovsky's *Kont͡sert dli͡a f-no s
          orkestrom No.1* [Piano Concerto No.1], per-
          formed by Rachmaninoff. He returned to Tif-
          lis in October 1915 to perform two concerts
          featuring his own works and works of
          Scriabin. Illustrations.

200.   Maine, Basil. "Conversation with Rachmani-
          noff." *Musical Opinion* 60 (October 1936):
          14-15.

          An unusually successful interview with the
          composer. Maine apparently relaxed Rach-
          maninoff, who was usually apprehensive about
          interviews, so that he expressed personal
          ideas that he never broached before. Rach-
          maninoff comments on his inner reaction
          while performing for a highly interested
          youthful audience and his reasons for not

performing for the radio. A tactful and
significant question asked by Maine was,
"How much of your power over audiences do
you attribute to the fact that you are a
creator, as well as interpreter of Music?"
Rachmaninoff's reply is thoughtful and
penetrating.

201. Martens, Frederick H. "The Modern Russian
Pianoforte Sonata." *Musical Quarterly* 5
(July 1919): 357-63.

Article is based (as noted) on an interview
with Sergei Prokofiev, but it is impossible
to differentiate material by Martens from
material by Prokofiev; it surely would be
of interest to know if the paltry representation of the Rachmaninoff sonatas described
here is the result of Prokofiev's bias of
the composer or simply Martens' impression
of the sonatas. Presumably, the article is
largely Martens', with some information
culled from Prokofiev. Martens' modern
Russian sonatas begin with Scriabin, Glazunov, Rachmaninoff, Medtner, Miaskovskiĭ, and
end with Prokofiev.

202. ———. "Sergei Rachmaninoff Talks of
Russia and America." *Musical Observer* 20
(April 1921): 11-12. Also in Russian,
"Govorit Sergeĭ Rakhmaninov." in *Sovetskaia
muzyka* 4 (1973): 96-98.

Rachmaninoff discusses topics such as the
Prelude in C-sharp Minor Op.3, No.2, other
pianists' interpretations of his works, his
admiration for Medtner's compositions, and
the popularity of his own music.

203. ———. *Rachmaninoff*. New York: Breitkopf
und Härtel, 1922, 25 p. ML 410 R12
OCLC 5301841

Biography of Rachmaninoff is one of a series of "Little Biographies" by Frederick Martens. The booklet contains a very concise biographical sketch and a description of several works. This mini-book served as an economical, readily available, general introduction to Rachmaninoff and his music. Illustrations, list of works.

204.   Maycock, Robert. "Rachmaninov the Symphonist." *Music and Musicians* 21 (July 1973): 40-48.

This useful in-depth study critically examines the three symphonies and offers a detailed motivic-thematic analysis of the Second Symphony. Maycock comments on the composer's structural and orchestral craftsmanship. He aptly compares critical appraisals of the composer, asserting that Rachmaninoff is not treated fairly, and laments at the infrequency of performance of the greater portion of his corpus. Illustrated, musical examples.

205.   McCabe, John. *Rachmaninov*. Sevenoaks: Novello, 1974. 32 p.   ML 410 R12 M2 ISBN 0-853-60059-7   OCLC 1230267

Biography and descriptive survey of selected works. In this concise work McCabe demonstrates sensitive perception of the composer. List of works, bibliography.

206.   Medveder, A. "'Velikiĭ muzykant' pis'ma S.V. Rakhmaninova, vospominaniia sovremennikov." [A great musician, letters of S.V. Rachmaninoff and reminiscences of his contemporaries] *Muzykal'naia zhizn'* No.6 (March 1958): 20-21.

A review of Zarui Apetian's *S.V. Rakhmaninova, pis'ma* and her volume, *Vospominaniia o Rakhmaninove*. Medveder is elated about these volumes by Apetian, proclaiming that the work offers the reader a better picture of Rachmaninoff the man and a better understanding of his personality. Especially important, says Medveder, are the letters to "Re" [Marietta Shaginian], Skalon, Zataevich, Vil'shau [Wilshaw], Slonov, and the reminiscences of Sof'ia Satina and Asaf'ev. There is an interesting letter quoted, written by Rachmaninoff (1923) to the son of Rimsky-Korsakov (Mikhail Nikolaevich), telling him how popular his father's works are in the USA. Medveder rightfully commends the work of Zarui Apetian.

207. ———. "O Rakhmaninove." [About Rachmaninoff] *Muzykal'naia zhizn'* No.6 (March 1973): 4-7. (an edition in honor of the 100th anniversary of Rachmaninoff's birth)

A compilation of Medveder, of recollections of the composer by several of his friends- M. Gromov, L.I. Prokof'eva, Gorky, and Medtner. There is an interesting arbitrary division of the composer's life into three periods- First, 1890-97 (16 Opp.) spanning the *Kontsert dlia f-no s orkestrom No.1* [Concerto for Piano and Orchestra No.1], *Aleko*, and the first performance of the *Simfoniia No.1* [Symphony No.1]; Second, 1900-17 (23 Opp.) spanning the *Kontsert dlia f-no s orkestrom No.2* [Concerto for Piano and Orchestra No.2] to the *Etiudy-Kartiny* [Etudes-tableaux] Op.39; Third 1917-43 (6 Opp.) spanning the *Kontsert dlia f-no s orkestrom No.4* [Concerto for Piano and Orchestra No.4], *Tri russkie pesni* [Three Russian Songs] Op.41, and the *Simfonicheskie tantsy* [Symphonic Dances]. It is stated that there are no well-defined borders or divisions in Rachmaninoff's artistic career. Gorky compares Rachmaninoff with Chekov, "a gentle talent."

208.	Mikhailov, M.K., and E.K. Frid, eds. *Russ-kaiā muzykal'naiā literatura*, vypusk IV, izd.2-e, pererabotannoe i dopolnennoe. [Russian musical literature, issue IV, sec. ed., revised and enlarged] Leningrad: Muzyka, 1969. 256 p. (SR p.177-234) ML 300 R8 F7

   A school textbook designed to familiarize the reader with works of Liādov, Glazunov, Taneev, Arenskiĭ, Kalinikov, Scriabin, and Rachmaninoff. The chapter on Rachmaninoff is written by Aleksei Kandinskiĭ and contains a brief biography followed by descriptions of several works, including *Preliūdiĭ* [Preludes] (Op.3, No.2; Op.23, Nos.2,3,5; Op.32, Nos.5,10,12); the *Kontsert dliā f-no s orkestrom No.2* [Concerto for Piano and Orchestra No.2]; *Romansov* [Songs] (Op.4, Nos.3,4; Op.8, No.4; Op.14, No.11; Op.21, Nos.5,6,7; Op.26, Nos.12,15); and *Aleko*. Illustrations, musical examples, no index.

209.	Mila, Massimo. "Rachmaninoff musicista mondano." [Rachmaninoff, fashionable musician] *Rassegna nazionale*, Terza Serie, 10 (1930): 113-18.

   Essay largely criticizing Rachmaninoff's compositional style. Mila claims that the composer intentionally writes in a style that is readily accepted by the public, and that even though Rachmaninoff is not strongly talented, he has original musicality. Rachmaninoff is a man with the Midas touch, in that everything he does spontaneously turns to beauty. The author vividly describes the *Valse* and *Nocturne* from Op.10, and the *Polichinelle* Op.3, No.4.

210.	Milstein, Jacov Iszakovics. "Az orosz Liszt-kutatás kevéssé ismert lapjai." [Lesser-known contributions in Russian-Liszt studies] *Magyar zene* 18 (December 1977): 354-61.

A useful study on the influence of Liszt on Scriabin, Rachmaninoff, Prokofiev, and Shostakovich. Rachmaninoff's Lisztian influences are manifested in his poetical program conceptions, as in the *Isle of the Dead*, *The Bells*, and the *Etudes-tableaux*, and in his expanded technical use of the instrument, employing all types of possibilities, including tone-based contrasts of registers.

211. Moiseiwitsch, Benno. "Sergei Rachmaninoff, 1873-1943." *Gramophone* 20 (May 1943): 169-70.

212. ―――. "Rachmaninoff Remembered." *Musical Courier* 164 (May 1962): 14-15.

213. ―――. "Reminiscences of Rachmaninoff." *Musical Journal* 21 (January 1963): 67-68.

These three articles are similar in content. Moiseiwitsch relates his first meeting Rachmaninoff in 1919, his continued friendship, the inspirational source for the *Prelude in B Minor Op.32, No.10*, the "creme de menthe" variation (24th variation of the *Rhapsody on a Theme of Paganini*), naming the variations (id.), and the author's touching account of his performance of the Second Concerto just after receiving notice that Rachmaninoff had died. There are other recollections. Illustrated.

214. Montagu-Nathan, Montagu. *Contemporary Russian Composers*. London: Palmer and Hayward, 1917. 329 p. ML 390 M68 OCLC 4770450

An historical survey of Russian music, with chapters dealing with the lives of nine Russian composers. A concise biography of Rachmaninoff is followed by commentary on his stylistic characteristics. Several works are described. Illustrations, index.

215. ———. "The Story of Russian Music: XV.-- Rakhmaninov." *Music Student* 10 (March 1918): 280-82.

This article appeared shortly after the author wrote his book *Contemporary Russian Composers* (1917), in which he views Rachmaninoff's life and comments on his stylistic tendencies. In this short article he admits that it is difficult to appraise a living composer, especially Rachmaninoff, for although he has shown himself to be a romanticist, we must wait for future works to see what direction he will take; then after there are additional works to examine, it may be possible to ascertain if he will be recognized as a master composer. Although Montagu-Nathan is apprehensive in his appraisal, he has no doubt about the composer's musicanship or craftsmanship.

216. ———. *A History of Russian Music*. 2d ed., rev. and corrected. London: Reeves, 1918. 346 p. (SR p.281-86) ML 300 M78 OCLC 1015291 (Reprint-- New York: Biblo and Tannen, 1969).

An account of the rise and progress of the Russian school of composers covering the period from Glinka to Stravinsky, with a survey of their lives as well as a description of their works. Montagu-Nathan's *History of Russian Music* is divided into four parts: Pre-Nationalists, Nationalists, decline of Nationalism, and the present movement. Several of Rachmaninoff's works are examined and part of the material presented is biographical. Appendixes, index.

217. Morgenstern, Sam. *Composers on Music.* New York: Pantheon, 1956. 584 p. (SR p.373-76) ML 90 M6 OCLC 378001 Also- London: Faber and Faber, 1956.

Composers on Music is an anthology of composers' writings on their own music and others' music, from Palestrina to Copland. Four segments from Riesemann's *Rachmaninoff's Recollections* (1934) are quoted. Reminiscences chosen attempt to prove that, although Rachmaninoff's outward manner was one of seriousness and gloom, his inner self was one of joy and contentment. Index.

218. Nadejine, Nicholas. "Rachmaninoff." *Gramophone* 12 (March 1935): 383.

A flattering review of Riesemann's recently published *Rachmaninoff's Recollections* (1934). Nadejine revels in the depiction of the pomp and splendor of old Russia, romantic descriptions with which Riesemann characteristically adorns his narrative. Nadejine summarizes parts of the Riesemann book in quasi-biographical style. Illustrated.

219. Nardony, Ivan. "The Art of Sergei Rachmaninoff." *Musical America* 16 (22 June 1912): 17.

A brief survey of contemporary Russian composers (of 1912)- a view of the two schools of Russian composers- influences- and a concise survey of selected works of Rachmaninoff. Of the *Isle of the Dead,* Nardony states, "The composer seems to have adopted the mood and mastered the eloquence of ultra-modern music." Nardony contends that the *Isle of the Dead* earned the composer a position in the first ranks of Russian classicists.

220. Nemenova-Lunts, M.S., ed. and trans. "Rakhmaninov o sebe." [Rachmaninoff, about himself] *Ogonek* No.12-13 (31 March 1943): 12.

Shortly after Rachmaninoff's death this article, which is based on material from Riesemann's book (1934), appeared in *Ogonek*. It is a recollection of Rachmaninoff's student days and of his artistic career. The article makes note of the fact that it is based on Vospominaniia Rakhmaninova [*Rachmaninoff's Recollections*] but fails to mention that it was written by Oskar von Riesemann. This gives the reader the impression that the material was written directly by Rachmaninoff. The misconception that Riesemann's *Rachmaninoff's Recollections, As Told to Oskar von Riesemann* is an autobiography was one reason why Rachmaninoff spoke adversely of the work.

221. Nest'ev, Israel Vladimirovich. *Prokofiev*. Translated from the Russian by Florence Jonas; with a foreword by Nicolas Slonimsky. Stanford, Calif.: Stanford University Press, 1971. (reprint of the 1960 ed.) 528 p.   ML 410 P865 N463   OCLC 602573   Also- Ann Arbor, Mich.: University Microfilms International, 1980.   OCLC 7120397   Also- in German, *Prokofjew: Der Kunstler und Sein*. Translated by Christa Schubert-Consbruch. Berlin: Henschel, 1962.   ML 410 P96 N46   OCLC 4559554   Also- in French, *Prokofiev*. Translated by Rostislav Hofmann. Paris: Editions du Chene, [1946]   OCLC 3337292

Nest'ev's book was originally published in Russia in 1957 by Gosudarstvennoe Muzykal'noe Izd-vo, in Moscow. It is an extension and elaboration of Nest'ev's earlier book, *Sergei Prokofiev, His Musical Life* (New York: Knopf, 1946). The author points out influences of Rachmaninoff in Prokofiev's music, Prokofiev's youthful opinion of Rachmaninoff and how that opinion changed in later years, and Rachmaninoff's estimation of Prokofiev and how that also differed in time. Illustrations, list of works (Prokofiev), indexes.

222. *The New Grove Dictionary of Music and Musicians.* 6th ed., ed. by Stanley Sadie. London: Macmillan; Washington, D.C.: Grove's Dictionaries of Music, 1980. 20 vols. ML 100 N48   ISBN 0-333-23111-2
OCLC 5676891

Grove makes amends to Rachmaninoff. The new edition of Grove's Dictionary contains a comprehensive survey of Rachmaninoff written by Geoffrey Norris. The biographical section is divided into four parts: early years through graduation from conservatory, failure of First Symphony to success of Second Concerto, the fruitful years, and his departure from Russia and the years abroad. Included are sections on Rachmaninoff the performer, and an overview of his compositions, list of works, and a bibliography of over 25 items. To illustrate the change of attitude towards Rachmaninoff and the re-evaluation that has evolved, compare this present survey with that of the 5th ed. of Grove's Dictionary which is extremely succinct and disparaging.

223. "A New Russia: Rachmaninoff as Pianist and Composer." *Boston Transcript*, 17 November 1909.

A review of Rachmaninoff's 16 November 1909 recital in Boston's Symphony Hall. The program consisted of his own works, including the First Sonata. The critic thought the music sounded more German than Russian. As in other reviews during this first tour in the USA, Rachmaninoff is treated as a curiosity (makes good copy); as a result, the major part of the reviews are concerned with his physical appearance and stage demeanor. The review contains an interesting comment, maintaining that while Rachmaninoff's tone was incisive, at no time did it have the resonance of another young Russian on the scene, Josef Léhvinne.

224.   Norman, Gertrude, and Miriam Shrifte, eds.
        and comps. *Letters of Composers: An
        Anthology 1603-1945.* New York: Knopf,
        1946. 442 p. (SR p.338-40) ML 90 N67
        OCLC 911392

        Collection of composers' letters, from
        Sweelinck to William Schuman. One Rachmaninoff letter is quoted, dated 5 May 1912, to
        Marietta Shaginian, the Russian poet and
        novelist in whom Rachmaninoff confided
        through correspondence (1912-17). Index.

225.   Norris, Geoffrey. "Rakhmaninov's Second
        Thoughts." *Musical Times* 114 (April 1973):
        364-68.

        A detailed examination of Rachmaninoff's
        revisions of the First Concerto, Third Symphony, and the Fourth Concerto. Norris'
        closing statement reflects the value of the
        revisions: "Not only did he achieve significant improvements to several of his first
        published thoughts, but also, in the case
        of the first concerto, transformed an early
        immature essay into a concise, spirited
        work." Illustrated, musical examples. See
        also, Robert Threlfall's "Rachmaninoff's
        Revisions and an Unknown Version of his
        Fourth Concerto" in *Musical Opinion* 96
        (February 1973): 235-37, and also, Fritz
        Butzbach's *Studien zum Klavierkonzert Nr.1,
        Fis-moll, Op.1 von S.V. Rachmaninov*
        (Regensburg: Gustav Bosse, 1979).

226.   ———. "Rakhmaninov's Student Opera."
        Musical Quarterly 59 (July 1973): 441-48.

        Norris examines the opera *Aleko* with
        special attention to the libretto (drawn
        from Pushkin's poem, "The Gypsies"). He
        finds this libretto, written by Vladimir
        Ivanovich Nemirovich-Danchenko, the principal weakness in *Aleko*. Norris examines in

detail the role of poet and librettist, early performances of the opera, the scenario, and the composer as an 18-year-old novice.

227. ————. *Rakhmaninov*. London: J.M. Dent, 1976. 211 p. ML 410 R12 N67 ISBN 0-460-03145-7 OCLC 2525693 Also- Totowa, N.J.: Littlefield, 1978. ISBN 0-8226-0701-8

Well-documented biography and critical analysis of Rachmaninoff's works. The *Musical Times* critic and Rachmaninoff scholar has divided his volume approximately in two equal parts, dedicating half to biographical material and half to critical examinations of the compositions. Norris' work is especially valuable for the investigation of the vocal works; the material on the operas, songs, and choral works is informative. This vocal genre well deserves special attention, since the piano works usually dominate any discussion of Rachmaninoff. As to Rachmaninoff's birthplace, Norris uses new information from V.N. Briant͡seva's "Gde rodilsi͡a S.V. Rakhmaninov?" in *Muzykal'nai͡a zhizn'* 19 (1969):20, which disputes Rachmaninoff's belief that he was born in Oneg. Norris' *Rakhmaninov* includes illustrations, a calendared conspectus, catalog of works, personalia, bibliography, and name index. Norris also wrote the Rachmaninoff entry for the *New Grove Dictionary* (1980) and collaborated with Robert Threlfall in the *Catalogue of the Compositions of S. Rachmaninoff* (London: Scolar Press, 1982).

228. ————. "Rakhmaninov's Apprenticeship." *Musical Times* 124 (October 1983): 602-05.

Norris examines Rachmaninoff's first phase as composer, beginning when he was 14 years old (1887) and composed a *Scherzo in D Minor* for orchestra, through 1896 and the *Moments musicaux Op.16*. He reflects on the composer's training in composition, the impact of his teachers, and the apparent influence of Tchaikovsky as demonstrated in early works, e.g., *Prince Rostislav* and *Aleko*. Norris cites the prominent use of the key of D minor in the works of Rachmaninoff, which Robert Walker, in his *Rachmaninoff: His Life and Times* (1980) also noted.

229.   O'Connell, Charles. *The Other Side of the Record*. New York: Knopf, 1947. 332 p. (SR p.157-71)   ML 65 02   OCLC 425407 Also- Westport, Conn.: Greenwood Press, 1970.   ML 65 02 1970   ISBN 0-837-12626-6 OCLC 145569

O'Connell, then musical director of RCA Victor, reflects in anecdotal style on the lives and careers of several international artists. He extols Rachmaninoff's judiciously controlled tone as being the best of the time. The author's reminiscences of the composer, both as musician and person, reveal the casual and intimate side of Rachmaninoff. Name index.

230.   Oliphant, E.H.C. "A Survey of Russian Songs." *Musical Quarterly* 12 (1926): 196-230.

Descriptive survey of some 600 Russian songs by 63 composers. Oliphant notes Tchaikovsky's influence on Rachmaninoff, comments on the difficulty of the accompaniments, use of traditional harmonies, and informs, "His technique is modern-German modified by Russian folk-music influence. He possesses considerable descriptive power and a sense of landscape..." Oliphant briefly regards songs, Op.4, Nos.4,5,8; Op.14, Nos.9,11; Op.21, No.1; and Op.26, No.7.

231. Olkhovsky, Andrey. *Music Under the Soviets: The Agony of an Art.* New York: Published for the Research Program on the USSR by F.A. Praeger, 1955. 427 p. ML 300.5 O4 OCLC 1299342 Also- London: Routledge and K. Paul, 1955. ML 300.5 O4 OCLC 223828 Also- Westport Conn.: Greenwood Press, 1975. ISBN 0-837-17856-8 OCLC 1094873

   A well-documented history of the Soviets' dictatorial management of USSR's musical environment. Olkhovsky, who was head of the history and theory department at the Kiev Conservatory from 1934 to 1942, states that Rachmaninoff as a conservative has been misunderstood in our time and that he and Scriabin were important in developing modernism in Russia. Bibliography, appendixes, name index, general index.

232. Orlova, Elena and Ekaterina Ruç'evskaĩa, eds. and comps. *Stranitsy istorii russkoi muzyki.* stat'i molodykh muzykovedov [Pages from the history of Russian music, articles by young musicologists] Leningrad: Muzyka, 1973. 183 p. ML 300 S92 OCLC 6524772

   Ten articles written on diverse musical subjects. The Rachmaninoff article "Rakhmaninov, Melodist" is written by L. Skaftymova. It traces the evolutionary stages of the composer's use of microthemes and points out the importance of melodies in his works, stating, "Melodies are the carriers of artistic content and are the basis of Rachmaninoff's musical thought." The *Kontsert dlĩa f-no s orkestrom No.3* [Concerto for Piano and Orchestra No.3] is used as an example of thematic development. Musical examples.

233. Ormandy, Eugene. "Sergei Rachmaninoff." *Russian Orthodox Journal* 17 (March 1944).

Ormandy relates Rachmaninoff's love of the Philadelphia Orchestra and the dedication of the *Symphonic Dances* Op.45 to the orchestra. Ormandy reveals that Rachmaninoff and two other great musicians (unidentified) were partly responsible for his becoming the director of the Philadelphia Orchestra upon Stokowski's resignation.

234.   "The Passing of a Giant." *Etude* 61 (May 1943): 291.

A farewell editorial to *Etude* magazine's good friend, Sergei Rachmaninoff. The composer gave more interviews to *Etude* than to any other periodical. The article presents a short summary of Rachmaninoff's career, comments on his friendship with the magazine, and laments the loss of the musical "Giant."

235.   Pasternak, Alexander. "Skryabin: Summer 1903 and after." *Musical Times* 113 (December 1972): 1169-74.

The Pasternaks discovered, quite by accident, that their dacha was near the Scriabins' dacha, located outside of Moscow. Their friendship began at that time. Pasternak, having heard Rachmaninoff, Busoni, and Scriabin perform, compares their approach to the instrument. An informative article, especially for those interested in the event when Rachmaninoff was criticized for his interpretation of Scriabin's music, which took place in November 1915. The article compares the two composer-pianists, revealing some of the disparity in their attitude and style.

236.   "Philharmonic Concerts, 1899." *Monthly Musical Record* (May 1899): 106.

Review of Rachmaninoff's first appearance in England (19 April 1899, Queen's Hall) in which he conducted an aria (sung by Miss C. Andray) from Borodin's *Prince Igor*, and his fantasy for orchestra *The Rock Op.7*, and played two piano solos: the *Elégie* and *Prelude* (the ubiquitous one) from Op.3. The reviewer was not favorable to Rachmaninoff's music, but did like his piano performance, with reservation, remarking that Rachmaninoff fared better as pianist, "although his touch is less elastic than some performers who have recently been heard in the country."

237. Piatigorsky, Gregor. *Cellist*. Garden City, N.Y.: Doubleday, 1965. 273 p. ML 418 P63 A3 OCLC 713394 (Reprint-- New York: Da Capo Press, 1976. OCLC 2072720) Also- in German *Mein Cello und ich und unsere Begegnungen*. Translated from the English by Elsa Winter, München: Deutscher Taschen- buch Verlag, 1975. OCLC 3085952

There are two anecdotal references to Rachmaninoff in *Cellist*, which is an account of Piatigorsky's life, supplemented with various reminiscences and correspondence. The two occasions recalled are when Piatigor- sky performed Rachmaninoff's *Sonata for Piano and Cello Op.19*, with the composer in the audience, and a performance of the *Trio élégiaque Op.9* with Piatigorsky, Horowitz, and Milstein, in the composer's home.

238. Piggott, Patrick. *Rachmaninov Orchestral Music*. Seattle, Wash.: University of Washington Press, 1974. 61 p. ML 130 R2 P5 ISBN 0-295-95308-X OCLC 1258794

In his introduction Piggott attempts to dispel some misconceptions concerning Rach- maninoff, such as that Rachmaninoff was primarily a piano composer, his orchestral music is pianistic, his music is cosmopolitan in style and not very idiomatically Russian. The orchestral compositions are discussed as to background, style, and orchestral techniques. Index.

239. ———. *Rachmaninov*. London: Faber and Faber, 1978. 110 p. ML 410 R12 P5 ISBN 0-571-10265-4 OCLC 4077092

Piggott had some input from Sof'i͡a Satina in writing this illustrated biography. He subsequently dedicated the book to her memory. There is descriptive commentary on Rachmaninoff's compositions as well as inclusion of musical examples of specific works being examined. Piggott gives special attention to the recurrent bell motive (passages influenced by the ringing of church bells) in Rachmaninoff's works, contending that his upbringing in the Novgorod region instilled a lasting influence on his music. Illustrated, musical examples, bibliography, (11 items), list of principal works, name-works index.

240. Plaskin, Glen. *Horowitz: A Biography of Vladimir Horowitz*. New York: William Morrow, 1983. 607 p. ML 417 H8 P6 ISBN 0-688-01616-2 OCLC 8763305

A large part of Plaskin's biography of Horowitz is based on material gathered from interviews, including some second-hand material; however, the friendship of Rachmaninoff and Horowitz is conveyed through several anecdotal accounts. Of interest are the stories of Rachmaninoff commiserating with Horowitz during Horowitz's first seclusion from the public and their collaboration in two-piano performances for their own pleasure. There are many comments made by Horowitz concerning Rachmaninoff. Illustrations, discography, list of repertoire, index.

241. Ponizovkin, I͡U. *Rakhmaninov- pi͡anist,
       interpretor, sobstvennykh proĭzvedeniĭ.*
       [Rachmaninoff- pianist, interpreter of
       his own works] Moskva: Muzyka, 1965.
       95 p. ML 410 R12 P6

   This valuable work is divided into four
main chapters: "Rakhmaninov i russkai͡a
muzykal'nai͡a kul'tura nachala XX stoletii͡a"
[Rachmaninoff and Russian musical culture
at the beginning of the 20th century];
"Interpretat͡sii͡a Rakhmaninovym sobstvennykh
proĭzedeniĭ" [Rachmaninoff's interpretations
of his own works]; "Osnovnye cherty Rakh-
maninovskogo ispolnitel'skogo stili͡a"
[the main characteristics of Rachmaninoff's
performing style] (which is subdivided into-
melodic intonation, rhythm, dynamics, and
performance plan); and "Pervai͡a chast'
tret'ego kont͡serta dli͡a f-no s orkestrom v
interpretat͡sii avtora" [first movement of
the Third Concerto for Piano and Orchestra
in Rachmaninoff's interpretation]. Ponizovkin examines and analyzes Rachmaninoff's
performance peculiarities and cleverly
illustrates the minute variances of tempo,
tone, dynamics, and rhythm in the score (the
article includes musical examples). Source
of interpretation is from Rachmaninoff's
performance of the Third Concerto with
Eugene Ormandy and the Philadelphia Orchestra
recorded in 1940. No index.

242. Porte, John F. "Gramophone Celebrities,
       XII.--Sergei Rachmaninoff." *Gramophone* 3
       (August 1925): 128-29.

   A review of several Rachmaninoff recordings.
Porte gives a short summation of the composer's education and his Russian musical
style. He states that at time Rachmaninoff's
touch is too heavy for works such as Chopin
waltzes, but in the larger works, as in the
Chopin *Sonata in B-flat Minor Op.35*, his
interpretations reveal insight. When asked
which recordings were his favorites, Rach-

maninoff replied, the Waltz by Grieg (Op.12, No.2, recorded in 1921) and Mendelssohn's Spinning Song (Op.67, No.4, probably the version recorded in 1920). Porte advises his readers to reserve copies of the recording of the Second Concerto because they sell as soon as they arrive. Note- only the second and third movements were available (those movements recorded in January 1924); the first movement was recorded later, in December 1924.

243. Prieberg, Fred K. "Sergei Rachmaninoff: Zum 100. Geburtstag des Komponisten." [On the 100th anniversary of the composer's birth] *Musikhandel* 24 (June 1973): 245-46.

Prieberg's anniversary article first appeared in Verlagsnachrichten von Boosey und Hawkes [Boosey and Hawkes Newsletter] earlier in 1973. The author notes how unfair and biased critics were (including those in the USSR) in regard to works of Rachmaninoff. Russian musicologist Igor Belza attempted to change the course of criticism by publishing, in Russia, a supportive article on the composer, when critical opinion of Rachmaninoff was unfavorable. His works were banned in the USSR from 1931 to 1934 but the Soviets eventually reclaimed the composer as their own without reservation during WWII, when the USA and USSR were allies. Prieberg contends that the composer was ill-treated by critics of both countries, whereas instead he should have received great acclaim from them. He maintains that Rachmaninoff ignored the critics' attitude and looked for approval from his public, which was his measure of success or failure.

244. Prokof'ev, Grigori. "VI Simfonicheskoe sobranie filarmonicheskogo obshchestva; ispolnenie Rakhmaninovym pervogo fortepiannogo konṯserta Chaĭkovskogo." [Sixth

Philharmonic concert; Tchaikovsky's First Concerto played by Rachmaninoff] *Russkiĭ vedomosti*, 292, 20 December 1911.

Review of the sixth concert of the 1911-12 season of the Simfonicheskoe Filarmonicheskogo Obshchestvo [Philharmonic Symphony Society] orchestra (Moscow), performed on 18 December 1911. Works of Bach, Corelli, Dukas, and Tchaikovsky were programmed. Rachmaninoff's interpretation of the Tchaikovsky *Kontsert dlià f-no s orkestrom No.1* [Concerto for Piano and Orchestra No.1] is related as differing at times from the traditional concept, but performed with deep inspiration and flawless execution. Conductor Aleksandr Il'ich Ziloti occasionally hindered the performance, success of the concerto belonged to Rachmaninoff. As encores, Rachmaninoff performed his *Elégie* Op.3, No.1 and *Preliùdiià* (Op.32, No.12).

245. ———. "Vtoroĭ simfonicheskiĭ kontsert sobranie filarmonicheskogo obshchestva - 20 oktiàbrià." [Second symphonic concert of the Philharmonic Symphony Society - 20 October] *Russkie vedomosti*, 245, 24 October 1912.

Review of the second concert of the 1912-13 season of the Simfonicheskoe Filarmonicheskogo Obshchestva [Philharmonic Symphony Society] orchestra (Moscow) with Rachmaninoff as conductor. Program consisted of the Mozart *Simfoniià G-moll* [Symphony in G Minor], Weber's *Uvertiùra Oberon* [Overture to Oberon], Arenskiĭ's *Variàtsiĭ na temu Chaĭkovskogo* [Variations on a Theme of Tchaikovsky], Tchaikovsky's *Kontsert dlià f-no s orkestrom No.1* [Concerto for Piano and Orchestra No.1] and the Liszt *Kontsert dlià f-no s orkestrom No.1* [Concerto for Piano and Orchestra No.1] (E-flat Major), both with Josef Hofmann as soloist. Grigori Prokof'ev was not happy with Rachmaninoff's tempi (as conductor) in the Mozart, or with

246. ———. "Tretiĭ simfonicheskiĭ kont͡sert filarmonicheskogo obshchestva - 27-go okti͡abri͡a." [Third symphonic concert of the Philharmonic Society - 27 October] *Russkie vedomosti,* 250, 30 October 1912.

Review of the concert given on 27 October 1912, in which Rachmaninoff conducted the Philharmonic (Moscow) in Mendelssohn's *Shchotlandskai͡a simfonii͡a* [Scottish Symphony], Grieg's *Liricheskai͡a si͡uita* [Lyric Suite], and Liszt's *Mazzepa* (Symphonic Poem). Grigori Prokof'ev disapproves of Rachmaninoff's choice of literature (much too ordinary), and wonders why he does not expand his orchestral repertoire with fresher material.

247. ———. "Pi͡atoe simfonicheskoe sobranie, kont͡sert filarmonicheskogo obshchestva, 1-go dekabri͡a." [Fifth symphonic concert, Philharmonic Society, 1 December] *Russkie vedomosti* 279, 4 December 1912, p.6.

Review of Rachmaninoff's final concert of the season as director of the Simfonicheskogo Filarmonicheskogo obshchestva [Philharmonic Symphony Society] Orchestra (Moscow). Works on the program: *Simfonii͡a No.2* [Symphony No.2] by Borodin, *Vesna* [Spring] by Glazunov, and *Secha pri kerzhent͡se* [Battle at the Kerzhentse] by Rimsky-Korsakov. Grigori Prokof'ev disliked the staid interpretation of the Borodin symphony, yet at the same time commented on the conductor's ability to ignite the orchestra in the work's dramatic passages. G. Prokof'ev appreciated the execution of the Glazunov and Rimsky-Korsakov works.

248. ———. "Kontserty S.V. Rakhmaninova."
(16-go i 18-go noiabria) [S.V. Rakhmaninoff concerts of the 16th and 18th of November] *Russkie vedomosti*, 266, 19 November 1915.

Rachmaninoff recital (16 November, Nezlobin Teatr, Moscow) of his own works, and his recital of Scriabin's works (18 November, Large Hall of the Polytechnical Museum, Moscow). Program of Rachmaninoff works (works mentioned in the review) included a pair of *Etiudy-Kartiny* [Etudes-tableaux] in F Minor and G Minor Op.33, *Preliudii Soch.23* [Preludes Op.23] Nos.10 and 5, and the *Sonata dlia f-no No.2* [Piano Sonata No.2] Op.36. The Scriabin program included *Sonata-fantaisie Op.19, Fantasia Op.28, Poème satanique Op.36, Sonata No.5 Op.53*, and several *Preliudii Op.11* and *Etiudy Op.42*. Unlike the unsatisfactory reviews (one by G. Prokof'ev in *Russkaia muzykal'naia gazeta*, 6 December 1915) that Rachmaninoff received during this season for his interpretations of Scriabin's music, this review is generally on the positive side. Critic Prokof'ev notes that Rachmaninoff and Scriabin's music are diametrically opposed and remarks that in interpreting Scriabin's piano works, Rachmaninoff made the counterpoint clear and could not have performed the Scriabin works any differently.

249. ———. "Tretii simfonicheskii kontsert S. Kusevitskogo." [Third symphonic concert of S. Koussevitzky] *Russkie vedomosti*, 277, 3 December 1915.

Review of a concert (30 November 1915, Nezlobin Teatr, Moscow) dedicated to works of Rachmaninoff, directed by Sergei Aleksandrovich Kusevitskii [Koussevitzky]. Koussevitzky conducted *Vesna* [Spring] Op.20, *Kontsert dlia f-no s orkestrom No.3* [Concerto for Piano and Orchestra No.3], and *Kolokola* [The Bells] Op.35. Grigori Prokof'ev was delighted with the cantatas and especially impressed with *Vesna* Op.20. Rachmaninoff was a colossal success as soloist in the concerto. Prokof'ev considered this concert one of Koussevitzky's finest performances.

250. ———. "Po povodu kont͡sertov Rakhmaninova iz svoĭkh proi͡zvedeniĭ i Skri͡abina." [On the occasion of Rachmaninoff's concert of his and Scriabin's works] *Russkai͡a muzykal'nai͡a gazeta*, 49, 6 December 1915, p.799.

Recitals in Moscow (16 and 18 November) featuring Rachmaninoff's own works on the 16th and Scriabin's on the 18th. This is the often-quoted review, in which critic Prokof'ev objects to Rachmaninoff's interpretation of Scriabin's piano music. Upon the death of Aleksandr Nikolaevich Skri͡abin [Scriabin] on 14 April 1915, Rachmaninoff announced that he would perform programs of his friend and colleague's music and give the proceeds to Scriabin's widow, who was now destitute. Prokof'ev did not like Rachmaninoff's *Sonata dli͡a f-no No.2* [Sonata for Piano No.2] as a musical work, but he was ecstatic in his descriptions of Rachmaninoff's performance of it. "He plays his own works with superhuman beauty," is a sample descriptive phrase used by G. Prokof'ev on Rachmaninoff's performance. As to the performance of Scriabin's music, it was a different story. Critic Prokof'ev contends that either Rachmaninoff did not want to capture the essence of Scriabin's music, or he was unable to do so. "When Skri͡abin's music floated in the clouds, Rachmaninoff brought it down to earth." Evidently his performance and interpretations of Scriabin's *Satanicheskoĭ poemy* [Satanic Poem] Op.36 and Second and Fifth Sonatas were pedantic in conception and dissimilar to Scriabin's unique palette of sonorities. Prokof'ev concludes with the remark that it pains him to realize that even the great talent of Rachmaninoff has limitations.

251.   ———. "Rakhmaninov igraet Skri͡abina."
       [Rachmaninoff plays Scriabin] Sovet͡skai͡a
       muzyka 3 (1959): 121-26.

   Critic Grigori Prokof'ev re-examines his
   recollection of the event that took place
   44 years ago, when Rachmaninoff performed
   Scriabin programs in memory of the composer-
   pianist. At these concerts Rachmaninoff
   was severely criticized for his interpretation of Scriabin's music. G. Prokof'ev was
   one of those critics who was troubled by
   the Rachmaninoff reading of Scriabin. The
   author now feels that there is room for
   different approaches to Scriabin's music,
   and that possibly Rachmaninoff purposely did
   not perform Scriabin as the composer himself
   would. One of the criticisms voiced at that
   time was that Rachmaninoff was too literate
   with Scriabin's line, and that he lacked the
   rubato that Scriabin employed in his playing.
   Illustrations.

252.   ———. "Zametki o Rakhmaninove." [Notes
       about Rachmaninoff] Sovet͡skai͡a muzyka 10
       (1959): 128-36.

   The author examines the Medtner-Rachmani-
   noff friendship; a complicated relationship
   with differing personalities. Grigori
   Prokof'ev remarks that despite Rachmaninoff's
   mission to propagandize Medtner's music, he
   only sporadically performed his friend's
   music. G. Prokof'ev also reflects on Rachmaninoff the pianist, commenting on his dili-
   gence in mastering the instrument, practice
   schedule, interpretive changes, and the con-
   stant quest for perfection. Illustrations.

253.   Prussing, Stephan. "Compositional Techniques
       in Rachmaninoff's 'Vespers, Opus 37'."
       Ph.D. diss., Catholic University, 1979.
       Ann Arbor, Mich.: University Microfilms
       International, 1980. 224 p. ML 410 R12
       P7   OCLC 9876039

Rachmaninoff's *Vespers* is observed in relation to the history of Russian church music; analyzed, and compared to the *Liturgy of Saint John Chrysostom Op.31*, and compared to church works by contemporaries of Rachmaninoff, namely Archangelskiĭ, Gretchaninov. Kastalskiĭ, Tchaikovsky, and Tschnokov. The work includes a biographical sketch of the composer and an overview of the background of *Vespers*. The fifteen settings are harmonically analyzed, with comparative observations; also included are commentaries on word texture, dynamics, and style. The author also discusses the chant derivations of the First Symphony. In conclusion, Prussing informs that *Vespers* is basically simple in harmonic structure, with the use of very little counterpoint, and asserts that *Vespers* is "superior to previous and contemporary efforts to compose church music with both propriety and inspiration." Musical examples, bibliography.

254. Rachmaninoff, Sergei. "My Prelude in C-sharp Minor." *Delineator* 75 (February 1910): 127.

   Rachmaninoff informally discusses the history of the *Prelude in C-sharp Minor Op.3, No.2*, stressing that the composition is absolute music, devoid of any romanticized story. He relates that he did not copyright the work, reveals his surprise at its widespread success, and includes a detailed account of his interpretation of the piece, pointing out technical problems, dynamic contrast, climaxes, and general mood of the composition.

255. ———. "Ten Important Attributes of Beautiful Pianoforte Playing." *Etude* 28 (March 1910): 153-54, Also- in Russian "Ispolnenie trebuet glubokikh razmyshleniĭ." [Performance demands deep reflection] in *Sovetskaĩa muzyka* 2 (1977): 78-84.

These are Rachmaninoff's ten commandments for skill in performance, which have been often quoted since this article appeared in print. The article refers to Rachmaninoff's new title, that of Supervisor General of the Imperial Conservatories of Russia, which was an appointment he received in 1909; with this position came the responsibility of inspecting the music conservatories in Western Russia, a responsibility he accepted in earnest. The composer expounds on the ten important points of being a consumate musician-pianist; they are: Forming the proper conception of a piece, Technical proficiency, Proper phrasing, Regulating the tempo, Character in playing, Significance of the pedal, Danger of convention, Real musical understanding, Playing to educate the public, and the Vital spark. In the discussion of technique, Rachmaninoff reveals some of the technical requirements used in examinations at the Russian conservatories. The article, though directed towards piano students and with very generalized comments, still is helpful to all. Those more sophisticated will find the occasional comments made by Rachmaninoff on Russian training, Rubinstein's approach, etc., to be very interesting.

256. ———. "National and Radical Impressions in the Music of Today and Yesterday." *Etude* 37 (October 1919): 615, Also- in Russian (abridged), "O russkom narodnom muzykal'nom tvorchestve." [concerning the art of Russian folk music] in *Sovetskaia muzyka*, sbornik chetvertyĭ, (1945): 52-58.

Rachmaninoff discusses formal music's link with folk music, the importance of melody in music, futurists and modern trends. He speaks with admiration of Medtner's works, remarking that they are fresh and modern, and that he cannot understand why Medtner's music is ignored. Rachmaninoff comments on Russian music of the past and future, the new trends, and notes how popular MacDowell's music is in Russia.

257. ———. "How Russian Students Work." *Etude* 37 (October 1919): 298.

Here are a few remarks made by Rachmaninoff concerning diverse musical topics: Slavs are apt to be lazy; Americans have far more patience; Chopin's music is comfortable to the hand; American audiences are more appreciative of the substantial and beautiful elements in music than many European audiences; Europe is suffering from a mania for cacophony; Americans are too practical to be fooled by such material. Rachmaninoff makes some startling comparisons.

258. ———. "New Lights on the Art of the Piano." *Etude* 41 (April 1923): 223-24.

Interesting interview in which Rachmaninoff divulges many of the Russian conservatory methods, especially technical training in use during his student tenure in conservatory. He stresses the need for technical training when the student is very young. He himself prefers scales and arpeggi, and recommends two hours' practice daily on technique. The Russian conservatory technical piano examination, given to students reaching the sixth class, is outlined by Rachmaninoff.

259. ———. "Some Critical Moments in My Career." *Musical Times* 71 (June 1930): 557-58, Also in French "La carrière d'un grand virtuose." [The career of a great virtuoso] in *Candide* No.338 (4 September 1930).

Rachmaninoff reflects on the life of the concert artist: how time-consuming the travel is and how the continuance of success dominates the entire life. Obtaining the first opportunity for recognition, and the need for assistance by the already successful are two important factors which aid the rise of new talent, informs Rachmaninoff. He tells of how helpful the support from Tchaikovsky and Tolstoĭ was in his career. He comments that with age one loses self-confidence, and that he rarely feels satisfied with what he is doing, recalling specifically one concert when everything was perfect: the instrument and its position on stage, lighting, the hall, audience reaction, acoustics, etc. The concert took place in Vienna (n.d.). Rachmaninoff concludes with a lament for his loss of homeland. The article is important for Rachmaninoff's recollections on his success and his discussion of topics he never previously broached. Note- A peculiarity in comparing the two versions of this article: in the *Musical Times*, the reference to *Aleko* is written as, "....my first opera, 'The Aleccot,'....," which represents the French spelling for the pronunciation of *Aleko*, while the reference to *Aleko* in *Candide* reads, "....mon premier opera 'The Aleccot'....," which looks like an English title. The article 'the' does not belong in either title and is especially out of place in the French version. Evidently both versions were prepared at the same time, and the bad judgement to use "The Alecott" to represent *Aleko* appeared verbatim in both versions.

260. ———. "The Artist and the Gramophone." *Gramophone* 9 (April 1931): 525-26, Also-in Russian "Khudozhnik i gramzapis'." *Muzykal'naĩa zhizn'* 6 (March 1973): 3-4.

Rachmaninoff states that recordings, with their modern recording methods, are far superior to radio transmission. He recalls when he first made records with the Edison Company in 1919; the sound was thin and tinkly, resembling a balalaika. Modern piano recordings do the pianist complete justice. Rachmaninoff disliked radio music and refused to perform for the medium.

261. ———. Interview by Florence Leonard. "Interpretation Depends on Talent and Personality." *Etude* 50 (April 1932): 239-40, Also- in Russian "Interpretat͡sii͡a zavisit ot talanta i individual'nosti." [Interpretation depends on talent and individuality] in *Sovet͡skai͡a muzyka* 4 (1973): 99-102.

Interpretation and its many facets are reviewed by Rachmaninoff. General subjects such as contrast, dynamic proportion, stylistic differences, rubato, the pedal, and technique are scrutinized. A great deal of attention is given to Chopin's works, noting interpretive practices. Rachmaninoff marvels at the greatness of his music, stating that Chopin today is more modern than many moderns. As in many of the *Etude* interviews of Rachmaninoff, the specter of Anton Rubinstein appears as the omnipotent pianist. Rachmaninoff often refers to Rubinstein's interpretations with the greatest fondness and admiration. Rubinstein was a major influence in Rachmaninoff's pianistic career.

262. ———. Interview by Norman Cameron. "The Composer as Interpreter." *Monthly Musical Record* 64 (November 1934): 201.

This substantive interview finds the composer in an introspective mood, willing to explore subjects that caught his interest. Rachmaninoff offers an in-depth reply to the question, "Given sufficient executive ability, should a composer prove the best interpreter of his own music?" The interpreter, composer, composer-interpreter, and composer-conductor, are posed in various comparative and evaluative attitudes on musical production. Two of the points made by Rachmaninoff: of the composer and interpreter, the composer possesses the greater imaginative gift and sensitivity towards musical coloring; the sense of musical color is a disadvantage to the composer-conductor when interpreting works of others. Rachmaninoff concludes the interview with a justification of his loss of the desire to compose: his separation from his musical roots, traditions, and background- a lament for his native land. A revealing and informative article.

263. ——. Interview by David Ewen. "Music Should Speak From the Heart." *Etude* 59 (December 1941): 804,849, Also- in Russian "Muzyka dolzhna idti ot serdtsa." [Music must come from the heart] *Sovetskaia muzyka* 4 (1973): 103-04.

This is perhaps Rachmaninoff's longest deliberation on the subject of "modern music." To Rachmaninoff, musical expression is simple, sincere, personal, and above all, from the heart, and he sets forth his musical credo in this interview. He completely disregards any experimental ventures in musical composition because this would be contrary to his creative nature. He states that he could never write in a radical vein, disregarding the laws of tonality or harmony. This is Rachmaninoff's conservative-traditional stance, which he often proclaimed and never modified. Rachmaninoff tells of his use of extra-musical sources for compositional inspiration, such as books, pictures, and poems. These sources, of course, are rarely disclosed and are subsidiary to the musical work. Young composers are urged to study the old masters before they venture in a new style.

264. "S.V. Rakhmaninov." *Moskovskie vedomosti*, 3 September 1904.

Announcement of Rachmaninoff's debut as conductor of the Bol'shoĭ Opera (evening of 3 September 1904) performing Dargomyzhski's opera *Rusalka*. The article makes mention of

Rachmaninoff's experience as conductor of operas with Savva Mamontov's Moskovskai͡a Chastnai͡a Russkai͡a Opera [Moscow Private Russian Opera] Company, performed at the Solodnikov Teatr, in Moscow 1897-98. A brief survey of the composer's conservatory study follows.

265. "Rachmaninoff Makes Debut in New York." *Musical America* (20 November 1909).

A review of Rachmaninoff's first concert in New York City (Carnegie Hall, 13 November 1909), in which he performed the Second Concerto with the Boston Symphony Orchestra under Max Fiedler. There follows a vivid description of the composer's physical appearance and a brief account of his performance.

266. "Rachmaninoff Arrives in America." *Musical Courier* 77 (14 November 1918): 8.

Informative article appeared only four days after the Rachmaninoffs arrived in the USA, following a ten-day journey by ship from Oslo. The composer was very direct with his responses. The inverview was held in the Hotel Sherry-Netherland, in New York City, where the Rachmaninoffs were temporarily staying; it was conducted in French. The composer tells of the unpleasantness under the Bolshevik regime- his escape to Stockholm- reasons for rejecting the conducting offer with the Boston Symphony Orchestra- why he came to America- his plans for revising the First Concerto (the only manuscript he had with him)- his thoughts concerning the political situation in Russia- and his first-hand view of the Armistice Day celebration in New York City. The interviewer was very astute in asking such pertinent questions.

267. "Rachmaninoff Returns to America: The Rachmaninoff of 1918." *Boston Transcript*, 20 November 1918.

An absorbing article written shortly after Rachmaninoff's arrival in New York City (10 November 1918). The interviewer relates the composer's flight from Russia and re-examines his various talents. Rachmaninoff at the time of this interview was recovering from a touch of the flu. The author noted a change in his appearance from the last time they met, 9 years previously: "his eyes were sunken and the bones in his face protrude upon his yellow skin." This change, as was explained, was due to the effects of flight, exile, and privation on the composer. Rachmaninoff comments informally on contemporary Russian composers- Medtner, Glazunov, Tcherepnin, Glière, Stravinsky, Prokofiev, and Scriabin.

268. "Rachmaninoff Opens His Tour in Providence, R.I.." *Musical America* 29 (21 December 1918): 33.

A review of Rachmaninoff's first recital in the USA after his separation from Russia and arrival from Oslo. He presented an out-of-town opening for the recital he was to play in Carnegie Hall on 21 December 1918. Rachmaninoff opened in Providence at the Strand Theater on 8 December 1918, performing Mozart's "Theme and Variations" (from *Sonata in A Major* KV 331), Beethoven's *Sonata Op.10, No.3*, a Chopin group, Rachmaninoff group, and the Liszt *Hungarian Rhapsody No.12*. The critic commented on the absence of mannerisms (performers at this time were expected to exhibit mannerisms), clear and certain technique, etc.

269. "Sergei Rachmaninoff." *Etude* 41 (October 1923): 662.

On the 40th anniversary of the *Etude* magazine, a question on the future of music was posed to several composers and performers. Rachmaninoff's response is predictable, stating that melody must be the integral foundation of all music; he decries the Futurists in Russia (and in other countries) because they turn their backs on the simple folk melodies of their lands. Note- Rachmaninoff speaks often about the Futurists; for a view of that movement (at the time the movement was waning) see "Futurism, a Series of Negatives" by Nicholas C. Gatty in the *Musical Quarterly* 2 (January 1916): 9-12.

270. "Rachmaninoff's Songs." *British Musician* 4 (May 1928): 72; and 4 (June 1928): 101-03.

Descriptive analysis of several songs, with emphasis on the Russian metrical form, verbal declamation, syncopated rhythms, and the general appreciation of Rachmaninoff's songs. Selected songs were chosen from the Collected Edition of Rachmaninoff Songs, recently published by Hawkes and Son.

271. "Sergei Rachmaninoff." *Musical Opinion* 54 (December 1930): 213.

Descriptive article, views the Russian heritage of the composer, the effect his exile has had on his creativity, his lack of interest in atonal music, and his first appearance in England. The article stresses that Rachmaninoff's music must not be neglected; his works need to be heard often.

272. "Rachmaninoff spielt für 'Pro Juventute'." [Rachmaninoff plays for "Pro Juventute"] *Sie und Er* 8 (1938): 166-67.

A Swiss pictorial article showing views of the Rachmaninoff villa "Senar" (name derived form SErgeĭ, NAtali︠a︡, Rakhmaninov) located in Hertenstein-bei-Luzern, Switzerland. The narrative accompanying the photographs explains that on 4 May 1938, Rachmaninoff was to perform a concert in the Zürcher Tonhalle [Zurich Recital Hall], donating the entire proceeds to the "Pro Juventute" program and the Swiss relief work for emigrant children. There are fascinating views of "Senar," showing the glass-enclosed terrace, and exterior view from Küssnachter Bucht [Kussnacht Bay], the covered trellis, dining room, and scenes of the composer with his wife and his grandchildren. The special photographs for *Sie und Er* were prepared by H.N. Niedecken.

273. "Rachmaninoff Festival: Series Marks 30th Anniversary of His Debut in U.S." *Newsweek* 14 (4 December 1939): 40.

An announcement of the "Rachmaninoff Cycle" concerts (26 November, 3 December, and 10 December 1939) given in Carnegie Hall. The article reveals the outcome of a Columbia Broadcasting System (CBS) poll, in which the public was asked what living composer's music will be performed 100 years from now; the result ranked Sibelius first, Richard Strauss second, and Rachmaninoff third, followed by Stravinsky, Prokofiev, and Shostakovich. Curious that four out of six are Russian composers.

274. "Rachmaninoff." *Time* 34 (18 December 1939): 56.

A short review of the concert at Philadelphia's Academy of Music, with the Philadelphia Orchestra directed by Rachmaninoff; the program included the Third Symphony and *The Bells*. Rachmaninoff made his conducting debut in the USA with the Philadelphia Orchestra in 1909, and now 30 years later, he again directs the orchestra in a concert that in two days (10 December 1939) would be repeated in Carnegie Hall, as part of the "Rachmaninoff Cycle," a series of three concerts dedicated to the composer. Note-He also performed as pianist, playing the first three concerti and the *Rhapsody on a Theme of Paganini*.

275.   "Rachmaninoff Days in Moscow." *Soviet Literature* 1 (1946): 67-68.

An account of an exhibition honoring Rachmaninoff, held in the State Central Museum of Musical Culture, in October 1945. Several papers were read at the Moscow Conservatory dealing with the life, creative art, and performances of Rachmaninoff. Participants included Bortnikova, Dobrokhotov, Pytovich, Protopopov, I͡akovlev, Gol'denveizer, Nezhdanova, Belza, and Livanova. There were also several concerts of Rachmaninoff's works given in his honor. For more detailed information on this exhibition and symposium in honor or Rachmaninoff see T.E. T͡sytovich's *S.V. Rakhmaninov, sbornik state i materi͡alov* (1947) and I.F. Belza's *S.V. Rakhmaninov i russka͡ia opera* (1947).

276.   "Sergei V. Rakhmaninov." *Vestnik* (published by the Los Angeles "R" Club, Chapter 155 Federated Russian Orthodox Clubs) 2 (March 1948).

Biographical sketch by an orchestral member (article is initialed I.O.) under Stokowski who watched Rachmaninoff perform during his last days. The author writes with great admiration and describes the composer's appearance at this concert as being physically weak and generally worn-out.

277.   "Rachmaninoff Fund Forced to Discontinue." *Musical America* 69 (June 1949): 4.

Reasons for the demise of the Rachmaninoff Fund are given. Inaugurated in 1943, the Rachmaninoff Fund was designed to provide career opportunities for young pianists through selection by national contests. Unfortunately there was only one competition held; prizes were awarded in 1948, after a delay caused by the inability of regional

juries to come up with the required talent.
The board of directors of the Rachmaninoff
Fund were hoping that the USSR would work
in conjunction with the USA competition and
hold a similar national contest, so that
winners could perform in each other's
country. No such competition developed in
the USSR. For a description of a newly
formed USSR Rachmaninoff competition in
1983 see Mikhail Gol'dshtein's "Rakhmaninovskiĭ konkurs v Moskve," in *Novoye russkoye slovo*, 72, 1 November 1983, p.4.

278. Rakhmaninova, Natalīa Aleksandrovna.
"S.V. Rakhmaninov." *New Review* (Novyĭ
zhurnal) No.100 (September 1970): 245-59,
and cont. in No.103 (1970): 137-52.

Recollections of Rachmaninoff by his wife
Natalīa, published in two successive editions
of *New Review*, which is published in New
York and written in Russian. The recollections are published in the above journal for
the first time, with permission of Sof'īa
Satina. The first part of the recollections
is divided into five sections- "Druz'īa-
muzykanty v Rossiĭ" [Friends and musicians
in Russia], "Kont͡sertnye poezdki po Amerike"
[Concert tours in America], "S.V.-pīanist,"
"S.V.-kompozitor." [S.V.-composer], and
"S.V.-dirizher" [S.V.-conductor]. Part two
contains chapters dealing with: "Kharakter
S.V." [Character of S.V.], "Senar i ot'ezd
iz Evropy" [Senar and the departure from
Europe], and "Bolezn' i smert' S.V." [Ill-
ness and death of S.V.]. Natalīa offers
interesting, intimate narrative of Sergei
Vasil'evich and his career; the recollections contain fascinating minutiae of the
composer. The first part of Natalīa's
recollections also appeared, in abbreviated
form, in *Muzykal'naīa zhizn'* No.6 (March
1973): 8-9, as "Vospominaniīa."

279.   "RCA to Gift Library of Congress With Rare
        Rachmaninoff Discs." *Variety* 190 (1 April
        1953): 78.

        An announcement of the presentation of a
        series of Rachmaninoff recordings, including
        several pre-electric recordings, by RCA Victor to the Library of Congress, for inclusion
        in the Rachmaninoff Archive.

280.   Reed, Peter Hugh. "Rachmaninoff Left Priceless Recordings." *Etude* 61 (June 1943):
        369,424.

        An evaluation of Rachmaninoff's recording
        legacy, a comment on his capabilities as
        pianist and composer, and a review of several
        recordings. Reed maintains that Rachmaninoff
        is by no means as great a composer as he is
        an interpreter. Reed has other reservations
        about how long his music will endure, or
        which compositions will survive. The critical attitude of Reed is typical of the prevalent consensus concerning Rachmaninoff's
        future role in music history.

281.   Reither, Joseph. "Chronicle of Exile."
        Tempo 22 (Winter 1951-52): 29-36.

        Reither includes a critical appraisal of
        Rachmaninoff biographies by Riesemann,
        Culshaw, Lyle and Seroff, a criticism of
        the composer by quasi-authorities, and a
        discussion of his career. The major subject
        Reither examines is Rachmaninoff's career
        as recording artist, describing his major
        recordings and those of other artists'
        interpretation of his music.

282.   Riesemann, Oskar von. *Rachmaninoff's
        Recollections*, Told to Oskar von Riesemann.
        Translated from the German manuscript by

Dolly Rutherford. London: Allen and
Unwin, 1934. Also- New York: Macmillan,
1934. 272 p. ML 410 R12 A22 OCLC
891073

An important pioneer biography-study of
Rachmaninoff that later was criticized for
being exaggerated and inaccurate. Supposedly
based on information culled from interviews
conducted with the composer in France
(Clairefontaine), although Sof'īā Satina
and Rachmaninoff later claimed that Riesemann
took no notes during the discussions.
Rachmaninoff was expecting a biography from
Riesemann, but instead the work had all the
appearances of an autobiography, which upset
him greatly. Fortunately, part of Riesemann's material was provided by Sof'īā
Satina, who supplied him with accurate biographical data. Rachmaninoff was chagrined
on first reading the work and insisted on
some revisions before publication; finally
he allowed the work to be published and
even included a feeble personal endorsement.
Despite the over-elaboration and other inherent faults, the Riesemann book did offer
an accurate overview of the composer's early
years and training, and filled an informational void concerning the enigmatic
composer-pianist. Riesemann's book served
as a source for many subsequent biographies
until new sources appeared- mainly the collected letters and other archival materials.
Illustrations, list of works (through Op.42),
name index.

283. Rosenfeld, Paul. "Rachmaninoff." *New Republic* 18 (15 March 1919): 208-10.

Rosenfeld's article, which examines Rachmaninoff's traditional-conservative compositional style, is largely deprecatory:
he does not make any subtle allusions to
Rachmaninoff's apparent anachronistic status;
he candidly expresses his displeasure with
the composer's lack of boldness, his overly

soft, sweet, elegiac writing, and his lack
of originality in melodic passages (they
have a "Mendelssohnian cast"), rhythms, and
harmonies, etc.. Rosenfeld cannot understand why Rachmaninoff continues to write
piano concerti in the old style (like Liszt
and Rubinstein) when the form is being treated differently by such composers as Brahms,
Stravinsky, and Scriabin, i.e., the virtuoso
concerto is being replaced by the concerto
which treats the piano as an orchestral
instrument. When Rosenfeld says something
complimentary (not often), it is stated in
a condescending, demeaning manner, as in this
remark: "Doubtless, M. Rachmaninoff is an
accomplished and charming workman. He is
almost uniformly suave and dextrous." This
text is also in Rosenfeld's *Musical Portraits:
Interpretations of Twenty Modern Composers.*
New York: Harcourt, Brace and Howe, 1920.
314 p.   ML 390 R78   OCLC 854294   (Reprint--
Freeport, N.Y.: Books for Libraries Press,
1968.   OCLC 449291)

284.   Roy, Basanta Koomar. "Rachmaninoff is
    Reminiscent." *Musical Observer* 26 (May
    1927: 16.

   Some of the questions posed to Rachmaninoff
in this interview: how have you gained recognition as a composer?, your sources of
inspiration?, what about other composers in
Russia?, does the personality of a musician
aid or hinder success?, and what is the musical future of this country? A large portion
of this interview is concerned with the composer's sources of inspiration and his novice
years as a composer. Rachmaninoff reiterates
his desire that the USA initiate a national
conservatory of music, where the most talented could be trained.

285.   Rubin, David. "Transformation of the Dies
    irae in Rachmaninov's Second Symphony."
    Musical Review 23 (May 1962): 132-36.

Rubin demonstrates through musical examples, references to the *Dies irae* theme (first phrase) in Rachmaninoff's music. He cites allusions to the motive in the Second Symphony, *Vocalise,* Third Symphony, *Symphonic Dances,* and Second Sonata, as well as mentioning the more obvious statements of the *Dies irae* made in the *Isle of the Dead, Rhapsody on a Theme of Paganini,* and the First Symphony. Many of the cited allusions to the motive are remote. Since Rachmaninoff's music is frequently based on sequential movement, the similarity to the *Dies irae* (first phrase of which is sequential) could be unrealistically construed as being extensive in his works.

286. Rubinstein, Arthur. *My Young Years.* New York: Knopf, 1973. 479 p. ML 417 R79 A3 ISBN 0-394-46890-2 OCLC 520585

Rubinstein relates the experience of hearing the "Saison russe" concerts in Paris (1907)- a series of concerts given at the Theatre de l'Opera featuring Russian music and musicians. Rachmaninoff conducted his *Spring* cantata Op.20 and performed the Second Concerto. Rubinstein reveals his impression of the series. Illustrated, name index.

287. ───. *My Many Years.* New York: Knopf, 1980. 626 p. ML 417 R79 A28 ISBN 0-394-42253-8 OCLC 5673961 Also- London: Cape, 1980. ML 417 R79 A28 1980 OCLC 6619951 Also- in German *Mein glückliches Leben.* Translated from the English by Günther Danehl. Frankfurt Am Main: Fischer, 1980. 792 p. ML 417 R79 A2815 ISBN 0-100-67602-5 OCLC 8999855

The second part of Rubinstein's autobiography. The author expresses his opinion of Rachmaninoff the musician and quotes many personal remarks made to him by the composer.

Rubinstein relates his impression of hearing Rachmaninoff perform. There is an interesting reminiscence of a social encounter between Stravinsky and Rachmaninoff. Illustrated, epilogue, name index.

288. Rüger, Christoph. "Ein Kunstler--zwei Leben." [One artist-two lives] *Musik und Gesellschaft* 23 (April 1973): 198-203.

Written on the 100th anniversary of the composer's birth, this article, which is largely biographical, focuses on Rachmaninoff's multiplicity of musical talent. The composer follows a great line of successful composer-pianists. Rüger contends that the Chaliapin friendship was influential to the character of Rachmaninoff's music: the cantilena-style melodic lines, use of middle register, phrasing, breath, etc. The article traces Rachmaninoff's brilliant career in the USA. Illustration.

289. Rummenhöller, Peter. "Zum Warencharakter in der Musik: Analyse von Sergej Rachmaninovs Prelude Op.32, Nr.1" [On music as a commodity: an analysis of S. Rachmaninoff's *Prelude Op.32, No.1*] *Zeitschrift für Musik Theorie* 4 (1973): 30-36.

A theoretical monograph which endeavors to employ analysis to ascertain social meaning in music. Rummenhöller states that despite Rachmaninoff's blindness towards innovative compositional trends (i.e., atonality and dodecaphony), he must not be overlooked. His music belongs to the standard repertoire and his influences are widely felt especially in the field of light music and film music; he presents a classic alternative to 20th century music, demonstrating the last unity of composer, interpreter, and public. As a concrete example of his theory, Rummenhöller analyzes the *Prelude in C Major*

Op.32, No.1, especially noting segments that
appear adapted, commercial in character,
archaical, and "window-dressed." Rummenhöller's treatise is philosophic in nature.
It is difficult reading; the author offers
many alternate convoluted explanations that
tend to confuse the reader.

290. Ryt͡sareva, M.G., ed. *Avtografy S.V. Rakh-
maninova:* v fondakh Gosudarstvennogo
T͡sentral'nogo Muzei͡a Muzykal'noĭ Kul'tury
Imeni M.I. Glinki: katalogspravochnik 2-oe
izdanie, rasshirennoe i dopolnennoe.
[Rachmaninoff's autographs in the State
Central Glinka Museum of Musical Culture:
catalog reference, 2d ed., supp. and enl.]
Moskva: Vsesoi͡uznoe Izdatel'stvo Sovet͡skiĭ
Kompozitor, 1980. 136 p.

This second edition of the *Avtografy S.V.
Rakhmaninova* supersedes Evgenii͡a Bortnikova's 1955 catalog of Rachmaninoff autographs. The autographs and other Rachmani-
novabilia are housed in the Fondakh S.V.
Rakhmaninova No.18 [Rachmaninoff Archive
No.18] of the Gosudarstvennogo T͡sentral'nogo
Muzei͡a Muzykal'noĭ Kul'tury Imeni M.I.
Glinki [State Central Glinka Museum of Musical Culture] in Moscow (initially opened in
1943). The second edition lists 566 entries,
some of which are annotated, including: manuscripts of works according to genre, author's
corrections, documents, dedications, photographs, and manuscript gifts. A second edition was necessary because of the accumula-
tion of materials in the Soviet Rachmaninoff
Archive. This expanded edition contains a
listing of new material from Sof'i͡a Satina
(donated in 1972), some 338 letters, documents pertaining to publishing, and microfilms of holdings from the USA Rachmaninoff
Archive, located in the Library of Congress.
This work is the result of Soviet scholars
striving to consolidate information from the
two major Rachmaninoff archives: the Library
of Congress and the Gos. T͡sentral'nyĭ Muzeĭ

Muzykal'noĭ Kul'tury Imeni M.I. Glinki.
Portrait, name, and work indexes. Note-
Zarui Apetĭan, in her important work *S. Rakhmaninov: literaturnoe nasledie*, 3 vols. published in 1978-80, also includes materials from the Library of Congress.

291. Sabaneyeff, Leonid. *Modern Russian Composers*. Translated from the Russian by Judah A. Joffe. New York: International Publishers, 1927. (Reprint-- Freeport, N.Y.: Books for Libraries, 1967. 253 p. ML 390 S123 M6 OCLC 854313)

A valuable study of the composer written by Russian music critic Leonid Sabaneyeff, who strives for a socio-psychological understanding of Rachmaninoff. Sabaneyeff points out that Rachmaninoff grew up in a milieu of moderation and conservatism; life in Moscow was one of "impenetrable pessimism" and the conservatory was proud of its conservative approach; this influence was reflected in his music. The author offers a descriptive perspective of the differences in the Moscow School and St. Petersburg School of composers, as well as presenting chapters on Rachmaninoff's mentor, Sergeĭ Ivanovich Taneev, and colleagues Aleksandr Nikolaevich Scriabin and Nikolaĭ Karlovich Medtner. No index.

292. Sabina, M. "Vospominaniĭa o Rakhmaninove." [Reminiscences of Rachmaninoff] *Sovetskaĭa muzyka* 2 (1958): 147-49.

A review of Zarui Apetĭan's *Vospominaniĭa o Rakhmaninove* (Moskva: Muzgiz, 1957, first ed.). The collection of reminiscences by diverse authors, compiled by Apetĭan, receives commendation from M. Sabina. The reviewer offers a suggestion that in subsequent editions Apetĭan trim and cut the repetition of facts related by several authors of the recollections. Since the first edition, *Vospominaniiā o Rakhmaninove* has undergone revision and enlargement in editions of 1961, 1967, and 1974. Apetīan's monumental work, *S. Rakhmaninov: literaturnoe nasledie* (3 vols.) published in 1978-80, also contains reminiscences, as well as articles, interviews, and the complete letters of Rachmaninoff.

293. Salazar, Adolfo. *Music in Our Time.* Trends in Music Since the Romantic Era. (A translation, with revisions, of *La Musica Moderna:* Las corrientes directrices en el arte musical contemporaneo. by Adolfo Salazar, Buenos Aires, 1944) Translation from the Spanish by Isabel Pope. New York: Norton, 1946. 367 p. ML 196 S252 OCLC 390672 Also- Westport, Conn.: Greenwood Press, 1970. ML 196 S252 OCLC 65324

An historical criticism and overview of contemporary musical styles. There are inaccuracies in the historical account of Rachmaninoff. Salazar states that Rachmaninoff made a reputation as a pianist before he became known as a composer. His musical career seems to prove just the opposite. Rachmaninoff's piano performances in Russia were foremost as promulgator of his own works, stressing his accomplishments as composer. Salazar also professes that Rachmaninoff's career as composer began shortly after he became professor in the conservatory (Moscow), when he wrote his opera *Aleko*. *Aleko* was written as a graduation project by Rachmaninoff, the <u>student</u>. Salazar, in describing Rachmaninoff's compositional style in *Francesca da Rimini*, believes that Rachmaninoff's music is detached from the unfolding drama on stage, in a manner similar to that developed later by films, where the stage action is directed toward visual appreciation, and the music furnishes the environmental mood. Musical examples, bibliography (includes foreign language books and periodicals dealing with the history of music), composer-composition index.

294. Salmond, Felix. "The Sonata of Rachmaninoff for Piano and Violoncello." *Strad* 26 (1915): 100-02, 155-57.

A thematic analysis of the *Sonata for Piano and Violoncello in G Minor Op.19* by cellist Felix Salmond. Salmond hopes that this article describing the sonata will aid in understanding and appreciating the work. He cannot understand why it is not performed more often, since in his opinion it is one of the finest sonatas ever written for the instrument. Of the third movement (Andante), he writes, "there is no slow movement in the literature of the violoncello music which surpasses it for sheer beauty and depth of feeling."

295. Satina, Sophia [Sof'ía Aleksandrovna Satina] "Communications." *Journal of the American Musicological Society* 21 (Spring 1968): 120-21.

Since it is persistently mentioned in the press that Rachmaninoff destroyed the manuscript of the First Symphony, Satina here writes a repudiation of that assumption. The composer's cousin and sister-in-law, Sof'ía Satina quotes several letters written by Rachmaninoff to his friends which mention the score of the symphony and his intention to correct and revise it. Satina informs that she was entrusted with the care of the desk where the score was kept, when Rachmaninoff left Russia in 1917. Shortly after Satina left Russia in 1921, the desk disappeared together with the score. Note-The score to the Symphony was eventually reconstructed (in 1946) from orchestral parts found in the Leningrad Conservatory and from the four-hand piano arrangement made by Rachmaninoff.

296.   ———. "S.V. Rakhmaninov: K 25-letiĩu so dnĩa konchiny." [S.V. Rachmaninoff: on the 25th anniversary of his death] *New Review* (Novy zhurnal) No.91 (June 1968): 115-29.

Written on the 25th anniversary of her cousin's death, published here for the first time, Satina relates reminiscences about Rachmaninoff. Of special interest is her recollection of the time when young Sergei moved in with the Satins, shortly after the break with his teacher Nikolai Sergeevich Zverev. Satina sets out to dispel some misconceptions about the composer: that he was unsympathetic to those who were needy and that he rarely read. Material is largely biographical, Satina always supplementing the account of the composer's life with interesting Rachmaninoff minutiae.

297.   Salzman, Eric. "Rachmaninoff, Da-Nyet." *Stereo Review* (May 1943): 66-69.

The pros and cons of Rachmaninoff's music. Interesting article examines the differing opinions and criticisms of Rachmaninoff and his music. Another article about differing opinions of the composer is "The Problem of Rachmaninoff" by Robin Hull, in *Musical Opinion* (April 1942).

298.   Schickel, Richard. *The World of Carnegie Hall*. New York: J. Messner, 1960. 438 p. ML 200.8 N52 C34 OCLC 592022 (Reprint-- Westport, Conn.: Greenwood Press, 1973. ISBN 0-837-16946-1 OCLC 632373)

Rachmaninoff is referred to several times in this history of Carnegie Hall. His first piano recital in the hall is observed- Stokowski conducting *The Bells*- and his last appearance in Carnegie Hall; also included are interesting remarks made by the composer regarding the American public. Illustrations, name index.

299.   Schindler, Kurt, trans. "An Authentic Biography of Rachmaninoff," especially translated from the Russian of I. Korzuchin by Kurt Schindler. *Etude* 37 (October 1919) 623-24.

A biographical survey of Rachmaninoff, with attention to his creativity. Schindler claims, "This biography has been read by the composer in person and is, therefore, accurate." Accurate?- not quite so: Rachmaninoff performed in the UK in 1899, not 1897, and he did not take up residence in Dresden (1906) to devote most of his time to pianistic concert activities, but instead expressly to work on composition, fruits of which were the *Isle of the Dead* (1907), *Sonata for Piano in D Minor Op.28* (1907), and the Second Symphony (1907). Despite the few inaccuracies, this short biography helped the many readers of *Etude* magazine understand the background of this complex personality, who was now being seen more and more on the concert stage.

300.   Schluessmayer, Gerhard. "Die Klavierwerke Rachmaninows." *Musikerziehung* 31 (June 1978): 252-57.

The author strives to familiarize the reader with the characteristics of Rachmaninoff's music through examination of selected piano works, and attempts to dispel the notion that his works are solely salon style in effect. Schluessmayer points out the composer's use of melodic lines that are comprised of small intervals (usually seconds) and their unusual length, his preference for minor keys, harmonic style, and his use of chromaticism and multiple melodic lines. The author gives a descriptive account of the solo piano works, and laments that many of the finest of these are never performed.

301.	Schonberg, Harold C. *The Great Pianists*.
	New York: Simon and Schuster, 1963. 448 p.
	(SR p.367-76) ML 397 S3 OCLC 563987

	This interesting volume on giants of the
	keyboard covers pianists from Mozart to
	Arthur Rubinstein and Horowitz. Rachmani-
	noff's technique, style and interpretations
	are vividly described by Schonberg in his
	personable style of discourse. Portions of
	letters by Shaginían, Medtner, and Rachmani-
	noff are quoted, as well as parts of reviews
	by Huneker and W.J. Henderson. Illustra-
	tions, name index.

302.	―――. *The Great Conductors*. New York:
	Simon and Schuster, 1967. 387 p. (SR
	p.301-02) ML 402 S387 G7 OCLC 600069
	Also- London: Gollancz, 1968. ML 402
	S387 G7 1968 OCLC 6417713

	Written in the style of Schonberg's pre-
	vious book, *The Great Pianists*. This study
	of conductors examines their styles, at-
	titudes, and techniques. Schonberg states
	that Rachmaninoff had the potential to be-
	come as great a conductor as he was a
	pianist. A letter describing Rachmaninoff's
	conducting, written by his friend Nikolaĭ
	Medtner, is quoted here. Illustrations,
	musical examples, name index.

303.	―――. *The Lives of the Great Composers*.
	rev. ed. New York: Norton, 1981. 653 p.
	(SR p.524-39) ML 390 S393 1981a OCLC
	8402674

	The author sketches Rachmaninoff's life,
	stressing his pianistic abilities and his-
	torical status. Schonberg quotes the last
	two paragraphs of the fifth edition of
	Grove's Dictionary of Music and Musicians
	to demonstrate the derogatory scholarly
	concensus of Rachmaninoff that was prevalent

at that time. Schonberg employs a personal, anecdotal style in his writing, making the composers more approachable and less formidable; this informal touch makes this a fine introductory study of the composers which can be subsequently amplified by further reading, and Schonberg offers an ample bibliography for just this purpose. Illustrations, bibliography (extensive), index.

304. ———. *Facing the Music*. New York: Summit Books (Simon and Schuster), 1981. 464 p. (SR p.335-38) ML 60 S382 ISBN 0-671-25405-5 OCLC 7204970

The book title is derived from Schonberg's experience writing for the *Musical Courier*, in which he wrote a column titled "Facing the Music." An interesting retrospect of Schonberg's career as *New York Times* critic, represented by a selection of his articles and Sunday pieces that originally appeared in the *Times* from 1960 to 1980. The article on Rachmaninoff titled "Did Rachmaninoff Collaborate with God?" appeared on 1 April 1973 and is in honor of the composer's birth centennial. Schonberg primarily views Rachmaninoff the pianist, along with commentary on his diverse musical talents. There is some comparison with Josef Hofmann. Schonberg always speaks with great admiration of Rachmaninoff and admits that of the Romantic pianists, Rachmaninoff and Hofmann are his favorites. The articles are interesting and enlightening. *Facing the Music* deserves reading. Index.

305. Scott, Michael. *The Record of Singing*. New York: Holmes and Meier, 1980. 262 p. ML 1460 S35 ISBN 0-841-90599-1 OCLC 5831677 Also- *The Record of Singing*. 3 vols., Published in conjunction with an album of records specially prepared by E.M.I.. London: Duckworth, 1977. ML 1700 S39x ISBN 0-715-61030-9 OCLC 3941833

An illustrated survey of the art of singing as it exists on records (78rpm period). A descriptive examination of artist singers, their métier and careers. Scott treats several national styles, including Russian. There is an interesting account of soprano Nina Pavlovna Koshits (known professionally as Nina Koshetz), 1894-1965, and her association with Rachmaninoff, which she claims was partly romantic. The *Six Songs Op. 38* were dedicated to Koshetz; she and Rachmaninoff performed them in Russia shortly after the songs were written. Scott describes her vocal style and comments briefly on Rachmaninoff's integrity of interpretation. Illustrated, glossary, bibliography, name index.

306. Serebriakov, P.A., and N.P. Rozhdestvenskaia. "Sovetskie ispolniteli o S.V. Rakhmaninove." [Soviet performers on S.V. Rachmaninoff] *Sovetskaia muzyka* 3 (1968): 71-74.

Soviet pianist and teacher Serebriakov and soprano Rozhdestvenskaia comment on the composer and his music. Serebriakov rarely assigns works of Rachmaninoff to his students because they require great technique and emotional maturity. Serebriakov, in repeatedly performing the works of Rachmaninoff, always discovers new and hidden nuances in the music. Soprano Rozhdestvenskaia recalls her preparation for the role of Francheska in *Francheska da Rimini* [Francesca da Rimini], to be performed in the fall of 1943; many Rachmaninoff concerts were scheduled at this time, in honor of his 70th birthday. Sadly, these dedicatory concerts were transformed into memorial programs because of the composer's death. This made the concerts very difficult emotionally for the performers, as Rozhdestvenskaia relates. Illustration.

307. Seroff, Victor Ilyich. "The Great Rachmaninoff." *Vogue* 101 (1 April 1943): 43,88.

An interview with Rachmaninoff. This piece for *Vogue* was prepared and in press when Rachmaninoff died on 28 March 1943. Rachmaninoff informally discusses his *Prelude in C-sharp Minor Op.3, No.2*, difficulty with the English language, educating young composers, American hospitality, superiority of American orchestras, and his Russian traits. Remarking on young composers and their experimentation, he adds, "The seed of the future music of America lies in Negro music. What character there is to work with!" It's unfortunate that Seroff did not pursue this response with an inquiry for further explanation- what type of Negro music had the composer heard to inspire this remark? Seroff comments on Rachmaninoff's practice schedule, physical appearance, and his love of American cars.

308. ―――. *Rachmaninoff*. New York: Simon and Schuster, 1950, 269 p. ML 410 R12 S4 OCLC 837786

A biography in narrative style, partly based on Riesemann's work of 1934 (*Rachmaninoff's Recollections*). Seroff's biography is one of the first to utilize an extensive number of letters in the text, offering a more intimate look at the composer. Seroff devotes a chapter to the Shaginiân-Rachmaninoff friendship, citing the letters that Rachmaninoff wrote to her between 1912 and 1917. The letters were previously published in 1943, in *Novy mir*. There is ample coverage of the Soviet boycott of Rachmaninoff's music, as well as inclusion of remarks on the change of attitude in the USSR after the composer's death, quoting S. Satina, K.A. Kuznetsov, G. Kogan, D. Zhitomirskii, and Grigori Prokof'ev. Seroff's biography is significant for its incorporation of the letters, the attention given Shaginiân, and

the view of USSR's renewed allegiance to
Rachmaninoff. Sources are not always documented (exclusive of the letters), and the
extensive bibliography that is included was
borrowed from T.E. T̂sytovich's substantial
bibliography in *S.V. Rakhmaninov*, sbornik
stateĭ i materĩalov (Muzgiz 1947). Seroff's
work includes illustrations, list of works
and bibliography.

309.   ———. "Notes on a Translation." *Saturday
         Review* 37 (31 July 1954): 53.

         A very irate Victor Seroff writes of a
         French translation of his book on Rachmaninoff (1950), claiming that he knew nothing
         of this translation until six weeks after
         its publication (surely his publisher Simon
         and Schuster knew of it). The incensed
         author accuses the translator of misquotation, falsification, omission, etc. In
         effect, this article publicly disassociates
         Seroff entirely from this French edition.
         Note- the suspect work is Victor Seroff,
         Rachmaninoff: traduit de l'anglais, par
         Michel Bourdet-Pleville, Paris: Laffont,
         1954.

310.   Shaginĩan, Marietta Sergeevna. "S.V. Rakhmaninov (Muzykal'no-psikhologicheskiĭ
         etĩud)." [S.V. Rachmaninoff (musical-
         psychological study)] *Trudy i dni* 4-5
         (July-October 1912): 97-114.

         Written at the time Shaginĩan ("Re") was
         corresponding with Rachmaninoff. She gives
         a comparative study of the arts, noting how
         music differs from the others. The reader
         senses a defensive attitude in Shaginĩan's
         portrayal of Rachmaninoff and his music. A
         sampling of her remarks: he should not be
         associated with Tchaikovsky's music because
         Rachmaninoff's music is entirely different;
         Rachmaninoff loves human elements of inspi-

ration; the *Kontsert dlia f-no s orkestrom No.2* [Concerto for Piano and Orchestra No.2] contains the essence of all his music; there is sex (eros) in his music, since the theme of *Francheska da Rimini* [Francesca da Rimini] is of powerful love; the music of Rachmaninoff is healing. Shaginian concludes with a poetic perspective, describing his music as spreading its roots in her native land; amidst decay it alone displays green leaves.

311. ―――. "S.V. Rakhmaninov k Re i S.V. Rakhmaninov, prilozhenie k pis'mam." [S.V. Rachmaninoff's letters to "Re" and annotations on Rachmaninoff's letters] *Novy mir* No.4 (1943): 105-13.

    Fifteen letters of Rachmaninoff to "Re" (Marietta Sergeevna Shaginian), the first dated 14 February 1912 and the last dated 26 January 1917. These letters, written to Shaginian, reveal Rachmaninoff's gentle, childlike nature. In this correspondence he opened his innermost thoughts and dreams to her alone. Here we find a fragile, vulnerable, and uncertain man. The letters are written in a very elegant, refined, and intimate style. Shaginian fills in the background of their friendship and describes the composer's great success in Russia; she tells that he was well-loved by the Russian youth. Seroff's work of 1950 and Bertensson and Leyda's work on Rachmaninoff (1956), examine the Shaginian-Rachmaninoff relationship and contain the letters in translation.

312. Shaporin, Iuri. "Otkrytie muzykal'nogo sezona; Kontserty Radiokomiteta." [Opening of the musical season: concerts organized by the (State) Radio Committee] *Literatura i iskusstvo* No.41 (7 October 1944): 1.

    Review of the opening orchestral concert (30 September 1944) of the 1944-45 season in Moscow. The Bol'shogo Simfonicheskogo

Orkestra [Bol'shoĭ Symphony Orchestra] and the Khora Vsesoiuznogo Radiokomiteta [Union Radio Committee Chorus] performed works by Taneev and two of his pupils- Scriabin and Rachmaninoff. Taneev's cantata *Ioann Damaskin* was performed, as well as Rachmaninoff's *Simfonicheskie tantsy* [Symphonic Dances] and Scriabin's *Poema ekstaza* [Poem of Ecstasy]. Composer Iuri Shaporin remarks that one can hear Russian folklore in the *Simfonicheskie tantsy* and that the movements could easily be described, or titled: I Choir, II Morning, and III Dance macabre. Illustration.

313. Siloti, Alexander [Aleksandr Il'ich Ziloti] "Many Roads to Artistic Playing." *Etude* 40 (May 1922): 299-300.

An interview with Ziloti, cousin and piano teacher of Rachmaninoff (from 1888-91). Ziloti began his studies at age ten with Nikolaĭ Sergeevich Zverov at the Moscow Conservatory, just as Rachmaninoff later did when he was twelve years old. In 1883 Ziloti began studying with Liszt and purportedly was one of his favorite pupils. In the interview, Ziloti reflects on his own training, remarking that Zverov was a true pedagogue, unlike Anton Rubinstein, who only overpowered his students with astonishing demonstrations. Ziloti used a straight-parallel-arm-to-keys approach to the instrument, similar to Liszt's keyboard attitude. Ziloti points out that Leschetizky's students played with arms at a lower level; students playing in either fashion play equally well, affirms Ziloti. Rachmaninoff, as expected, did not discuss in any great detail his piano study; therefore it might help to investigate pedagogical references made by his teachers, in order to understand Rachmaninoff's pianistic approach. Illustration.

314. Sin'kovskaiā, N. "Nachalo odnoĭ tvorcheskoĭ druzhby." [Beginning of a creative friendship] Sovetskaiā muzyka 5 (1978): 97-100.

Commentary on Tchaikovsky's interest in and support of young composers. Despite his busy schedule, Tchaikovsky always made time to appraise works of promising composers; he felt it was his duty. After completing his Siuite [Suite] for orchestra in January 1891, Rachmaninoff sent the work to Tchaikovsky for his perusal and opinion. Sin'kovskaiā discusses this composition.

315. Sjöberg, Lars. "100-Årsjubilaren Rachmaninov älskad och missförstådd." [Rachmaninoff's centennial jubilee- loved and misunderstood] Musikern No.5 (May 1973): 13.

Sjöberg asks these questions: what is Rachmaninoff's legacy to the new generation of musicians who no longer encounter him as brilliant pianist and interpreter of his own works, and can his music help us see the man behind the virtuoso? He suggests that pianists study and perform the *Preludes* and the *Etudes-tableaux*, in order to discern the essential, most intimate Rachmaninoff. Sjöberg points out the composer's inclination to dark colors, concern with death (use of *Dies irae*), and the application of imagery in his works.

316. Skurko, Evgeniiā Romanovna. "Zhanrovye istoki variāntnogo metoda S. Rakhmaninova." [Genre sources of descriptive methods of S. Rachmaninoff] Sovetskaiā muzyka 6 (1978): 103-07.

The author informs that Rachmaninoff's use of long, slow melodic lines, as in the *Simfonicheskie tantsy* [Symphonic Dances] and the romansy [songs], is derived from church music of the 16th and 17th centuries and is a descriptive element in his music. The influences of bells, heard so often in his childhood, is evident in his music. Skurko concludes that these and other descriptive methods are important in the development of Rachmaninoff's music. Illustration and musical examples.

317. Smith, Carleton. "Pianos for Two, Rachmaninoff, the piano buster, and Hofmann, the piano builder, are the top performers." *Esquire* 6 (September 1936): 94,206-09.

Interesting article describes Rachmaninoff and Hofmann as private men, lacking in eccentricity, and notes that both perform without the gimmicks and tricks so often used by the theatrical pianists of the past. Rachmaninoff's somber, melancholic, stone-faced visage is depicted by Smith; yet he also observes the loving, mischievous, and child-like attitudes that were not easily apparent, but that were often revealed to his family and close friends. Smith discusses Rachmaninoff's background, stage demeanor, pianistic style, sarcasm, and his dilemma in managing three careers. An interesting comparison of the two consumate artists who happened to be the closest of friends.

318. Sokolova, Ol'ga Ivanovna. *Simfonicheskie proizvedeniia S.V. Rakhmaninova.* [Symphonic works of S.V. Rachmaninoff] Putevoditeli po russkoĭ muzyke [Guides in Russian music] Moskva: Gosudarstvennoe Muzykal'noe Izd-vo, 1957. 133 p. ML 410 R119 S683 OCLC 5207929

A descriptive examination and survey of Rachmaninoff's orchestral works, including *Iunosheskaia simfoniia* [Youth symphony] an early unfinished symphony in D Minor (1891), *Kniaz' Rostislav* [Prince Rostislav], *Simfonicheskaia fantaziia "utes"* [Symphonic fantasy "The Rock"], *Tsyganskoe kaprichchio* [Capriccio bohémien], *Pervaia simfoniia* [First Symphony], *Vtoraia simfoniia* [Second Symphony], *Ostrov mertvykh* [Isle of the Dead], *Tret'ia simfoniia* [Third Symphony], and the *Simfonicheskie tantsy* [Symphonic Dances]. Sokolava examines the diverse developmental stages of Rachmaninoff's orchestral writing, from the first youthful attempts to the mature, outstanding, later works. His symphonic style is compared to Borodin, Rimsky-Korsakov, and Tchaikovsky- a style represented by the Russian lyric-dramatic idiom. Musical examples, no index.

319.   Solovtsov, Aleksandr. *S.V. Rakhmaninov.*
Moskva, Leningrad: Gosudarstvennoe
Muzykal'noe Izd-vo, 1947. 113 p.

Well-documented biography, divided into four chapters: "Zhiznennyi put'" [Rachmaninoff's life in general],"Tvorcheskaia deiatel'nost'"[his creative work], a list of works, and a bibliography (28 items) including works by Grigori Prokof'ev (reviews), Riesemann, Asaf'ev, Belza, and Lipaev. A detailed account of Rachmaninoff's life in Russia, with less regard for the years after 1917. Illustrated, list of works, bibliography.

320.   ———. *Vtoroi i tretii fortepiannye kontserty Rakhmaninova.* [Rachmaninoff's Second and Third Piano Concerti] v pomoshch' slushateliu muzyki [an aid for listeners of music] Moskva, Leningrad: Gosudarstvennoe Muzykal'noe Izd-vo, 1950. 19 p.

A descriptive analysis of the Vtoroi i tretii fortepiannye kontserty [Second and Third Piano Concerti]. Solovtsov writes that Rachmaninoff's concerti, especially the second and third, fuse two great gifts: the composer's marvelous symphonism and his splendid pianism. Musical examples, no index.

321.   Sorabji, Kaikhosru Shapurji. *Mi Contra Fa:
        The Immoralisings of a Machiavellian
        Musician.* London: Porcupine Press, 1947.
        247 p.   (SR p.170-77)   ML 60 S699   OCLC
        4889013

        The "diabolus in musica" title is expected
        of this outspoken, enigmatic composer, who
        banned all public performances of his own
        works in 1940 (since lifted). Sorabji
        defends Rachmaninoff against critics and
        pundits who critically assaulted the composer.
        He hurls an avalanche of verbal invectives
        on these journalists and historians; in no
        way does he conceal his anger.

322.   South, M'Jean. "The Development of Russian
        Pianist-Composers Through the Conservatory
        System: St. Petersburg and Moscow (1862-
        1917)." Master's thesis, Brigham Young
        University, 1970.   106 p.   (SR p.76-89)
        ML 734 S6   OCLC 3064369

        Prokofiev, Rachmaninoff, and Scriabin are
        the principal pianist-composers examined in
        this work. South presents a chapter on
        early Russian music and an interesting per-
        spective of the Rubinsteins (Anton and
        Nikolaĭ) and their respective conservatories
        in St. Petersburg and Moscow. Material on
        Rachmaninoff is largely biographical.

323.   Sutton, Wadham. "A Theme of Paganini."
        Musical Opinion 94 (March 1971): 287-88.

        Sutton examines settings of Paganini's
        24th Caprice for Violin by Brahms, Rachmani-
        noff, Schumann, Blacher, Lutoslawski, and
        Thalben-Ball. He discusses the technical
        problems encountered in writing variations
        on a theme, remarking that Paganini's theme
        has a fatal allure to the unimaginative
        composer because of its essential flexibility.
        Sutton explains that because of Rachmaninoff's

sensitivity to orchestral sonorities and because of his personal brand of organization, he is at home with variation forms and therefore successful in his setting of the theme in the *Rhapsody on a Theme of Paganini*.

324. Suvalova, M.P. "Panikhida na mogile Sergeĩa Rakhmaninova." [Memorial service at the grave site of S. Rachmaninoff] *Novoye russkoye slovo* (Russian Daily), 14 April 1983, p.5.

   The Suvalov family makes a yearly pilgrimage in April to the Rachmaninoff grave site located in the Kensico Cemetery, Valhalla, New York. Suvalova describes the site- a large granite cross with two benches, surrounded by a natural fence of rhododendrons- and offers a touching account of a memorial service at the site, complete with choir, priest, and visitors. Illustration.

325. Sveshnikov, A. "Geniĭ russkoĭ muzyki." [Genius of Russian music] *Ogonek* No.14 (March 1973): 9-11.

   An emotional reminiscence by Sveshnikov (friend of Rachmaninoff) written for the centennial anniversary of the composer's birth. The author touches upon Rachmaninoff's musical gifts, keen ear, excellent memory, and creative energy. Sveshnikov, having heard Rachmaninoff perform in person, regrets that recordings do not do him justice. He contends that had Rachmaninoff not died in 1943, he would have returned to Russia.

326. Swan, Alfred. "The Present State of Russian Music." *Musical Quarterly* 13 (January 1927): 29-38.

Swan examines Stravinsky, Prokofiev, Rachmaninoff, Medtner, and Miaskovskiĭ (as well as reflecting on Scriabin), commenting on their individual trend-setting accomplishments and their influence on the art. The author sadly confirms that while exile proved to be productively beneficial for Stravinsky and Prokofiev, Rachmaninoff and Medtner fared not so well. Swan remarks that Rachmaninoff lived in the wrong era; his nature was more suited to a quiet, constructive period, but unfortunately the upheaval of the times took its toll emotionally and silenced his writing. A good overview of the period.

327. ―――. *Music 1900-1930.* New York: Norton, 1929. 86 p. ML 197 S8 OCLC 862252

A critical historical survey of music and musicians from 1900 to 1930. The author's subjects are the French School, Scriabin, Stravinsky, music in England, and the Moscow School, with attention to two of Taneev's pupils, Rachmaninoff and Medtner. Swan traces Rachmaninoff's exile from Russia, examines his style of composition, and observes native Russian qualities in his music. Name index.

328. ―――. "Russian Liturgical Music and its Relation to Twentieth-Century Ideals." *Music and Letters* 39 (July 1958): 265-74.

In searching for the modern link among Russian secular composers who write in the religious mode (mainly those influenced by the old znamenny chant), Swan points out the importance of Rachmaninoff's *Liturgy of Saint John Chrysostom Op.31*, and *Vespers Op.37*. *Vespers* draws primarily upon later chants (Kiev and Greek) while the composer retains the nobility of the znamenny chant. Swan asserts that with this work, Rachmaninoff brings Russian church music into 20th century practices.

329.   ———. *Russian Music and its Sources in Chant and Folk-Song.* London: John Baker, 1973. 234 p. ISBN 0-212-98421-7 OCLC 748613 Also- New York: Norton, 1973. 234 p. (SR p.147-54 and 171-76) ML 300 S92 OCLC 702069

The dissimilarities between Rachmaninoff and Scriabin, and influencing factors in Rachmaninoff's life are examined by Alfred Swan. He also gives a detailed description of Rachmaninoff's particular Russian sonority. Swan, a good friend of the composer, studied in St. Petersburg. Illustrations, musical examples, appendixes, bibliography, index.

330.   Swan, Alfred, and Katherine Swan. "Rachmaninoff: Personal Reminiscences." *Musical Quarterly* 30 (January 1944): 1-19, and continued in 30 (April 1944): 174-91, Also- in Russian "Vospominaniĩa o Rakhmaninove" [Recollections of Rachmaninoff] translated from English by K. Danko (article in abridged form), *Sovetskaĩa muzyka,* sbornik chetvertyĭ, (1945): 104-32.

A fascinating and valuable account of the Swans' visits with the Rachmaninoffs at their various summer residences; summer 1928 in Viller-sur-mer in Normandy, 1929-31 at Clairefontaine (near Paris), and the Rachmaninoff Villa "Senar" (name derived from SErgei NAtalia Rachmaninoff) in Switzerland. The Swans offer an informative and vivid narrative of the Rachmaninoff family at leisure. There are off-hand remarks made by the composer concerning Medtner, Taneev, Rimsky-Korsakov, Tolstoĭ, Chekov, and Gorky. Rachmaninoff also recollects his student days in conservatory. The authors reveal the side of Rachmaninoff that was hidden from the general public and was solely reserved for his close friends and family. Here we have him at play and in casual conversation. Portions of letters by Medtner, Konĩus [Conus], and Rachmaninoff are quoted. Illustrations, musical examples.

331.   "Tagore on Russia- The 'Circle of Russian
         Culture' Challenges Some of His
         Statements." *New York Times*, 15 January
         1931, p.24BQ.

   An indignant response by the "Circle of
   Russian Culture" (group organized to foster
   intellectual interchange among the Russian
   immigrants in New York) represented here and
   signed by Iwan I. Ostromislensky, Sergei
   Rachmaninoff, and Count Ilya L. Tolstoy.
   The article was written to give the public
   a view different from that of Rabindranath
   Tagore, who had praised the activities of
   the Bolsheviki. The three signatories
   refute Tagore's view of the Soviet system,
   and in turn describe the oppression, torture,
   and hardship inflicted on the masses. Shortly after this critical statement was published, Rachmaninoff's works were banned in
   the USSR. See "Kolokola zvoniāt, ob odnom
   kont͡serty v konservatoriĭ" by L.,E. in
   Verchernaiī͡a Moskva (9 March 1931), for the
   repercussion of the *New York Times* article.

332.   Taubman, Howard. "Musical Triple-Threat."
         Colliers 104 (16 December 1939): 54,61-62.

   An anecdotal article, primarily about Rachmaninoff on concert tours: the typical day
   of a concert, what the artist has for break-
   fast, his penchant for cherry malted milk
   floats, the chore of travelling, etc..
   Absorbing article for those interested in
   the minutiae of Rachmaninoff's life. Five
   years after this article, Taubman wrote a
   similar article on Vladimir Horowitz, also
   for *Colliers* (13 April): 65-66.

333.   ————. *Music on My Beat: An Intimate Volume
         of Shop Talk*. New York: Simon and Schuster,
         1943, 267 p. ML 65 T3 OCLC 385493
         (Reprint-- Westport, Conn.: Greenwood Press,
         1977. OCLC 2644597)

There are several references to Rachmaninoff in this volume of "intimate shop talk" as Taubman describes his book. These are a few of the subjects covered by the author's observations: Rachmaninoff's performance of the revised version of the *Prelude in C-sharp Minor Op.3, No.2*, his concert fees, and the concert proceeds given to the Russian War Relief. Name Index.

334. ———. "'Anya,' a Sentimental Musical." *New York Times*, 30 November 1965, p.48.

Review of "Anya," a musical (performed on Broadway) based on the story of Anastasia, with music by Rachmaninoff, including sections from the Second Concerto ("This is My Kind of Love." and "If This is Goodbye"), *Prelude in C-sharp Minor* ("That Prelude"), and the *Vocalise* ("Little Hands"). Taubman generally pans the musical while mentioning that Rachmaninoff's music is the most distinguished part of "Anya." One shudders to think what Rachmaninoff would have thought of this adaption.

335. Taylor, Deems. *Music to My Ears*. New York: Simon and Schuster, 1949. 288 p. MT 6 T23 OCLC 921574 Also- London: Home and Van Thal, 1951. MT 6 T23 1951 OCLC 1969641

Music to My Ears is based on material from a series of radio talks for the afternoon concerts of the New York Philharmonic (on the Columbia Broadcasting System [CBS]). The piece on Rachmaninoff was presented shortly after his death. Taylor describes Rachmaninoff's stage demeanor, pianistic skill, and classification as composer. Name index.

336.   Thiman, Eric H. "A Note on Rachmaninoff's
        Preludes." *Musical Opinion* 49 (September
        1926): 1199-1200.

        Thiman views the fame of the *Prelude in
        C-sharp Minor* and comments on the excellence
        of the not-so-famous remaining preludes,
        subtly urging the musician reader to discover
        these preludes and possibly perform them.
        The most striking feature of Rachmaninoff's
        style is its extraordinary sonority and
        warmth, remarks Thiman, who also strongly
        asserts that it is time to displace the usual
        hackneyed Chopin group in favor of a selec-
        tion of Rachmaninoff preludes. Thiman's
        article includes a concise description of
        each prelude of Opp.23 and 32.

337.   Thompson, Kenneth. *A Dictionary of Twentieth-
        Century Composers (1911-1971).* London:
        Faber and Faber, 1973. 666 p. ML 118 T5
        ISBN 0-571-09002-8 OCLC 641607 Also-
        New York: St. Martin's Press, 1973. 666 p.
        (SR p.405-19) ML 118 T5 1973 OCLC 715438

        A catalog of works of 32 international
        composers. Thompson presents an accurate
        listing of Rachmaninoff's compositions, in-
        cluding data on completion dates, instru-
        mentation, first performance, first English
        performance, first English broadcast per-
        formance, and first publisher of work. A
        general bibliography containing 79 entries,
        and a biographical sketch of the composer
        are included.

338.   Thompson, Oscar. "Rachmaninoff: An Estimate,"
        His Strongest Compositions Merit Continuing
        Place - His Power as a Pianist. *New York
        Sun*, 3 April 1943.

        Thompson wrote this article shortly after
        the composer's death, offering his convic-
        tion of Rachmaninoff's artistic values. He
        speculates on various factors of Rachmani-

noff's career; Thompson wonders what would have happened if Rachmaninoff had accepted the conductorship of the Boston Symphony Orchestra when it was offered him; would he have composed more? Thompson was very impressed by Rachmaninoff's prowess as conductor and professes that he would have admirably upheld the Boston Symphony Orchestra's prestige as director of the orchestra. Thompson does give an estimate, as the title states, of Rachmaninoff's historical destiny: he does not believe that Rachmaninoff will long be remembered as pianist extraordinaire, or that all his large works will continue to be performed, but he specifies certain works that might survive. Reviewing Thompson's evaluations after some forty years, one finds his prophecies only partly accurate.

339.   Threlfall, Robert. *Sergei Rachmaninoff: His Life and Music*. London: Boosey and Hawkes, 1973. 74 p. ML 410 R12 T5 ISBN 0-851-62009-4 OCLC 749990

A great amount of information is packed into this slim volume. Largely biographical and descriptive, it offers an effective overview of the man, composer, and pianist. Illustrations, musical examples, list of principal works, no index.

340.   ———. "Rachmaninoff's Revisions and an Unknown Version of His Fourth Concerto." *Musical Opinion* 96 (February 1973): 235-37.

Threlfall reviews revisions made by Rachmaninoff of the Third Symphony, several piano pieces, *The Bells*, Second Sonata, First Concerto, and the Fourth Concerto. The primary concern of the article is to examine three versions of the Fourth Concerto: the autograph version of 1926, the

1928 published version (by TAIR), and the further revised version of 1944 (published by Charles Foley). The concerto, which was begun before Rachmaninoff departed from Russia, later received reworking from the composer while he maintained his international concert career. Threlfall points out differences in the various versions, and notes that each version is slightly compressed in length. Threlfall's research on the Fourth Concerto, explained in more detail, is presented in Threlfall and Norris' *A Catalogue of the Compositions of S. Rachmaninoff*, London: Scolar Press, 1982. Norris also examines Rachmaninoff revisions in "Rakhmaninov's Second Thoughts" in *Musical Times* 114 (April 1973): 364-68.

341. Threlfall, Robert, and Geoffrey Norris. *A Catalogue of the Compositions of S. Rachmaninoff*. London: Scolar Press, 1982. 218 p. ML 134 R12 T5 ISBN 0-85967-617-X OCLC 8321847

A collaboration of two British Rachmaninoff scholars who became acquainted in 1973, during the Rachmaninoff centenary year. Both were preparing similar research material on revisions of the Fourth Concerto. They effectively joined forces to prepare this comprehensive catalogue of the composer's works. The catalogue includes the following information: title of work, completion date, dedication, texts, key, compass (songs), instrumentation, MSS (sources traced), publication, first performance, recordings (only Rachmaninoff's), arrangements, and notes. This valuable volume contains a wealth of information and should prove to be the definitive catalogue of Rachmaninoff's works. The authors have included copious detailed information on the publication, the historical background, and manuscript locations of specific compositions. The work is thoroughly documented. *A Catalogue of the Compositions of S. Rachmaninoff* is a welcome scholarly contribution to the

understanding of Rachmaninoff and his
creativity. Illustrations, musical examples,
appendixes, name and title index.

342.   Tideböhl, Ellen von. "Sergez Rachmaninoff."
       Musical Record 36 (1 July 1906): 148-49.

       Description and review of the premiere
       performance of the operas *The Miserly Knight*
       (translated here as "Covetous Knight") and
       Francesca da Rimini, both performed at the
       Imperial Theater (Bol'shoĭ) in Moscow on
       11 January 1906. Besides giving a concise
       plot description, Tideböhl vividly portrays
       the staging, costumes, and musical effects
       of the operas. The music to *Miserly Knight*
       is noted as being in a broad Wagnerian
       style, with declamation for the singers and
       rich orchestration in which chromatic
       elements abound. The two operas made a
       favorable impression on the public. Tideböhl
       states, "Rachmaninoff has once more confirmed
       his position as a first-rate composer."

343.   ———. "A Vocalise by Rachmaninoff."
       Musical Courier 72-14 (1916): 42.

       Review of the premiere vocal performance
       of the *Vocalise*, sung by the dedicatee of
       the work, Antonina Vasilievna Nezhdanova,
       with Rachmaninoff accompanying her, on the
       sixth Koussevitzky Symphony Concert, 24
       January 1916. She also performed an aria
       from *Francesca da Rimini* and other
       Rachmaninoff songs. An interesting note is
       that Koussevitzky, as reported by Tideböhl,
       first performed the *Vocalise* himself, at the
       fourth Koussevitzky Symphony Concert, as a
       self-transcribed version for contrabass.
       So, it seems that the very first performance
       of the *Vocalise* actually was as a transcrip-
       tion for contrabass. Tideböhl states, "The
       performances of both artists [Koussevitzky
       and Nezhdanova] were admirably alike in their

breadth and subtlety," and of the contrabass arrangement, "One would scarcely believe that the big instrument could realize such soft and delicate sounds!"

344. Toombs, Elizabeth O. "America Must Have a National Conservatory, says Rachmaninoff." *Good Housekeeping* 74 (February 1922): 132-34.

Rachmaninoff compares musical education in Russia and the USA. He observes that good teachers are the great lack in America's musical development. There is a need for a government-supported National Conservatory in this country. Rachmaninoff goes on to give an extended explanation of the Russian conservatory system, offering suggestions for its adaptability in the USA. This would allow equal opportunity to the talented regardless of the parents' income. Rachmaninoff offers advice to students: study the lives of the great composers, obtain the best teacher, and attend concerts often. He comments on the fact that students in Russia are able to attend orchestra rehearsals free, noting that American students miss this type of concert entirely, since they are not able to afford symphony concert seats. In this interview with Elizabeth Toombs, Rachmaninoff displays unusual enthusiasm in revealing his convictions on musical education. Illustration.

345. Tretiakova, Liliia Sergeevna. *Stranit͡sy russkoĭ muzyki: russkai͡a klassicheskai͡a muzyka na rubezhe XIX-XX vv*. [Pages of Russian music: Russian classical music at the turn of the 19th-20th century] Moskva: Znanie, 1979. 158 p. (SR p.111-34)
ML 300 T73   OCLC 6376825

An historical overview of composers at the end of the 19th century: Tchaikovsky and Rimsky-Korsakov, composers of the Belaiev

Circle (St. Petersburg composers), Liadov, Glazunov, Taneev, and Kalinnikov; and composers at the beginning of the 20th century: Scriabin and Rachmaninoff. Chapter on Rachmaninoff is an account of his years in Russia, training with Zverov, Tchaikovsky influence, early compositions, Dresden period, friendship with Chaliapin, Chekov, Tolstoĭ, etc.. Tretiakova includes the comment that Rachmaninoff accumulated riches overseas but lost the desire to write because of the separation from his homeland. Illustrations, bibliography, no index.

346. Trubnikova, Anna Andreevna. "Sergeĭ Rakhmaninov." *Ogonek* (7 April 1946).

A portion of Anna Trubnikova's reminiscences of Rachmaninoff (also in Zarui Apetian's *Vospominaniia o Rakhmaninove*, Moskva, 1974). Trubnikova (cousin to Rachmaninoff) gives a first-hand account of the composer's youthful years. She relates that when Sergei was six years old, he and his grandfather (Arkady Aleksandrovich Rakhmaninov) played four-hand Beethoven pieces together, notes that his mother (Liubov Petrovna Rakhmaninova) gave him piano lessons when he was four years old, comments on the influences of the Novgorod region in his music, remembers the time when Sergei was a student (age nine) at the St. Petersburg Conservatory and lived with the Trubnikovs, mentions the presence of Rachmaninoff's grandmother (Varvara Vasil'evna Rakhmaninova) at the first staged performance of *Aleko* (27 April 1893), remarks on the failure of the First Symphony. There are other intimate disclosures of lesser importance.

347. Tsukkerman, V. "Zhemchuzhina russkoĭ liriki." [Pearls of Russian lyricism] *Sovetskaia muzyka* 1 (1965): 25-35.

Detailed harmonic and melodic analysis of the second movement (adagio sostenuto) of the *Kontsert dlia f-no s orkestrom No.2* [Concerto for Piano and Orchestra No.2]. The author offers an interesting descriptive analysis illustrating the harmonic similarities of this movement to Tchaikovsky and Borodin works. Tsukkerman affirms that Rachmaninoff's lyricism is based on the transformation of folk elements, both Russian and Eastern (oriental)--the latter element appearing often in his music. Tsukkerman speaks of this movement with great admiration, stating that this is Rachmaninoff's finest lyric display.

348.   Tsytovich, Tamara Erastovna, ed. *S.V. Rakhmaninov*, sbornik statei i materialov, trudy Gosudarstvennogo Tsentral'nogo Muzeia Muzykal'noi Kul'tury, tom I. [S.V. Rachmaninoff, collection of articles and materials, works of the State Central Museum of Musical Culture, book I] Moskva, Leningrad: Muzgiz, 1947. 270 p.

Materials and investigations dealing with the life and artistic achievement of Rachmaninoff, presented in a symposium held in the Tsentral'nogo Muzeia Muzykal'noi Kul'tury [Central Museum of Musical Culture] in Moscow on 17-25 October 1945. Lectures on diverse topics pertaining to Rachmaninoff were delivered by prominent Soviet musicologists, and are published in this volume. Author and subject: Igor Belza- "S.V. Rakhmaninov i russkaia muzykal'naia kul'tura" [S.V. Rachmaninoff and Russian musical culture], Evgeniia Bortnikova- "S.V. Rakhmaninov zhizn' i tvorchestvo v dokumentakh i materialakh 1873-1917" [S.V. Rachmaninoff's life and artistic work in documents and materials 1873-1917], Tamara Tsytovich- "Neopublikovannye fortepiannye sochineniia Rakhmaninova" [Unpublished piano works of Rachmaninoff], B. Dobrokhotov (two topics)- "Opernye zamysly S.V. Rakhmaninova" [Rachmaninoff's operatic projections] and

"Neopublikovannye kamernye ansambli S.V. Rakhmaninova" [Unpublished chamber music of Rachmaninoff], V. Protopopov- "Pozdnee simfonicheskoe tvorchestvo S.V. Rakhmaninova" [Later symphonic works of S.V. Rachmaninoff], L. Mazel'- "O liricheskoĭ melodike Rakhmaninova" [Lyric melodies of Rachmaninoff], and V. I︠A︡kovlev- "Rakhmaninov-dirizher" [Rachmaninoff the conductor]. The volume concludes with the inclusion of over 60 letters (Pis'ma S.V. Rakhmaninova k N.S. Morozovy" [Letters of Rachmaninoff to N.S. Morozov]) of Rachmaninoff to Nikita Semenovich Morozov, a colleague who graduated with him in composition from the Moskovskai︠a︡ Konservatorii︠a︡ [Moscow Conservatory]. Letters date from June 1900 to January 1925. Contains a list of works, list of dedicatees of Rachmaninoff's works, list of authors of texts and libretti, bibliography (extensive: around 250 items arranged by genre, including 20 English language entries), musical examples, portrait, and errata. See also- *S.V. Rakhmaninov i russkai︠a︡ opera, sbornik stateĭ*, edited by Igor Belza, which is also a collection of monographs by several authors on the subject of Rachmaninoff's operas, presented for this same series of symposia on the composer.

349. Vachnadze, M. "V Senare - u Rakhmaninovykh." [In Senar - at Rachmaninoffs'] *Sovet︠s︡kai︠a︡ muzyka* 2 (1979): 107-08.

A reminiscence of Vachnadze's visit to Rachmaninoff's Villa "Senar" in Hertenstein, Switzerland in 1946. He describes the estate in vivid detail- Rachmaninoff's studio with his desk and piano, favorite chair, the lake view (Lake Lucerne), the garden view, etc.. Vachnadze always refers to the composer with adulation. For actual views of "Senar" see the pictorial article, "Rachmaninoff spielt für 'Pro Juventute'" in *Sie und Er* 8 (1938): 166-67.

350.   Vactor, David Van. "New Works in Chicago."
        Modern Music 19 (January-February 1942):
        122.

   Review of contemporary works performed by
   the Chicago Symphony Orchestra under Frederick Stock during the 1941-42 season.
   Vactor has complimentary words for the *Symphonic Dances Op.45* performed by the Chicago
   Symphony Orchestra, stating that Rachmaninoff's craftsmanship is organized in a
   masterly fashion. This is the only article
   in *Modern Music* that deliberates on a work
   of Rachmaninoff, otherwise he is only mentioned in reference to other contemporary
   composers.

351.   Varro, Margit. "Rachmaninoff e Stravinsky,"
        Considerazione sulle due autobiografie.
        (translated from the German by Adolfo
        Gardelli) *Musica d'oggi* 19 (January 1937):
        3-8.

   A comparative representation of these two
   diverse musicians based on Riesemann's *Rachmaninoff's Recollections* (1934) and Stravinsky's *Chroniques de ma vie* (1936). Varro
   considers the Riesemann work an autobiography
   of Rachmaninoff, as the title implies, which
   was a misconception that greatly irritated
   Rachmaninoff. Based on material found in
   Chronicles and *Recollections*, Varro compares
   the life and music of Rachmaninoff and
   Stravinsky. Some of Varro's observations:
   both composers came from musical families;
   Stravinsky started studying theory and composition when he was 18 while Rachmaninoff
   finished studying at that age; Stravinsky is
   cosmopolitan and not tied to any country
   while Rachmaninoff has strong attachments to
   his native land, etc. The divergence of
   these two Russian composers is so vast it is
   of little consequence to compare them.

352.   Vasilenko, Sergeĭ. "Moĭ vospominaniĭa o
        dirizherakh." [My recollections of the
        conductors] Sovetskaĭa muzyka 1 (1949):
        92-97.

   Vasilenko, himself a conductor, recalls
many conductors during his career; some of
those are Tchaikovsky, Arenskiĭ, Anton Rubinstein, Ippolitov-Ivanov, Safanov, Richard
Strauss, and Rachmaninoff. Vasilenko wonders
where Rachmaninoff acquired the practical
knowledge necessary for conducting an
orchestra, noting that suddenly he appeared,
conducting with assurance and authority. He
points out that Rachmaninoff's superior
musical talent lent itself easily to this
particular musical skill, along with the
assistance of an enormous innate physical
aptitude. Vasilenko contends that Rachmaninoff was not just an artist-conductor but a
creator-conductor, who could extract hidden
meanings in the music, aspects that only a
composer could perceive. Rachmaninoff's
success as a conductor in Russia grew rapidly
after his debut conducting operas for Savva
Mamontov's Moskovskaĭa Chastnaĭa Russkaĭa
Opera [Moscow Private Russian Opera] company
in 1897.

353.   ———. Sergeĭ Vasil'evich Rakhmaninov
        1873-1943. Leningrad: Muzykal'noe Izd-vo,
        1961. 106 p. ML 410 R12 V3

   A popular, well-illustrated biography
directed towards Russian youth. Vasilenko
vividly describes Rachmaninoff's life and
creativity, stressing that the composer was
truly Russian in his compositions and that
he lost the stimulus to compose after he
departed from his homeland. Vasilenko
maintains that Rachmaninoff was the last Russian composer to complete the line of musicians writing in classical traditions. Note-
the term "classical" in Russian musical ter-
minology does not denote music of the 18th
century, but implies the musical period span-
ned by Glinka and Rimsky-Korsakov, or gener-

ally, composers of the 19th century. Illustrations, musical examples, list of works, no index.

354. Vasil'ev, Evgeniĭ. "S.V. Rakhmaninov, k desiatiletii͡u so dni͡a smerti." [S.V. Rachmaninoff, on the 10th anniversary of his death] *Vozrozhdenie* (La renaissance), Literaturno-politicheskii͡a tetradi (January-February 1954): 123-38.

Vozrozhdenie, subtitled "La renaissance," is a Russian literary-political publication, formerly published in Paris. Vasil'ev composes an adulatory article on the 10th anniversary of the composer's death. He highly praises Rachmaninoff, comments on the assistance and encouragement that Rachmaninoff received from the Satin family, discusses the failure of the First Symphony, offers a brief biographical sketch of the composer, views Rachmaninoff the landowner of "Ivanovka," and expounds on the musical talents of Rachmaninoff. Illustrations.

355. Volkov, Oleg. "I dym otechestva - dorozhnye zametki." [Smoke of the native land- notes on a trip] *Nash sovremennik* 6 (1969): 105-12.

A descriptive narrative of the author's trip to "Ivanovka," which at times evokes the image of Rachmaninoff dwelling in his natural surroundings. Volkov utilizes exaggerations concerning the composer and too often lingers on patriotic aspects. He suitably describes the forming of the Ivanovka Muzeĭ - komnata S.V. Rakhmaninova [Ivanovka Rachmaninoff Museum Room] (in 1968), the history of Tambov, and the "Ivanovka" estate.

356. "Volynskaía, N. "Rakhmaninov i Bunin."
      [Rachmaninoff and Bunin] "Golos Rodiny i
      zhurnal *Rodina*" 3 (1973): 6-8.

      Article in honor of the composer's cente-
      nary anniversary of his birth. It is printed
      in a literary supplement to the newspaper,
      Rodina, published by Izdanie Sovetskogo
      Komiteta po Kul'turnym Svíazíam s Sooteches-
      tvennikami za Rubezhom [Soviet Committee for
      Cultural Relations with Compatriots Abroad].
      Volynskaía compares the common artistic
      elements of Rachmaninoff and Ivan Alekseevich
      Bunin. Bunin was the first Russian author
      to receive the Nobel Prize in literature, in
      1933. Rachmaninoff used several of Bunin's
      verses for his songs. They were close
      friends, and both left their native land in
      middle age to spend a large part of their
      lives abroad. The works of Bunin and Rach-
      maninoff reflect classic simplicity and
      clarity.

357. Waldo, Fullerton. "Rachmaninoff's The Bells."
      Outlook 124 (25 February 1920): 318-19.

      An informal review of the first performance
      of *The Bells* in the USA, with the Philadelphia
      Orchestra and chorus under Stokowski, perform-
      ed on 6 February 1920. Waldo carefully ob-
      served Rachmaninoff's reaction to the perform-
      ance (the composer was seated in a box) and
      relates his observations. Rachmaninoff also
      performed his Third Concerto at this concert
      and Waldo offers a vivid depiction, "he play-
      ed with the heroic energy of a blacksmith
      who handles only Percherons and the gentleness
      of a visiting nurse with a new baby." Waldo
      was impressed with *The Bells* and assured of
      its permanence in the repertoire.

358. Walker, Robert. *Rachmaninoff: His Life and
      Times*. Tunbridge, Kent (Eng.): Midas Books,
      1980. 133 p. ML 410 R12 W32 ISBN 0-85936-
      111-X OCLC 7307930 Also- Neptune, N.J.:
      Paganiniana, 1981. OCLC 8334254

Rachmaninoff Bibliography 285

An illustrated documentary of Rachmaninoff's life and times. Rachmaninoff's life is depicted against a concurrent account of Russian historical events. This historical background is helpful in understanding Rachmaninoff's early environment and cultural heritage. Walker contributes an informative historical overview, with data on Rachmaninoff's career as recording artist, tracing it from its inception in 1919. Since this work is directed primarily towards the general reader and music appreciator, sources are not documented. Illustrations, name index.

359.   Walsh, Stephan. "Flawed but a Genius." *Music and Musicians* 16 (August 1968): 32-33, 54.

A critical appraisal of Rachmaninoff and his music. The author writes that part of Rachmaninoff's lack of confidence in his works was caused by psychological disturbances, and Walsh sets out to examine these emotional setbacks, including the family separation and the failure of the First Symphony. He discusses the composer's large-scaled works versus the small structures, with attention to the miniature piano pieces, comparing the latter with Schumann and Chopin. Walsh contends that Rachmaninoff was more at ease composing the small forms, but was constricted in the large works because of his use of preconceived patterns. Walsh offers interesting perceptive evaluations, to which some may take exception.

360.   ———. "Sergei Rachmaninoff." *Tempo* No.105 (June 1973): 12-21.

A highly perceptive and imaginative article by Stephan Walsh on the development of Rachmaninoff's compositional style. Walsh traces stylistic innovations in the composer's works from the First Symphony to the *Symphonic Dances*. There is concern for the psychological problems of the composer, also present in Walsh's article "Flawed but a Genius" in *Music and Musicians* 16 (August 1968): 32-33. This present monograph is important for its attention to the comparative analysis of the Corelli Variations and the Paganini Rhapsody, examination of typical harmonic modulations, comparisons with Tchaikovsky, view of the critical assailment leveled at the composer, and Rachmaninoff's stylistic development. A useful study. Musical examples.

361. Waters, Edward N. "Music." *United States Library of Congress Quarterly Journal of Current Acquisitions* 9 (November 1951): 39-42.

Announcement of the acquisition of scores, letters, reviews, lists, articles, etc., by the Library of Congress from the Rachmaninoff family. Natalĩa Rakhmaninova (the composer's wife) felt the Library of Congress was the most fitting institution to house the Archives, since it was free of political and commercial interests. A list of autograph manuscripts (some 21 compositions) presented to the Library of Congress is included in the article.

362. Werth, Alexander. "The Rachmaninov Enigma." *New Statesman and Nation* 50 (17 September 1955): 318-19.

Werth examines Rachmaninoff's reticent and defensive personality, commenting on the correspondence with Marietta Shaginĩan ("Re"), where he reveals his innermost feelings, and quoting a letter to Nikita Semenovich Morozov (22 October 1901) which reveals doubts about his music. Werth comments that after going through 600 pages of the collected letters

(Zarui Apetĩan's ed. *Rakhmaninov: Pis'ma,* Moskva: Muzykal'noe Izd-vo, 1955), there is no mention of modern composers such as Prokofiev or Stravinsky, only a few references to Scriabin and Richard Strauss. Werth was making a point of Rachmaninoff's insular attitude towards modern music. A study of the Rachmaninoff personality.

363. Wile, Raymond R. "The Edison Recordings of Serge Rachmaninoff." *American Record Guide* 40 (February 1977): 11-12.

A listing of the 10 Edison records (8 pieces) made by Rachmaninoff in April 1919. These were Rachmaninoff's first recordings. Wile includes the comments made by the recording engineers as to the quality of the takes. Interesting to understand the problems that existed in the early stages of the recording industry. An upright piano was used for maximum sound collection, for these were acoustic recordings, where the sound had to be directed into a recording horn. Compositions recorded included pieces by Mozart, Scarlatti-Tausig, Chopin, Liszt, and Rachmaninoff (his first recording of the ubiquitous *Prelude in C-sharp Minor Op.3, No.2*).

364. Williams, Richard. "Two Somber Men and a Rhapsody." *House Beautiful* 96 (November 1954): 20,32,34.

Curious similarities between Paganini and Rachmaninoff are revealed. Both men were strange in appearance, each had a trance-like preoccupation, and both were masters of their instruments. Williams notes that these two morose, reserved men collaborated, in a sense, in the creation of the *Rhapsody on a Theme of Paganini*. Illustrated.

365.   Wooldridge, David. *Conductor's World*. New
        York: Praeger, 1970. 379 p. ML 457 W65
        OCLC 67090

        An historical criticism of orchestras,
        conductors, and their interpretations. The
        references to Rachmaninoff relate to: Mahler's
        conducting the Third Concerto with Rachmani-
        noff as soloist, cuts in the clarinet melody
        of the Second Symphony, Koussevitzky con-
        certs, association with Stokowski and
        Ormandy, etc. Performances of the Third
        Symphony are critically compared. Illustra-
        tions, musical examples, discography,
        orchestral layouts, name index.

366.   Yasser, Joseph. "Progressive Tendencies in
        Rachmaninoff's Music." *Tempo* 22 (Winter
        1951-52): 11-25. Also- in Russian, *New
        Review* (Novyĭ zhurnal) 6 (1943): 325-40.

        This is a slightly revised version (foot-
        note information is incorporated into the
        text) of the article previously published in
        English in *Musicology* Vol.2, No.1 (1948).
        Yasser endeavors to clarify common mis-
        conceptions about Rachmaninoff's traditional
        perspective. He delves into Rachmaninoff's
        attitude towards modern music in detail.
        Quotations from critics and colleagues are
        aptly used to demonstrate that many of the
        composer's early works show modernism for
        their time. Yasser specifically traces the
        effect and repercussion of the First Symphony
        premiere performance, and from there notes
        gradual progressive transformation in his
        works. A valuable study on Rachmaninoff's
        stylistic evolution.

367.   ―――. "Symphony Post-Mortem." *New York
        Times*, 28 March 1948, p.x7.

        Yasser presents an abridged translation of
        Rachmaninoff's letter to Aleksandr Viktorovich

Zataevich, dated 6 May 1897, concerning the premiere performance of his First Symphony (15 March 1897). In this article, Yasser endeavors to shed new light on Rachmaninoff's reactions to that disastrous performance, which devastated the composer. The contents of the letter to Zataevich were not commonly known at the time this article appeared. Yasser specifically focuses attention on Rachmaninoff's concluding statement in the letter, in which he says he might destroy the score of the symphony. The comments made by Yasser in regard to Rachmaninoff's final statement imply that the destruction of the score is a fait accompli. This article, and the attention given to the score, is possibly one of the reasons why Sof'i͡a Satina eventually published a repudiation of this hypothesis of the score's destruction. The article title "Symphony Post-Mortem" refers to the impending first New York performance of the symphony on 30 March 1948, performed from a reconstructed score (orchestral parts found in Leningrad and the four-hand piano version score). See Sof'i͡a Satina's "Communications," in the *Journal of the American Musicological Society* 21 (Spring 1968): 120-21, for information on the disappearance of the score.

368.   ─────. "The Opening Theme of Rachmaninoff's Third Piano Concerto and its Liturgical Prototype." *Musical Quarterly* 55 (July 1969): 313-28.

In 1935, Yasser wrote Rachmaninoff asking him if the opening theme of the Third Concerto had been borrowed from Russian national sources, either secular or liturgical. Rachmaninoff's reply, which is often quoted in works about the composer, was that this theme is borrowed neither from folk-song forms nor from church sources. Yasser maintains that Rachmaninoff at one time (c.1893) heard an old Russian Orthodox chant, used in vesper service at the Kievan-Petchersk Lavra of the

Assumption; this is the chant which Yasser uses as the possible liturgical source, and he asserts that this chant was implanted in the composer's subconscious mind, only to emerge 16 years later, after "several somnigenic phases of internal regeneration," transformed into the opening theme of his Third Concerto. Yasser charts out the two themes, comparing them. Musical examples.

369. Zelina, Marina, and E.E. Levina. *Russkaia klassicheskaia muzyka*: rekomendatel'nyĭ ukazatel' literatury v pomoshch' samoobrazovaniiu molodezhi. Moskva: Izdatel'stvo, "Kniga." 1971. 174 p. (SR p.129-39, 159-60) ML 120 R8 Z4 OCLC 9136322

A bibliographic reference book addressed to Soviet youth and those interested in the arts. Sections devoted to lives and works of composers from Glinka to Scriabin. An introductory essay on Rachmaninoff is followed by a list of his works, an annotated bibliography (7 entries), and a list of recordings made by Rachmaninoff of compositions other than his own. There is also a short chapter mentioning artists who painted portraits of Rachmaninoff- L. Pasternak, V. Rossinskiĭ, K. Somov, Boris Chaliapin- and C. Konenkov, who sculpted a bust of Rachmaninoff in 1925 for Steinway Hall. Author and title indexes.

370. Zetel, I. "Iz perepiski N. Metnera i S. Rakhmaninova." [Selections from correspondence between Medtner and Rachmaninoff] *Sovetskaia muzyka* 11 (1961): 76-88.

Series of 22 letters by Medtner and Rachmaninoff to each other, dated from 8 June 1922 to 12 January 1939. There is a great deal of discourse about each other's music in the letters and the two men often exchanged scores for criticism and opinion; since they were close friends the response was usually favorable, but this was a way of exchanging viewpoints and reinforcing each other's confidence in their work. Explanatory comments on the letters are included.

371. Zhitomirskiĭ, Daniel. "Fortepiannoe tvorchestvo Rakhmaninova." [Piano artistry of Rachmaninoff] Sovetskaia muzyka, sbornik chetvertyĭ, (1945): 80-104.

Descriptive analysis, with attention to style, of the Vtoraia i tret'ia Kontserty [Second and Third Concerti], with references to several piano solos. Zhitomirskiĭ affirms that Rachmaninoff was important to the development of Russian piano music and that he is a direct continuation of traditions set by Glinka and Tchaikovsky. Illustrated, musical examples.

372. ―――――. "Russia Honors Memory of Rachmaninoff." Musical Courier (15 January 1946); 36-37.

Zhitomirskiĭ reports on the festival sponsored by the Central Music Museum (T͡sentral'nyĭ Muzeĭ Muzykal'noĭ) in honor of Rachmaninoff. Activities included a revival of the First Symphony (from a recently reconstructed score), series of symposia featuring Igor Belza, who presented the introductory speech, and Evgenii͡a Ermolaevna Bortnikova of the museum staff, who read a paper, and presentation of information on unpublished compositions, such as the Russian Rhapsody for two pianos (1891), the first Trio élégiaque (1892), and several movements of two unfinished string quartets. Displays of Rachmaninoff's works were set up in the Round Hall of the Moscow Conservatory and manuscripts and scores of the composer's grandfather, Arkady Aleksandrovich Rakhmaninov, were also on exhibition. Four concerts dedicated to the music of Rachmaninoff were performed. For detailed information of the proceedings (briefly reported here by Zhitomirskiĭ) and texts of the papers read at the symposia see: T.E. T͡sytovich's *S.V. Rakhmaninov, sbornik stateĭ i materi͡alov,* trudy Gosudarstvennogo T͡sentral'nogo Muzei͡a Muzykal'noĭ Kul'tury, Moskva: Muzgiz, 1947, and *S.V. Rakhmaninov i russkai͡a opera,* sbornik stateĭ, edited by Igor Belza.

373.   ———, ed. *Muzika XX veka: ocherki v dvukh chasti͡akh.* [Twentieth century music: sketches in two parts] Moskva: Muzyka, 1976. 2 vols. ML 300.5 M935 OCLC 5517882

Volume One of this two-part historical survey of 20th century music covers the period 1890-1917. A collection of monographs on important composers of this century: Rimsky-Korsakov, Rachmaninoff, Scriabin, Puccini, Mahler, Debussy, Ravel, Strauss, Janacek, and DeFalla. This two-volume series is prepared by the Leningradskiĭ Gosudarstvennyĭ Institut Teatra, Muzyki i Kinomatografiĭ Ministerstva Kul'tury [Leningrad State Institute of Theater, Music, and Cinematography, Ministry of Culture]. Volume One considers development of major genres. References to Rachmaninoff in Volume One are generalities: influence of Tchaikovsky, the composer's development of classical traditions, his epic-symphonic style, and his ability to preserve tradition without altering its foundation, yet infusing it with his own unique qualities. Volume Two contains a monograph by I͡uri Keldysh dealing with the composer's artistic achievements, Russian tradition, Rachmaninoff's style, his major works, and his ability to convey human emotions. Extensive bibliography lists over 130 items, including 30 English language sources. Name and composition indexes.

374. Zschorlich, Paul. "Rachmaninoff: Klavierabend von Rachmaninoff - 3, Philharmonisches Konzert unter Wilhelm Furtwängler." [Rachmaninoff's piano recital - Third Philharmonic concert under Wilhelm Furtwängler] *Deutsche Zeitung* (Berlin), 23 November 1928.

A glowing review of Rachmaninoff's 9 November 1928 Berlin recital and the 11-12 November 1928 Berlin Philharmonic program with Furtwängler conducting. It was duly noticed that Rachmaninoff had not performed in Berlin for some time (since 1908). Impressions of the concerts related by Zschorlich pertain to Rachmaninoff's dignity of stage deportment, mission in composition, command of the instrument, grace and elegance in performing, and the grandeur of his personage. On the recital Rachmaninoff performed a Chopin group (Fantasy, Rondo, two Etudes, a Nocturne, Waltz, and the *Scherzo Op.39*), a Rachmaninoff group (four Preludes), Bach-Busoni and Liszt (Dante Sonata). Zschorlich did not consider the Third Concerto a strong work, although he noted the second movement as revealing the true Rachmaninoff spirit. At one point in the review Zschorlich takes a jab at composers in Germany, stating that Rachmaninoff was "clearly above all those who call themselves composers in Germany."

375. ———. "Serge Rachmaninoff: Sein Klavier-Abend- Sein neues Klavierkonzert." [S. Rachmaninoff: His piano recital - His new piano concerto] *Deutsche Zeitung* (Berlin), 17 December 1930.

Review of Berlin concerts given on 5 December 1930 (recital) and 7-8 December 1930 (Philharmonic concert). These were Rachmaninoff's last concerts in Germany. Zschorlich was very much impressed by Rachmaninoff's performance of Schumann's *Davidsbündlertänze*. Among his comments: "a kaleidoscope of perceptions and moods," "delicate dreaminess," "congenial and finely declaimed," and "tonally satisfying." Zschorlich had similar glowing comments about the Liszt group that he performed (*Etude in D-flat Major*, *Valse-impromptu*, and *Carnaval de Pesth*). Rachmaninoff also programmed 5 *Etudes-tableaux* from Op.33 (Nos.1,3,4,5,6) which Zschorlich did not appreciate, stating that he would rather have heard some of the lesser-known Preludes. Rachmaninoff's performance of the Fourth Concerto with the Berlin Philharmonic under Bruno Walter received a mixed review; Zschorlich commended the pianistic writing and the beauty of the second movement, but noted a lack of consistency in structure in the first and third movements. "Needless to say," he adds, "Rachmaninoff was a most persuasive interpreter of his piano concerto."

References

Albrecht, Otto E. 1953. *A Census of Autograph Music Manuscripts of European Composers in American Libraries*. Philadelphia, Penn.: University of Pennsylvannia Press.

Apeti͡an, Zarui. 1978-80. *S.V. Rakhmaninov: literaturnoe nasledie*, 3 vols. Moskva: Sovetskiĭ Kompozitor.

BBC Music Library Piano and Organ Catalogue. 1965. London: British Broadcasting Corp.

BBC Music Library Song Catalogue. 1966. London: British Broadcasting Corp.

Bennett, John R., comp. 1981. *Melodiya: A Soviet Russian L.P. Discography*. Westport, Conn.: Greenwood Press.

Bertensson, Sergei, and Jay Leyda (with the assistance of Sophia Satina). 1956. *Sergei Rachmaninoff: A Lifetime in Music*. New York: New York University Press.

Dictionary Catalog of the Music Collection - Boston Public Library. 1972. Boston, Mass.: G.K. Hall.

Farish, Margaret K., ed. 1979. *Orchestral Music in Print*. Philadelphia, Penn.: Musicdata.

Horecky, Paul. 1962. *Basic Russian Publications*. Chicago: University of Chicago Press.

Kammerer, Rafael. 1966. "The Golden Art of Sergei Rachmaninoff." *American Record Guide*. (October): 156-65.

Lang, Christoph. 1973. "Der Pianist Sergej Wassiljewitsch Rachmaninoff." *Oesterreichische Muzikzeitschrift* 28: 425-32.

Library of Congress Music, Books on Music, and Sound Recordings. 1953-. Washington D.C.: Library of Congress.

Library of Congress National Union Catalog. 1953-.
   Totowa, N.J.: Rowman and Littlefield.

Marco, Guy A. 1975. *Information on Music: A Handbook of Reference Sources in European Languages* Vol.1, Basic and Universal Sources. Littleton, Col.: Libraries Unlimited.

Marco, Guy A., and Sharon P. Ferris. 1984. *Information on Music: A Handbook of Reference Sources in European Languages* Vol.3, Europe. Littleton, Col.: Libraries Unlimited.

The Music Index. 1949-. Detroit, Mich.: Information Coordinators, Inc..

Nardone, Thomas R., ed. 1976. *Classical Vocal Music in Print*. Philadelphia, Penn.: Musicdata.

New Grove Dictionary of Music and Musicians. 6th ed., ed. by Stanley Sadie. 1980. London: Macmillan: Washington, D.C.: Grove's Dictionaries of Music.

The New York Public Library - Dictionary Catalog of the Music Collection. 1964. Boston, Mass.: G.K. Hall.

Norris, Geoffrey, 1976. *Rakhmaninov*. London: J.M. Dent.

Répertoire international de littérature musicale (RILM Abstracts). ed. by Barry S. Brook, 1967-. New York: International RILM Center.

Rytsareva, M.G., ed. 1980. *Avtografy S.V. Rakhmaninova*. Moskva: Sovetskiĭ Kompozitor.

Schwarz, Boris. 1972. *Music and Musical Life in Soviet Russia*. Bloomington, Ind.: Indiana University Press (1983).

Thompson, Kenneth. 1973. *A Dictionary of Twentieth-Century Composers (1911-1971)*. New York: St. Martin's Press.

Threlfall, Robert, and Geoffrey Norris. 1982. *A Catalogue of the Compositions of S. Rachmaninoff*. London: Scolar Press.

References

T͡sytovich, Tamara Erastovna, ed. 1947. *S.V. Rakhmaninov, sbornik stateĭ i materi͡alov.* Moskva, Leningrad: Muzgiz.

Walker, Robert. 1980. *Rachmaninoff: His Life and Times.* Tunbridge Wells, Kent (Eng.): Midas Books.

Wile, Raymond R. 1977. "The Edison Recordings of Serge Rachmaninoff." *American Record Guide* (February): 11-12.

Illustrations

Plate 1. Photograph of Rachmaninoff (1885-86) presented to his friend Matveĭ Leont'evich Presman. (Courtesy Izdatel'stvo "Muzyka")

Plate 2. Moscow Conservatory piano pedagogue Nikolaĭ Sergeevich Zverev with his special students of 1885 - from left, Matveĭ Leont'evich Presman, Sergei Vasil'evich Rachmaninoff, Leonid Aleksandrovich Maximov, and Zverev. (Courtesy Izdatel'stvo "Muzyka")

Plate 3. Announcement of the first complete and staged performance of *Aleko* at the Bol'shoĭ Teatr on 27 April 1893. The announcement states: "The artists of the Imperial Theaters will stage for the first time, *Aleko*, opera in one act, music by S.V. Rakhmaninov, libretto based on A.S. Pushkin's poem 'T͡sygane' [Gypsies], by Vl.I. Nemirovicha-Danchenko." The cast of gypsy dancers is listed, followed by the names of the principal singers performing the roles of Aleko (Mr. Korsov), Molodoĭ t͡sygan [young gypsy] (Mr. Klement'ev), and Zemfira (Mrs. Deisha-Sionit͡skai͡a). (Courtesy Izdatel'stvo "Muzyka")

Plate 4. Rachmaninoff with his dog Levko in the Tambov area. 1899. (Courtesy Izdatel'stvo "Muzyka")

Plate 5. The composer out on a fishing trip. 1901. (Courtesy Izdatel'stvo "Muzyka")

Plate 6. The composer at the age of 30. (Courtesy Izdatel'stvo "Muzyka")

Plate 7. Announcement of the first Moscow performance of the *Simfonii͡a e-moll, soch. 27* [Symphony in E Minor Op.27] in the Large Hall of the Moscow Conservatory on 2 February 1908. The announcement states: "Fifth Symphony Concert under the conductorship of S.V. Rakhmaṇinov with the participation of A.V. Nezhdanovoĭ and S.V. Rakhmaninova. Program - First Part, S.V. Rakhmaninov *Simfoniia̅ e-moll, soch.27* (v pervy raz' [for the first time])." Second part of the program (not mentioned in this announcement) consisted of Rachmaninoff's Second Concerto performed by the composer (conducted by Anatoliĭ Andreevich Brandukov) and a group of songs sung by Antonina Vasil'evna Nezhdanova. (Courtesy Izdatel'stvo "Muzyka")

Plate 8. Rachmaninoff driving his prized possession with cousins of the Rachmaninoff family, Natalii̅a̅ Nikolaevna Lanting and Anna Andreevna Trubnikova. c.1912. (Courtesy Izdatel'stvo "Muzyka")

Plate 9. Rachmaniṇoff in concert, from a drawing by V. Rossinskiĭ. 1917. (Courtesy Izdatel'stvo "Muzyka")

Plate 10. The Rachmaninoffs' visa to enter the USA, registered by the American Consulate General in Copenhagen, Denmark on 17 September 1918 and granted on 24 October 1918. There was ample evidence of Rachmaninoff's intent to work in the USA by performing concerts. He had various documents from Frederick Cabot of the Boston Symphony Orchestra Association, Henry Wolfsohn Concert Bureau, Steinway Company, and Modest Altschuler supporting his artistic position. Notice that Rachmaninoff uses 2 April 1873 as his date of birth. This birth date is also inscribed in the granite cross that marks his grave. Actually, he was born on 20 March 1873 in the Old Style (Julian) calendar, which converts to 1 April 1873 in the New Style (Gregorian) calendar. Regardless, many sources use the 2 April date.

The acquisition of this visa to the USA represents a major step in breaking with the past, a step that took courage, and certainly Sergei and Natalia deliberated seriously before making this decision. This move to the USA, thought to be temporary until the political turmoil settled in

Russia, proved to be permanent. Rachmaninoff never returned to his beloved homeland. (Courtesy of the representatives of the Rachmaninoff estate)

Plate 11. Rachmaninoff in California. June 1919. (Courtesy Izdatel'stvo "Muzyka")

Plate 12. Natalia and Sergei at their Villa "Senar" overlooking Lake Lucerne, Switzerland. c.1932. (Courtesy Izdatel'stvo "Muzyka")

Plate 1.

Plate 2.

Цѣна 5 коп.

18  93.

ИМПЕРАТОРСКІЕ Московскіе Театры.

БОЛЬШОЙ ТЕАТРЪ

ПРОГРАММА.

Во Вторникъ, 27-го Апрѣля, Артистами ИМПЕРАТОРСКИХЪ Театровъ представлено будетъ, ВЪ ПЕРВЫЙ РАЗЪ:

Опера въ 1 дѣйствіи. Музыка соч. С. В. Рахманинова.

Либретто по поэмѣ А. С. Пушкина „Цыгане" Вл. И. Немировича-Данченко.

Танцы поставлены г. ДОМАШОВЫМЪ.

ЦЫГАНСКІЕ ТАНЦЫ:

ЦЫГАНКИ:—г-жи Бармина, Ермолова, Пукирева 2, Востокова, Дьякъ, Сворцова, Бакеркина, Егорова, Тимоѳеева, Морозова, Иванова 3, Крылова 2 и восп-ца Гельцеръ.

ЦЫГАНЕ:—гг. Домашевъ, Литавкинъ 1, Бекъ, Новиковъ, Пановъ, Хомяковъ, Литавкинъ 2, Сидоровъ, экст. учен. Морозовъ и Щегловъ.

ДѢЙСТВУЮЩІЕ·

Алеко . . . . г. Корсовъ.
Молодой цыганъ . . . . г. Клементьевъ.
Земфира . . . . г-жа Дейша-Сіоницкая.

Программа перваго представленія оперы «Алеко»

Plate 4.

Plate 5.

Plate 6.

19 08  № 1497.

Московское Филармоническое Общество.

Въ Субботу, 2-го Февраля,
въ большомъ залѣ
МОСКОВСКОЙ КОНСЕРВАТОРІИ
ПЯТОЕ СИМФОНИЧЕСКОЕ СОБРАНІЕ,
подъ управленіемъ **С. В. Рахманинова**, съ участіемъ
А. В. Неждановой и **С. В. Рахманинова**.

ПРОГРАММА.

Отдѣленіе I-е.

1. С. В. Рахманиновъ. Симфонія e-moll, соч. 27 (въ 1-й разъ).
    a) Largo. Allegro moderato.
    b) Allegro molto.
    c) Adagio.
    d) Allegro vivace.

Антрактъ **20** минутъ.

Программа концерта
С. В. Рахманинова совместно с А. В. Неждановой

Plate 8.

Plate 9.

(Form No. 228.)
(Established July, 1917.)

DECLARATION OF ALIEN ABOUT TO DEPART FOR THE UNITED STATES.
Erklæring af Udlænding, som agter at reise til De Forenede Stater.
(See General Instruction No. 535.)

AMERICAN CONSULATE GENERAL   COPENHAGEN, DENMARK   Sept. 17th 1918.
                                                      Date — Dato

I _Sergei Rachmaninoff_, _artist_, a Citizen or subject
Jeg   Name of declarant — Navn   Occupation — Beskæftigelse   en Borger eller Undersaat

of _Russia_   bearer of passport No. _6118_, dated _October 17/25 1918_;
af   Name of country — Nation   indehaver af pas Nr. _84/64_   dateret

issued by _The Russian Consulate General_, am about to go to United States, accompanied by
udstedt af   Name of office — Navn af autoritet   _Copenhagen_ at reise til de Forenede Stater, ledsaget af

Wife,   _Natalie Rachmaninoff_   , born at _Tambow, Russia_ _May 26, 1877_
Hustru,   Full name — Hele navnet   født i

Sons under 16 years of age as follows: — Følgende sønner under 16 aars alder:

_____ , born at _____, _____
    Name — Navn   født i   Date — Dato

_____ , born at _____, _____
                          født i

And daughters under 21 years of age as follows: — Og følgende døttre under 21 aars alder:
Irene Rachmaninoff   , born at ~~Tambow~~ Moscow, Russia May 14, 1903
    Name — Navn   født i   Date — Dato
Tatiana Rachmaninoff   Tambow   born at ~~Moscow~~, Russia ~~June 21~~, 1907
                                                                July 4

1. I was born at _Nowgorod_ on _April 2th 1873_;
   Jeg var født i   Place — Sted   den   Date — Dato
2. My father was a citizen or subject of _Russia_ of the _Russian_
   Min fader var borger eller undersaat af   af den
   race, my mother was born a citizen or subject of _Russia_ of the
   race, min moder var født som borger eller undersaat af   af den
   Russian race;
          race;
3. (a) I last resided at _Copenhagen_, _____ 7, Gentofte_ on _Sept. 17th 1918_
   Jeg boede sidst i   Place — Sted   Address — Adr.   Date — Dato
   (b) I have resided in or visited the following countries within the past five years: _Russia, U.S.A.,_
   Jeg har boet i eller besøgt de følgende lande i de sidste fem aar: Places, addresses
   Denmark.
   and dates — Steder, adresser og datum
4. I have _____ previously resided in the United States as follows:
   Jeg har   tidligere boet i De Forenede Stater paa følgende steder:
   _1909 - 1910_   _as through-passengers._
   Dates — Datum   Place and Address — Sted og Adresse   Object of residence — Grunden for opholdet
5. I intend to depart for the United States on the date, from the port, and on the steamship as follows:
   Jeg agter at reise til de Forenede Stater paa den dato, fra den havn og med det dampskib nævnt nedenunder:
   November   _Kristiania_   _N A L's Damper_
   Date — Dato   Port — Havn   Steamship — Dampskib
6. I name the following, with addresses, as references:
   Jeg giver følgende personer, med deres adresser, som referencer:
   (a) _Musikforlag Vilh. Hansen, Gothersgade, Copenhagen._
       In the country from which declarant starts — I det land, fra hvilket ansøgeren begynder sin reise
   (b) _Wolfsohn Musical-Bureau, New York._
       In the United States — I de Forenede Stater

(OVER

7. I expect to go to the United States for **to give concerts,reference:Henry Wolfsohn,Bureau,**
   Jeg agter at reise til de Forenede Stater for — Object of visit — Grunden for reisen
   New York City.

   as shown by **various telegrams, from Dabot,Boston,Steinway,N.Y.,Modest**
   som bevises ved **Altschouler,N.Y.** — proofs of object — Dokumenter eller andre beviser af grunden til reisen

   to reside at **one of the hotels in New York** for a period of **one year.**
   at bo i — City, street and number — By, gade og nummer — for en periode af

8. I have informed myself of the provisions of section 3, Immigration Act of February, 5, 1917, and am convinced that I am eligible for admission into the United States thereunder.;
   Jeg har gjort mig selv bekendt med bestemmelserne af paragraf 3 af indvandringsloven af 5te Februar 1917, og er overbevist om, at jeg er derunder adgangsberettiget til de Forenede Stater;

9. (a) I realize that, if I am one of a class prohibited by law from admission into the United States, I will be deported or detained in confinement in the United States, and (b) I am prepared to assume the risk of deportation and of a compulsory return trip in case of my rejection at an American port.
   (a) Jeg forstaar, at hvis jeg kommer under en af de klasser, som er forbudt af loven til at faa adgangsberettigelse til de Forenede Stater, vil jeg blive hjemsendt eller holdt indespærret i de Forenede Stater, og (b) jeg er forberedt paa at antage resikoen af at blive hjemsendt og af tvungen retur i til ælde af at jeg bliver nægtet adgang til en Amerikansk havn.

2456   *Serge Rachmaninoff*   Ser no. 698
Signature of declarant — Ansøgerens underskrift

Subscribed and sworn to before me this **17th** day of **September, 1918**
Month and year — Maaned og aar

American Vice Consul   **Am. Vice Consul**
Official signature — Original underskrift

$1 FEE STAMP

N.B.—The taking of this declaration and visaing of the bearer's passport give no assurance that the bearer is not excludible from the United States under section 3 of the Immigration Act of February 5, 1917. The decision in each case must be made by the immigration authorities in the United States.

N.B.—Udskrivningen af denne erklæring og viseringen af ihændehaverens pas giver ingen sikkerhed for, at ihændehaveren ikke bliver udelukket fra de Forenede Stater under paragraf 3 af indvandringsloven af 5te Februar 1917. Afgørelsen i enhver sag maa tages af indvandrings autoriteterne i de Forenede Stater.

VISA GRANTED
See Department's telegram **24 OCT. 1918**
Remarks by official taking declaration:

Exhibits letter from the American Legation in Copenhagen in which declarant has been offered conductorship of Boston Symphony Orchestra, through Mr. Frederick P. Cabot, president of the association.

Sympathy letter will follow.

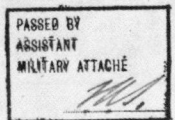

PASSED BY ASSISTANT MILITARY ATTACHÉ

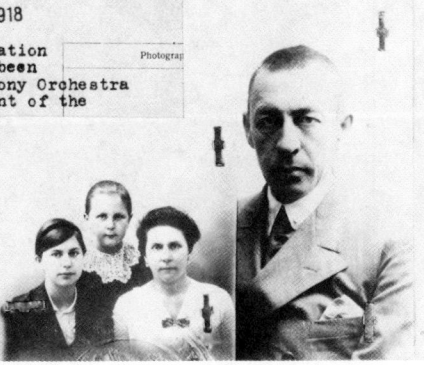

Plate 11.

Plate 12.

Author Index

(Numbers are item numbers in the bibliography proper)

Abraham, Gerald 1
Albin, M. 2
Aldanov, M. 3
Aldrich, Richard 4
Alekseev, Aleksandr Dmitrievich 5-7
Alekseeva, Ekaterina Nikolaevna 8
Apetian, Zarui 9-13
Aranovskiĭ, Mark Genrikhovich 14
Arnold, Elliot 15
Asaf'ev, Boris Vladimirovich [pseudonym Igor Glebov] 12, 16-20

Baca, Richard 21
Bachauer, Gina 22
Baker, Harry Jay 23
Bakst, James 24
Bazhanov, Nikolaĭ Danilovich 25
Beckett, Henry 26
Belaiev, Victor Mikhailovich 27
Belousov, V. 28
Belza, Igor Fedorovich 29-30, 348
Berkov, V. 31
Bertensson, Sergei 12, 32-33, 80
Blumberg, Marc 34
Bobykina, Irina 35
Bogdanov-Berezovskiĭ, Valer'ian Mikhailovich 36-37
Bokshchanina, Evgenii͡a A. 38

Boldt, Kenwyn Guy 39
Borisov, Leonid 40
Bortnikova, Evgenii͡a Ermolaevna 41-42, 348
Bowers, Faubion 43
Boyd, Malcom 44
Braggiotti, Mary 45
Brewerton, Eric 46
Brian͡tseva, V.N. 47-50, 190
Brower, Harriette 51
Bukinik, Michael 52
Bunimovich, Vladimir 53
Burke, Harry R. 54
Butzbach, Fritz 55

Calvocoressi, Michel D. 56-57
Cameron, Norman 262
Carples, Esther 58
Chaliapin, Fedor Ivanovich 59
Charton, Jean Marie 60
Chasins, Abram 61-62
Chekov, Mikhail Aleksandrovich 12, 63
Chernikhin, Jacob 64
Chertok, S. 82
Citkowitz, Israel 65
Conus, Olga 66
Cooke, Deryck 67
Coolidge, Richard 68
Culshaw, John R. 69-74, 124

Daniel, Oliver   75
Davidson, Gladys   76
Davies, Laurence   77
"Devilish Discords."   78
"Distinguished Russian Composer."   79
Dobrokhotov, B.   348
Dobuzhinskiĭ, Mstislav Valariānovich   12, 80-81
Dolinskiĭ, M.   82
Downes, Olin   83-86

Eberle, Merab   87
Eberlein, Dorothee   88
Emeliānova, N.N.   89
Engel, I͡Uliĭ Dmitrievich   90-93
Espina, Noni   94
Estrin, Morton   95
Evans, May Garrettson   96
Ewen, David   97, 263

Fagan, Keith   98
Farwell, Arthur   99
Faurot, Albert   100
Flanagan, William   101
Frank, Jonathan   102
Frankenstein, Alfred   103
Frid, E.L.   208
Friskin, James   104
Freundlich, Irwin   104
Froud, Nina   59

Gaisberg, Frederick   105-06
Gakkel', L.   107
Gitel'makher, V.   108
Glebov, Igor, see Asaf'ev, Boris Vladimirovich
Glinsky, M.   109
Goddard, Scott   110
Gol'denveizer, Aleksandr Borisovich   12
Gol'dshtein, Mikhail   111

Goldsmith, Harris   112
Gozunpud, Abram Akimovich   113-14
Gray-Fisk, Clinton   115
Greenawalt, Terrence Lee   116
Gronowicz, Antoni   117
Grove, Sir George   118

Hanley, James   59
Hanson, Elisabeth   119
Hanson, Lawrence   119
Harris, Jr., George   120
Hazen, David   121
Henderson, A.M.   122
Henderson, Mrs. A.M.   122
Hill, Edward Burlingame   123
Hill, Ralph   124
Hinson, Maurice   125-27
Hodgson, Leslie   128
Hofmann, Michel-Rostislav   129-31
Holcman, Jan   132
Holt, Richard   133
Hopkins, Antony   134
Howes, Frank   135-36
Hughes, Rupert   137
Hull, Robin   138

I͡Agolim, B.S.   30
I͡Akovlev, V.   30, 348
Isaev, N.   139

Jacobson, Robert   140
Johnson, Harrison   141
Jong, W.C. De   142

Kagen, Sergius   143
Kalashnikov, Dmitriĭ   144
Kammerer, Rafael   145-46
Kandinskiĭ, Alekseĭ   147-49, 208
Kardinar, N.   150

Author Index

Kashkin, Nikolaĭ 151-54
Kehler, George 155
Keldysh, I͡uriĭ Vsevolodovich 156-58, 373
Khentova, Sof'i͡a 159
Khubov, Georgiĭ Nikitich 160
King, William G. 161
Kogan, Grigori 162-65
Kolodin, Irving 166
Koltypina, G.B. 167
Konen, Valentina 168
Konii͡us, Olga Nikolaevna, *see* Conus, Olga
Korzuchin, I. 299
Kozhin, Nikolaĭ 169
Kramer, Walter A. 170
Kupferberg, Herbert 171
Kurenko, Marii͡a 172-73
Kuznet͡sov, Konstantin 174-77

L., E., "Kolokola zvoni͡at'. . ." 178
La Magra, Anthony James 179
Lang, Christoph 180
Larson, Richard 181
Legge, Robin 183
Leonard, Florence 11, 261
Leonard, Richard 97, 137, 184
Levasheva, Olga E. 185
Levina, E.E. 369
Leyda, Jay 32
Liebling, Leonard 186
Lipaev, Ivan 205
Lipman, Samuel 188-89
Lissa, Zofia 190
Livanova, Tamara Nikolaevna 30
Lochner, Louis Paul 191
Loftis, Eric Kenneth 192
Lvov, L. 193
Lyle, Watson 194-97

Mach, Elyse 198
Machavarilliĭ, M. 199
Maine, Basil 200
Martens, Frederick 11, 201-03
Maycock, Robert 204
Mazel', L. 348
McCabe, John 205
Medveder, A. 206-07
Mikhailov, M.K. 208
Mila, Massimo 209
Milstein, Jacov Iszakovics 210
Moiseiwitsch, Benno 211-13
Montagu-Nathan, Montagu 182, 214-16
Morgenstern, Sam 217

Nadejine, Nicholas 218
Nardony, Ivan 219
Nemenova-Lunts, M.S. 220
Nest'ev, Israel Vladimirovich 221
New Grove Dictionary of Music and Musicians (1980) 222
Newmarch, Rosa 118
"New Russia: Rachmaninoff as Pianist and Composer." 223
Nezhdanova, Antonina Vasil'evna 12
Norman, Gertrude 224
Norris, Geoffrey 222, 225-28, 341

O'Connell, Charles 229
Oliphant, E.H.C. 230
Olkhovsky, Andrey 231
Orlova, Elena 232
Ormandy, Eugene 233

"Passing of a Giant." 234
Pasternak, Alexander 23
"Philharmonic Concerts, 1899." 236
Piatigorsky, Gregor 237
Piggott, Patrick 238-39
Plaskin, Glen 240
Ponizovkin, I͡u. 241
Porte, John F. 242
Presman, Matveĭ Leont'evich 12
Prieberg, Fred K. 243
Prokof'ev, Grigori 244-52
Protopopov, V. 348
Prussing, Stephan 253

Rachmaninoff, Sergei Vasil'evich 254-63
"Sergei Rachmaninoff." 269, 271, 274
"Rachmaninoff Arrives in America." 266
"Rachmaninoff Days in Moscow." 275
"Rachmaninoff Festival . . ." 273
"Rachmaninoff Fund Forced to Discontinue." 277
"Rachmaninoff Makes Debut in New York." 265
"Rachmaninoff Opens His Tour in Providence, R.I.." 268
"Rachmaninoff Returns to America." 267
"Rachmaninoff's Songs." 270
"Rachmaninoff spielt für 'Pro Juventute'." 272
"Sergei V. Rakhmaninov." 264, 276
Rakhmaninova, Natali͡a Aleksandrovna 12, 278

"RCA to Gift Library of Congress. . ." 279
Reed, Peter Hugh 280
Reither, Joseph 281
Riesemann, Oskar von 217, 282
Rosenfeld, Paul 283
Roy, Basante Koomar 284
Rozhdestvenskai͡a, N.P. 306
Rubin, David 285
Rubinstein, Arthur 286-87
Ruc'evskai͡a, Ekaterina 232
Rüger, Christoph 288
Rummenhöller, Peter 289
Ryt͡sareva, M.G. 290

Sabaneyeff, Leonid 291
Sabina, M. 292
Salazar, Adolfo 293
Salmond, Felix 294
Salzman, Eric 297
Satina, Sof'i͡a Aleksandrovna 12, 33, 80, 295-96
Schickel, Richard 298
Schindler, Kurt 299
Schluessmayer, Gerhard 300
Schonberg, Harold D. 301-04
Scott, Michael 305
Serebri͡akov, P.A. 306
Seroff, Victor Ilych 307-09
Shagini͡an, Marietta Sergeevna 12, 310-11
Shaporin, I͡uri 312
Shrifte, Miriam 224
Siloti, Alexander 313
Sin'kovskai͡a, N. 314
Sjöberg, Lars 315
Skaftymova, L. 232
Skalon, Vera Dmitrievna 12

Author Index

Skurko, Evgeniia Romanovna 316
Smith, Carleton 317
Sokolova, Ol'ga Ivanovna 318
Solovt͡sov, Aleksandr 319-20
Sorabji, Kaikhosru Shapurji 321
South, M'Jean 322
Sutton, Wadham 323
Suvalova, M.P. 324
Sveshnikov, A. 325
Swan, Alfred 12, 16, 326-30
Swan, Katherine 330

"Tagore on Russia. . ." 331
Taubman, Howard 332-34
Taylor, Deems 335
Thiman, Eric 336
Thompson, Kenneth 337
Thompson, Oscar 338
Threlfall, Robert 339-41
Tideböhl, Ellen von 342-43
Toombs, Elizabeth O. 344
Tret͡iakova, Liliia Sergeevna 345
Trubnikova, Anna Andreevna 12, 346
T͡sukkerman, V. 347
T͡sytovich, Tamara Erastovna 348

Vachnadze, M. 349
Vactor, David 350
Varro, Margit 351
Varvat͡si, E.V. 30
Vasilenko, Sergeĭ 352-53
Vasil'ev, Evgeniĭ 354
Volkov, Oleg 355
Volynskai͡a, N. 356

Waldo, Fullerton 357
Walker, Robert 358
Walsh, Stephan 359-60
Waters, Edward N. 361
Werth, Alexander 362
Wile, Raymond R. 363
Williams, Richard 364
Wooldridge, David 365

Yasser, Joseph 366-68

Zelina, Marina 369
Zetel, L. 370
Zhitomirskiĭ, Daniel 371-73
Ziloti, Aleksandr Il'ich, see Siloti, Alexander
Zschorlich, Paul 374-75

Index of Proper Names

(N.B., Numbers preceded by "p." refer to page numbers; all other numbers are item numbers in the bibliography proper.)

Academy of Music (Philadelphia) 274
Aleksandrova, Nadezhda Aleksandrovna p.45
Altani, Ippolit p.31
Altschuler, Modest Isaakovich p.5, p.29, p.300
Ampico Corporation p.93
Anastasia 334
Andray, C. 236
Anosov, N. p.23
Apetîan, Zarui 206, 292, 362
Apukhtin, Aleksei Nikolaevich p.45, p.47-48
Arakshvile [Arakishvili], Dmitri Ignat'evich 38
Archangelskiĭ, Aleksandr Andreevich 253
Arenskiĭ, Anton Stepanovich p.8, p.11, p.23, p.67, 7, 43, 52, 208, 245, 352
Armenia (SSR) 38
Asaf'ev, Boris Vladimirovich 206
Azerbaijan (SSR) 38

Babin, Victor p.66
Bach, Johann Sebastian 103, 244, 374
Backhaus, Wilhelm 145
Bal'mont, Konstantin Dmitrievich p.43, p.55, p.59, 56, 121, 173, 178
Beethoven, Ludwig van 4, 54, 65, 67, 103, 141, 268, 346

Beethoven String Quartet p.28, p.30
Behr, Franz p.14
Beketova, Ekaterina A. p.48
Belwin-Mills p.4
Belyĭ, Andreĭ. see Bugayev, Boris
Belza, Igor Fedorovich 243, 275, 319, 372
Berlin Philharmonic 374-75
Bertensson, Sergei 168, 311
Beverly Hills 32, 40
Bizet, Georges p.18
Blacher, Boris 323
Blok, Aleksandr Aleksandrovich p.59
Blom, Eric 118
Böcklin, Arnold p.25
Bolsheviki 331
Bol'shogo Simfonicheskogo Orkestra 312
Bol'shoĭ Imperial Theater p.68, 90, 93, 114, 140, 151, 153, 156, 174, 264, 312, 324, p.299
Boosey and Hawkes p.4
Borisov, Leonid 10
Borodin, Aleksandr Porfir'evich 114, 153, 156, 182, 236, 247, 318, 347
Bortnikova, Evgeniĭa Ermolaevna 275, 290, 372
Boston Symphony Orchestra 34, 265-66, 338, p.300

Boudoir Theatre (Eng.) 182
Bourdet-Pleville, Michel 309
Brahms, Johannes 283, 323
Brandis, E. 40
Brandukov, Anatoli Andreevich p.29-31
Brant, Ada p.65
Breitkopf und Härtel p.3
Briantseva, V.N. 227
Briusov, Valeri I͡akovlevich p.59
Bugayev, Boris [pseud. Andrei Belyĭ] p.59
Buketoff, Igor p.32
Bunin, Ivan Alekseevich p.52-53, 173, 356
Busoni, Ferruccio 52, 141, 145, 235, 374

Cabot, Frederick p.300
Caillet, Lucien p.61-62
Carnegie Hall 4, 34, 73, 83, 265, 268, 273-74, 298, 365
Casals, Pablo p.63-64, p.85, p.89
Chaliapin, Boris 369
Chaliapin, Fedor Ivanovich p.47, p.54-57, 40, 59, 63, 82, 106, 114, 165, 169, 288, 345
Chateau de Corbeville 60
Chekov, Anton Pavlovich p.51, 63, 207, 330, 345
Chicago Symphony Orchestra p.69, 350
Chopin, Frederic François p.67-68, 14, 141, 190, 242, 257, 261, 268, 336, 359, 363, 374
Circle of Russian Culture 331

Clairfontaine 60, 63, 282, 330
Coates, Albert, see Kouts, Al'bert
Colonne, Edouard 91
Columbia Broadcasting Co. 273, 335
Concertgebouw Orchestra of Amsterdam p.26
Copeland, Fanny 121
Copland, Aaron 217
Copyright Convention p.3
Corelli, Arcangelo 244
Cui, César Antonovich 76, 78, 156
Culshaw, John R. 281

Dahl, Nikolaĭ p.5, 129
Dallapiccola, Luigi 44
Damrosch, Walter p.6, p.26
Danehl, Günther 287
Danilin, Nikolaĭ p.35
Danko, K. 330
Dante Alighieri p.32
Dargomyzhski, Aleksandr Sergeevich 151, 185, 264
Davidova, Marii͡a p.43
Debussy, Claude 373
DeFalla, Emanuale 373
Deisha-Sionitzkai͡a, Marii͡a p.43, p.299
De Pachmann, Vladimir 145
Dobrokhotov, B. 275
Dresden, 150, 299, 345
Dubensky, Arkady p.62
Dukas, Paul 244
Dvořák, Antonin 115

Edison Company p.93, 260, 363
Einerling, A. [pseud. G. Galina] p.49-50, p.53

Index of Proper Names 311

Electric Exposition 52
Elgar, Edward 115
Elman, Mischa p.64, p.86
Essentukakh (USSR) 82
Estonia (SSR) 38
Etude (magazine) 13, 234, 261, 269, 299

Farrar, Geraldine p.64
Fauré, Gabriel 130-31
Feivel, Berthold 121
Fet, Afansy, see Shenshin, Afanasy Afanas'evich
Fiedler, Max 265
Field, John 53
Figurov, Petr 82
Fischer, Carl p.3
Fokine, Mikhail 68
Foley, Charles p.3
Freundlich, Irwin 125
Frisken, James 125
Furtwängler, Wilhelm 180, 374

Galina, G., see Einerling, A.
Georgia (SSR), tours of 38, 199
Gershwin, George 15
Gingold, Josef p.65
Giuio, Zhan-Mari [Jean-Marie Guyot] p.47
Glazunov, Aleksandr Konstantinovich p.11, p.18, p.24, 19, 47, 88, 201, 208, 247, 267, 345
Glière, Reinhold p.89, 267
Glinka, Mikhail Ivanovich 14, 53, 93, 129, 185, 216, 353, 369, 371
Godowsky, Leopold p.14, 145
Goethe, Johann Wolfgang von p.43

Gol'denveiser, Aleksandr Borisovich p.12, p.79-80, 12, 275
Golenishchev-Kutuzov, Arensiĭ Arkad'evich p.41, p.49-52
Golenishchev-Kutuzov, Ol'ga Andreevna p.41
Golovanov, N. 160
Gorky, Maksim 59, 106, 207, 330
Gorshanova, Marîa 82
Gosudarstvennoe Muzykal'noe Izd-vo p.4, 221
Gosudarstvennaîa Biblioteka SSSR Imeni V.I. Lenina 82
Gosudarstvennyĭ Simfonicheskyĭ Orkestr SSSR 2, 160
Gosudarstvennyĭ T͡sentral'nyĭ Muzeĭ Muzykal'noĭ Kul'tury Imeni M.I. Glinki 8, 41-42, 55, 275, 290, 348, 372
Grainger, Percy 145
Grekov, Nikolaĭ p.37
Gretchaninov, Aleksandr 253
Grieg, Edvard 55, 91, 242, 246
Grigorovich, Karl Karlovich p.87
Gromov, M. 207
Grove, Sir George, *Dictionary of Music and Musicians* (1955) 303
Gunther, Felix p.65
Gutkheil [Gutheil], Karl Aleksandrovich p.3
Gutkheil [Gutheil], Marîa Ivanovna p.44

Handel, George Frideric 145
Hawkes and Son 270
Heifetz, Jascha p.62-63

Heine, Heinrich p.41-42
Heking, A. p.86
Hemingway, Ernest 40
Henderson, William James 301
Hertenstein 272, 349
Hofmann, Josef p.6, p.87, p.90, 80, 145, 245, 304, 317
Hofmann, Michel-Rostislav 221
Holby, Lee p.62
Horowitz, Vladimir 32, 85, 198, 237, 240, 301, 332
Hugo, Victor p.32
Huneker, James Gibbons 301
Hupfer, William 26

Iakovlev, L.G. p.42, 275
Iaroshchevskiĭ [Yaroshevsky], Adol'f Adol'fovich p.41
Igumnov, Konstantin Nikolaevich p.13, p.88
International Musical Festival (Lucerne) 122
Ianova, M. p.39
Ippolitov-Ivanov, Mikhail 352
Isaakian, Averik p.59
Ivanova, Mariia Aleksandrovna p.49
Ivanovka 28, 36, 89, 144, 354-55
Ivanovka Muzeĭ 355
Ivanovskiĭ, A.N. p.44

Jacquet, H. Maurice p.61
Janáček, Leoš 373
Joffe, Judah A. 291
Johnson, Edna Ruth 117
Jonas, Florence 221

Kalinikov, Vasili Sergeevich 208, 345
Kastal'skiĭ, Aleksandr Dmitrievich 253
Kensico Cemetery (N.Y.) 324
Kerr, Russell 137
Kerzin, Arkady Mikhailovich p.50
Kerzina, Mariia Semenovna p.50
Khachaturian, Aram Il'ich 44, 129
Khomiakov, Aleksei Stepanovich p.52, p.56
Khora Vsesoiuznogo Radiokomiteta 312
Kiev Conservatory 231
Kievan-Petchersk Lavra 368
Kirkora, G. p.66
Klement'ev, Lev p.299
Klokacheva, Anna Georgievna p.45
Knoxville (Tenn.) 155
Kogan, Grigori 308
Kol'tsov, Aleksei Vasil'evich p.44, p.51, p.54
Komissarzhevskaia, Vera Fedorovna p.56
Konenkov, C. 369
Konius [Conus], Boris Iul'evich Eduardovich 66, 87, 159
Konius [Conus], Iuliĭ Eduardovich p.29-30, p.65, 330
Konius [Conus], Lev Eduardovich 66, 87
Konius [Conus], Olga Nikolaevna 66, 87
Korinfskiĭ, Apollon Apollonovich p.55
Korsov, Bogomir p.299
Koshits [Koshetz], Nina Pavlovna p.58, 82, 93, 305

Index of Proper Names

Koussevitzky, Sergei
  Aleksandrovich p.3,
  p.61, 82, 85, 92, 249,
  343, 365
Kouts [Coates], Al'bert
  178
Krein, David p.29
Kreisler, Fritz p.17-18,
  p.31, p.63-64, p.96,
  p.102, 177, 191
Kreitser, Elena I͡ul'evna
  p.48
Kri͡ukova, V. p.63-64
Kruglikov (critic) 156
Kruglov, Aleksandr p.50
Kunin, I. 93
Kurenko, Marii͡a 140
Küssnachter Bucht (Lake
  Lucerne) 272
Kuznet͡sov, Konstantin A.
  308
Kvast-Hozap, Frieda p.87

Lamm, Pavel A. 126, 164
Langer, E. p.79
Lanting, Natali͡a Niko-
  laevna p.49, p.300
Latvia (SSR) 38
Lavrovskai͡a, Elizaveta
  Andreevna p.41-42,
  p.45
Lebedine (USSR) 108
Leningrad Conservatory
  295
Leningr͡adskiĭ Gosudarst-
  vennyĭ Institut Teatra,
  Muzyki i Kinomatografiĭ
  Ministerstva Kul'tury
  373
Leonard, Richard 192
Leonardi, L. p.60
Leoncavallo, Ruggero 183
Lermontov, Mikhail
  I͡ur'evich p.34, p.36-
  37, 173
Leschetizky, Theodor
  Osipovich p.12, 313

Leyda, Jay 168, 311
Lhévinne, Josef p.9,
  p.84, p.87, 52, 223
Li͡adov, Anatol
  Konstantinovich 88,
  208, 345
Library of Congress
  p.8-9, 8, 13, 55, 279,
  290, 361
Lipaev, Ivan 319
Liszt, Franz p.19, p.67,
  4, 14, 54, 103, 130-31,
  141, 210, 245-46, 268,
  283, 313, 365, 374
Lithuania (SSR) 38
Litvin, Felii͡a Vasil'evna
  p.58
Livanova, Tamara Nikolaevna
  275
Liven, Aleksandra Andreevna
  p.48
Lodyzhenskai͡a, Anna
  Aleksandrovna p.24, p.39
Lodyzhenskiĭ, Pyotr
  Viktorovich p.24
Lodyzhenskiĭ, Vladimir
  p.34
Longyear, Rey 192
Lotarev, Igor' Vasil'evich
  [pseud. Igor Severi͡anin]
  p.59
Lutoslavski, Witold 323
Lyle, Wilson G. 196, 281
Lysikova, Evdokii͡a N.
  p.40, 108

MacDowell, Edward 51, 256
Maeterlinck, Maurice p.32,
  41
Mahler, Gustav 44, 91,
  365, 373
Maikov, Apollon Nikolaevich
  p.56
Mamontov, Savva Ivanovich
  p.68, see also Moskov-
  skai͡a Chastnai͡a Russkai͡a
  Opera

Marinskiĭ Opernyĭ Teatr
  178
Maximov, Leonid Alek-
  sandrovich p.79, p.81,
  p.299
Mazzi, Antoinette 25
McCormack, John p.31
Medtner, Nikolaĭ
  Karlovich p.6, 11, 16,
  47, 87, 102, 124, 201-
  02, 207, 252, 256, 267,
  291, 301-02, 326-27,
  330, 370
Meĭ, Lev Aleksandrovich
  p.48
Meichik, M. p.86
Melodiya p.94
Mendelssohn, Felix p.19,
  242, 246, 283
Mengelberg, Josef Willem
  p.26
Merezhkovskiĭ, Dimitriĭ
  Sergeevich p.39, p.51
Metropolitan Opera Co.
  81
Mezhdunarodnīa Kniga p.4
Miaskovskiĭ, Nikolaĭ 44,
  88, 201, 326
Miller, Philip L. 33
Milstein, Nathan 237
Minskiĭ [Vilenkin],
  Nikolaĭ Maksimovich
  p.45
Morozov, Nikita Semenovich
  p.34, 37, 348, 362
Moscow Conservatory, *see*
  Moskovskaīa Konserva-
  toriīa
Moskovskaīa Chastnaīa
  Russkaīa Opera p.68,
  140, 264, 352
Moskovskaīa Konservatoriīa
  p.67-68, 41, 45, 52, 64,
  87, 111, 155, 178, 185,
  275, 291, 293, 313, 322,
  348, 372, p.299

Moskovskiĭ Khudozhestv-
  enniĭ Teatr 32, 81
Moskovskiĭ Sinodal'nyĭ
  Institut 111
Mozart, Wolfgang Amadeus
  p.68, 54, 245, 268,
  301, 363
Musical Courier 304
Musset, Alfred de p.48,
  129
Mussorgsky, Modest Petro-
  vich p.19-20, 31, 93
Muzgiz, *see* Muzykal'noye
  Gosudarstvennoye
  Izdatel'stvo
Muzyka p.4
Muzykal'noye Gosudar-
  stvennoye Izdatel'stvo
  p.4

Nadson, Semen Īakovlevich
  p.47, p.49
Nationalists 137, 216,
  219
Neidecken, H.N. 272
Nekrasov, Nikolaĭ Alek-
  seevich p.34
Nemirovich-Danchenko,
  Vladimir Ivanovich
  p.31, 226, p.299
Newmarch, Rosa 303
New York Philharmonic
  191, 335
New York Times 304
Nezhdanova, Antonina
  Vasil'evna p.58, 12,
  30, 275, 343, p.300
Nezlobin Teatr 248-49
Nikisch, Arthur 91
Novgorod (USSR) 239,
  346

Olfer'eva, M.V. p.42
Oneg (USSR) 48
L'Opera (Paris) 60, 286

Index of Proper Names

Orlev (conductor)   p.33
Ormandy, Eugene   p.27,
  p.107-08, 78, 83, 171,
  241, 365
Ornat͡skai͡a, Anna D.   p.46
Ostromislensky, Iwan I.
  178, 331

Pabst, Pavel Avgustovich
  p.10, 52
Paderewski, Ignace Jan
  145
Paganini, Niccolò   323,
  364
Pailleron, Edouard   p.37
Palais de Chaillot   60
Palestrina, Giovanni
  Pierluigi da   217
Pasternak, L.   369
Perry, Harold   p.61
Petrograd   109
Philadelphia Orchestra
  p.27, p.32, p.68-69,
  p.107-08, p.113, 15, 40,
  78, 83, 171, 233, 241,
  274, 353, 365
Piatigorsky, Gregor   237,
  319
Pleshcheev, Alekseĭ
  Nikolaevich   p.41
Plevit͡skai͡a, Nadezhda
  p.113
Poe, Edgar Allan   p.26,
  56, 96, 121, 178
Polonskiĭ, I͡akov Petrovich
  p.53, p.56, p.58
Polytechnical Museum
  (Moscow)   248
Pope, Isabel   293
Presman, Matveĭ
  Leont'evich   p.15, p.22,
  12, p.299
Pribytkova, Zoi͡a
  Arkad'evna   p.44
Pring, S.W.   27
Prokof'ev, Grigori   308
Prokof'eva, L.I.   207

Prokofiev, Sergei
  Sergeevich   88, 119,
  201, 210, 221, 267,
  273, 322, 326, 362,
  influence of Rachmani-
  noff   119, 221
Protopopov, V.   275
Providence (R.I.)   268
Puccini, Giacomo   67, 373
Pushkin, Aleksandr Sergeevich   p.31, p.37, p.40,
  p.54-55, 173, 182,
  p.299
Pytovich (lecturer)   275

Queen's Hall (London)
  196, 236

Rachmaninoff Cycle (1939)
  83, 171, 273-74
Rachmaninoff Memorial
  Fund   45, 85, 111, 277
Radio Corporation of
  America   p.93-94, 111,
  229, 279
Rakhmaninov, Arkady
  Aleksandrovich (grand-
  father)   53, 346, 372
Rakhmaninov, Vasili
  Arkad'evich (father) -
Rakhmaninova, Irina
  Sergeevna (daughter)
  p.3, 159, 161
Rakhmaninova, Li͡ubov
  Petrovna (mother)   346
Rakhmaninova, Natali͡a
  Aleksandrovna (wife)
  p.10, 8, 45, 70, 72,
  74
Rakhmaninova, Tati͡ana
  Sergeevna (daughter)
  p.3, 66, 87, 159, 161
Rakhmaninova, Varvara
  Vasil'evna (grandmother)
  346
Rakhmanova, Mari͡a   82

Index of Proper Names

Ratgauz [Rathaus], Daniil
  Maksimovich p.38,
  p.44, p.47, p.54
Ravel, Maurice 373
"Re," *see* Shaginian,
  Marietta Sergeevna
Rebner, Wolfgang p.66
Red Army 17, 40, 139,
  159, 333
Reisman, Alexander p.60
Respighi, Ottarino p.60-61, 44
Richter, Sviatoslav 160
Riesemann, Oskar von 1,
  37, 166, 175, 196, 217-18, 220, 281, 308, 319,
  351
Rimsky-Korsakov, Mikhail
  Nikolaevich p.21, p.24,
  76, 88, 114, 156, 169,
  206, 247, 318, 330,
  345, 353, 373
Riverside Drive (N.Y.)
  15, 32, 51, 58, 161
Roberts, Charles J. p.61
Romanov, Konstantin
  Konstantinovich p.34
Rose, Leonard p.65
Rosenthal, Moriz 145
Rossinskii, V. 369,
  p.300
Rostovtsova, Liudmila,
  see Skalon, Liudmila
  Dmitrievna
Rubinstein, Anton
  Grigor'evich 52, 125,
  137, 255, 261, 283, 313,
  322, 352
Rubinstein, Arthur 301
Rubinstein, Nikolai
  Grigor'evich 322
Rüger, Christof 158
Russkoye Muzykal'noye
  Obshchestvo p.68, 92
Russo, Feka Iakovlevna
  40
Rutherford, Dolly 282

Sabaneyeff, Leonid 149
Sadie, Stanley 222
Safonov, Vasily Il'ich
  p.5, p.24, 352
St. Louis Municipal
  Auditorium 54
St. Petersburg Conservatory 322, 346
Saison russe 60, 286
Sakhnovskii, Iurii
  Sergeevich p.39, p.44
Satin, Vladimir Aleksandrovich p.50
Satina, Natalia Aleksandrovna p.40, p.46,
  p.49, *see* also
  Rakhmaninova, Natalia
  Aleksandrovna
Satina, Sof'ia Aleksandrovna p.43, 8, 12, 25,
  37, 50, 80, 89, 175-77,
  206, 239, 278, 282, 290,
  308, 367
Sauer, Emil von 145
Schindler, Kurt p.36
Schneider, Edwin p.31
Schonherr, M. p.62
Schubert, Franz p.21-22,
  p.68, 31, 136
Schubert-Consbruch, Christa
  221
Schuman, William 224
Schumann, Robert p.67,
  54, 323, 359, 375
Scriabin, Aleksandr
  Nikolaevich p.67, 16,
  43, 47, 52, 87, 92-93,
  184, 199, 201, 208, 210,
  231, 235, 267, 283, 291,
  312, 322, 326-27, 345,
  362, 369, 373
Semonovo (USSR) 48
Senar 15, 19, 73, 122,
  272, 278, 330, 349,
  p.301
Seroff, Victor Ilych
  281, 311

Severianin, Igor', see
  Lotarev, Igor'
  Vasil'evich
Shaginian, Marietta
  Sergeevna p.55, 12, 37,
  175, 206, 224, 301, 308,
  362
Shefer', A.N. p.64
Shelley, Percy Bysshe
  p.43
Shenshin, Afanasy
  Afanas'evich [pseud.
  Afanasy Fet] p.36,
  p.39, p.43, p.57
Shevchenko, Taras
  Grigor'evich p.42, p.52
Shostakovich, Dmitri 129,
  210, 273
Sibelius, Jan 273
Sikorskii, I.I. 80
Siloti, Alexander, see
  Ziloti, Aleksandr Il'ich
Simfonicheskii Orkestr
  Vsesoiuznovo Radio-
  komiteta 160
Simfonicheskoe Filarmon-
  icheskoe Obshchestvo
  244-47
Skalon, Liudmila
  Dmitrievna (Liudmila
  Rostovtsova) p.9, 25,
  36
Skalon, Natalia Dmit-
  rievna p.9, 13, 24,
  36, 206
Skalon, Vera Dmitrievna
  p.9, 12, 14, 22, 36,
  206
Slonimsky, Nicolas 221
Slonov, Iurii 82
Slonov, Mikhail Akimovich
  p.32, p.36, p.39, p.41,
  37, 41, 108, 206
Smith, John Stafford
  p.22
Smolenskii, Stepan
  Vasil'evich p.35

Sobinov, Leonid Vital'-
  evich p.55-57
Soiuz Pisatelei SSSR 10
Soiuz Sovetskikh Kompoz-
  itorov SSSR 85
Solodnikov Teatr 264
Sologub, Fedor Kuz'mich,
  see Teternikov, Fedor
Somov, Evgeni Ivanovich
  80
Somov, K. 80, 369
Sorgenstein, Samuel 117
Sovetskii Kompozitor p.4
Sovetskii Komitet po
  Kul'turnym Sviaziam s
  Sootechestvennikami za
  Rubezhom 169, 356
Spalding, C. 80
Stanislavskii, Konstantin
  Sergeevich p.54
Steinway, J. 80
Steinway Company p.300
Steinway Hall (N.Y.) 369
Sterl, Robert 150
Stevenson, Ronald 44
Stock, Frederick 350
Stokowski, Leopold p.6-7,
  p.27, p.36, p.107, 75,
  171, 233, 276, 298, 357,
  365
Strand Theater (R.I.) 268
Strauss, Richard 93, 273,
  352, 362, 373
Stravinsky, Igor Fydorovich
  76, 88, 216, 267, 273,
  283, 287, 326-27, 351,
  362
Struve, Nikolai Georgievich
  p.25, 150
Svetlanov, E. 2
Swan, Alfred p.59-60, 192
Sweelinck, Jan Pieterszoon
  224
Symphony Hall (Boston)
  223
Synodical Choir p.33-35,
  111

Tagore, Rabindranath 331
TAIR p.3
Tambovskiĭ Oblastnoĭ
  Institut Usovershen-
  stvovaniĭa Uchiteleĭ
  144
Taneev, Sergeĭ Ivanovich
  p.11, p.25, p.90, 7,
  43, 47, 52, 114, 177,
  208, 291, 312, 327,
  330, 345
Taubmann, Otto p.65
Taylor, Deems 51, 137
Tchaikovsky, Modest Ilich
  p.32
Tchaikovsky, Peter Ilich
  p.9, p.22, p.30, p.56,
  p.67-68, 14, 31, 47,
  53, 57, 76, 90, 114-15,
  130-31, 137, 145, 156,
  160, 162, 174, 199, 230,
  244-45, 253, 259, 310,
  314, 318, 345, 347, 352,
  371
Tcherepnin, Aleksandr
  Nikolaevich 267
Teternikov, Fedor [pseud.
  Fedor Kuz'mich Sologub]
  p.59
Thalben-Ball, George 267
Tiutchev, Fedor Ivanovich
  p.46, p.51, p.53, p.57
Tkhorzhevskiĭ, M. p.47
Tolstoĭ, Alekseĭ
  Konstantinovich p.23,
  p.33-34, p.37-38, p.40,
  p.44, p.50, 173
Tolstoĭ, Ilya L. 178, 331
Tolstoĭ, Lev Nikolaevich
  59, 259, 330, 345
Toscanini, Arturo 161
Tourel, Jennie 140
Trubnikova, Anna Andreevna
  p.300
Trubnikova, Ol'ga
  Andreevna p.49
Tschnokov (composer) 253
T͡sentral'nyĭ Gosudarstv-
  ennyĭ Arkhiv Okti͡abr'-
  skoĭ Revoli͡ut͡sii 139

T͡syganov, Nikolaĭ
  Grigor'evich p.34
T͡sytovich, Tamara E.
  37, 308
Turgenev, Ivan 182

Ukrain (SSR) 38

Verlagsnachrichten von
  Boosey und Hawkes 243
Vi͡azemskiĭ, Petr Andree-
  vich p.46
Victor Talking Machine
  Company p.93
Vilenkin, Nikolaĭ M., see
  Minskiĭ, Nikolaĭ
  Maksimovich
Viller-sur-mer 330
Vil'shau [Wilshaw],
  Vladimir p.66, 37, 139,
  163, 196, 206
Vrubel', Nadezhda Ivanovna
  p.48
Vsesoi͡uznoye Obshchestvo
  Kul'turnoĭ Svi͡azi s
  Zagranit͡seĭ 17, 177
Vsesoi͡uznyĭ Konkurs Imeni
  Rakhmaninova 111

Wagner, Richard 31, 90,
  189, 342
Walker, Robert 228
Walter, Bruno 375
War Memorial Opera House
  (San Francisco) 103
Waters, Edward p.9
Weber, Carl Maria von
  245
Weingartner, Felix p.91
Winter, Elsa 237
Wolfsohn Concert Bureau
  p.300
Wood, Henry J. p.61

Ysaÿe, Eugène p.84, p.87

Index of Proper Names

Zataevich, Aleksandr
  Viktorovich   p.11,
  41, 206, 367
Zhitomirskiĭ, Daniel
  308
Zhukovskiĭ, Vasiliĭ
  Andreevich   p.49
Ziloti, Aleksandr Il'ich
  p.5, p.12, p.34, p.63-
  64, p.66, p.80, p.84,
  p.86-88, 52, 89-91, 244
Zürcher Tonhalle   272
Zveda   10, 40
Zverev, Nikolaĭ Sergeevich
  43, 52, 129, 296, 313,
  345, p.299
Zweig, Stefan   142

Index of Rachmaninoff's Compositions

(N.B., Numbers preceded by "p." refer to page numbers; all other numbers are item numbers in the bibliography proper)

"Again I am Alone" Op.26, No.9, see *Ia opiat' odinok*
"Again You Leapt, My Heart", see *Opiat' vstrepenulos' ty serdtse*
Albumleaf (Marguerite) p.21
Akh, ty, Van'ka Op.41, No.2 p.36
Aleko p.3, p.31, 38, 76, 114, 140, 147, 156, 174 182-83, 199, 207-08, 226, 228, 259, 293, 346, p.299
All-Night Vigil Op.37, see *Vsenoshchnoe bdenie*
"All Once I Gladly Owned" Op.26, No.2, see *Ves otnial u menia*
"All Things Depart" Op.26, No.15, see *Prokhodit vse*
Angel Op.15, No.6 p.34
Apple Tree, O Apple Tree p.59
Arion Op.34, No.5 p.55
"At the Gate of Holy Abode," see *U vrat obiteli sviatoi*
Au Op.38, No.6 p.59

Barcarolle Op.10, No.3, see *Sem' p'es*
"Before My Window" Op.26, No.10, see *U moego okna*
"Before the Image" Op.21, No.10, see *Pered ikonoi*
"Believe Me Not, Friend" Op.14, No.7, see *Ne ver' mne drug*
Belilitsy rumenitsy vy moi p.36, p.60
Bells, The, Op.35, see *Kolokola*
"Beloved, Let Us Fly" Op.26, No.5, see *Pokinem*
"Be Praised" Op.15, No.1, see *Slav'sia*
"Brooding" Op.8, No.3, see *Duma*
Brooklet (Schubert) p.21
Bumble Bee (Rimsky-Korsakov) p.21
Buria Op.34, No.3 p.55
"By the Grave" Op.21, No.2, see *Nad svezhei mogiloi*

Capriccio on Gypsy Themes Op.12, see *Kaprichchio na tsyganskie temy*
"Captivity" Op.15, No.5, see *Nevolia*
C'etait en avril p.37
Cherez rechku Op.41, No.1 p.36

Chetyre p'esy (1887) p.7
Chetyre improvizatsii p.11
Chetyrnadtsat' romansov Op.34 p.54
"Child, Thou Art as Beautiful as a Flower" Op.8,
   No.2, see *Ditia, kak tsvetok, ty prekrasna*
Chorus of Spirits, see *Khor dukhov*
"Christ is Risen" Op.26, No.6, see *Khristos*
"Come Let Us Rest" Op.26, No.3, see *My otdokhnem*
*Concert pour le piano avec accompagnement d'orchestre
   Op.1* p.4-5, 27, 35, 55, 68, 83, 124, 131, 181,
   197, 207, 225, 266, 274, 340
Concerto (1889), see *Kontsert* (1889)
Concerto for Piano and Orchestra No.1, see *Concert
   pour le piano avec accompagnement d'orchestre Op.1*
Concerto for Piano and Orchestra No.2, see *Deuxième
   concert pour le piano avec accompagnement
   d'orchestre Op.18*
Concerto for Piano and Orchestra No.3, see *Troisième
   concert pour le piano avec orchestre Op.30*
Concerto for Piano and Orchestra No.4, see *Quatrième
   concert pour le piano avec orchestre Op.40*

"Daisies" Op.38, No.3, see *Margaritki*
Davno l', moi drug Op.4, No.6 p.41
"Day to Night Comparing Went the Wind Her Way" Op.34,
   No.4, see *Veter pereletnyi*
Desiat' preliudii Op.23 p.12, p.61-62, p.66, 93, 99,
   179, 208, 248, 315, 336
Deus meus p.33
*Deuxième concert pour le piano avec accompagnement
   d'orchestre Op.18* p.5, 5, 18, 19, 24, 34, 37, 65, 68,
   93, 124, 133, 142, 148, 160, 181, 207-08, 213, 222,
   242, 265, 274, 286, 310, 320, 334, 347, p.300
Deuxième Sonate pour piano Op.36 p.15, 93, 198, 201,
   248, 250, 285, 340
"Discord" Op.34, No.13, see *Dissonans*
"Dissonance" Op.34, No.13, see *Dissonans*
Dissonans Op.34, No.13 p.58
Ditia, kak tsvetok, ty prekrasna Op.8, No.2 p.41,
   p.66
"Do You Remember This Evening?", see *Ty pomnish' li
   vecher*
"Dream, The" Op.8, No.5, see *Son Op.8, No.5*
"Dream, The (Dreams)" Op.38, No.5, see *Son Op.38, No.5*
Duma Op.8, No.3 p.42
Dva proshchaniia Op.26, No.4 p.51
Dve chasti iz kvarteta (1889) p.28, 372
Dvenadtsat' romansov Op.14 p.43

Index of Rachmaninoff's Compositions 323

Dvenadtsat' romansov Op.21   p.47
Dve p'esy Op.6   p.29, p.62, 108

Elegicheskoe trio (1892)   p.29, 372
Elegicheskoe trio Op.9   p.30, 199, 237
Elégie Op.3, No.1, see *Morceaux de fantaisie* Op.3
Esmeralda   p.32, 35
Est' mngo zvukov Op.26, No.1   p.50
Eti letnie nochi Op.14, No.5   p.44
Etudes-tableaux Op.33   p.15, p.60-62, 14, 93, 103, 133, 162, 164, 190, 210, 248, 315, 375
Etudes-tableaux, Neuf Op.39   p.16, p.60-61, 14, 103, 133, 162, 164, 207, 210, 315

Fantasia-Suite No.1 Op.5, see *Fantaziia. Siuita No.1*
Fantasticheskaia p'esa   p.11
Fantaziia. Siuita No.1 Op.5   p.9, 108
"Fate" Op.21, No.1, see *Sud'ba*
Fifteen Songs Op.26, see *Piatnadtsat' romansov*
"Floods of Spring" Op.14, No.11, see *Vesennie vody*
"Flower Has Faded, The," see *Uvial tsvetok*
Fontan Op.26, No.11   p.53
"For Long Has Brought Little Consolation" Op.14, No.3, see *Davno v liubvi*
"Fountain " Op.26, No.11, see *Fontan*
Four Improvisations, see *Chetyre improvizatsii*
Four Pieces (1887), see *Chetyre p'esy*
Fourteen Songs Op.34, see *Chetyrnadtsat' romansov*
Fragments   p.17
"Fragments from de Musset" Op.21, No.6, see *Otryvok iz Miusse*
Francheska da Rimini Op.25   p.32, 76, 90, 113, 140, 147, 152, 293, 306, 310, 342-43
From the Gospel of St. John, see *Iz evangeliia ot Ioanna*
Fugetta   p.7

Godunov, Boris, see *Monologi*
Gopak (Mussorgsky)   p.19
Grianem-ukhnem   p.38

"Harvest of Sorrow" Op.4, No.5, see *Uzh ty, niva moia*
"Heart's Secret" Op.26, No.1, see *Est' mngo zvukov*
"He Took All From Me" Op.26, No.2, see *Ves otnial u menia*

Hopak (*Gopak;* Mussorgsky) p.19
"How Everyone Loves Thee" Op.14, No.6, see *Tebi͡a tak li͡ubi͡at vse*
"How Fair This Spot" Op.21, No.7, see *Zdes' khorosho*
"How Few the Joys" Op.14, No.3, see *Davno v li͡ubvi*
"How Long My Friend" Op.4, No.6, see *Davno l', moĭ drug*
"How Painful For Me" Op.21, No.12, see *Kak mne bol'no*
Humoreske Op.10, No. 5, see *Sem' p'es*
Hungarian Rhapsody No.2 (Liszt) p.19

I͡a byl u neĭ Op.14, No.4   p.44
I͡a ne prorok Op.21, No.11   p.50
I͡a opi͡at' odinok Op.26, No.9   p.52-53
I͡a tebe nichego ne skazhu   p.36
I͡a zhdu tebi͡a Op.14, No.1   p.43
"I Came to Her" Op.14, No.4, see *I͡a byl u neĭ*
"I Have Grown Fond of Sorrow" Op.8, No.4, see *Poli͡ubila i͡a na pechal' svoi͡u*
"I Implore Pity" Op.26, No.8, see *Poshchady i͡a moli͡u*
Ikalos' li tebe   p.46
"In My Garden" Op.38, No.1, see *Noch'i͡u v sadu u meni͡a*
"In My Soul" Op.14, No.10, see *V moeĭ dushe*
"In the Silence of the Secret Night" Op.4, No.3, see *V molchan'i nochi tainoĭ*
"In the Soul of Each of Us" Op.34, No.2, see *V dushe u kazhogo iz nas*
"I Remember That Day" Op.34, No.10, see *Seĭ den' i͡a pomni͡u*
"I Shall Tell Nothing," see *I͡a tebe nichego ne skazhu*
Isle of the Dead Op.29, see *Ostrov mertvykh*
"Isle, The" Op.14, No.2, see *Ostorovok*
Italian Polka, see *Polka italienne*
"It Cannot Be" Op.34, No.7, see *Ne mozhet byt'*
"I Wait for Thee" Op.14, No.1, see *I͡a zhdu tebi͡a*
Iz evangelii͡a ot Ioanna   p.60

Kak mne bol'no Op.21, No.12   p.50
Kakoe schast'e Op.34, No.12   p.57-58
Kaprichchio na tsyganskie temy dli͡a orkestra Op.12   p.24, 20, 318
K deti͡am Op.26, No.7   p.52, 230
Khor dukhov   p.33
Khristos Op.26, No.6   p.52
K neĭ Op.38, No.2   p.59
Kni͡az' Rostislav   p.23, 228, 318
Kolokola Op.35   p.26, 44, 56, 93, 96, 98, 121, 148-49, 178, 184, 210, 249, 274, 298, 340, 357

Index of Rachmaninoff's Compositions 325

Kol'tso Op.26, No.14   p.54
Kolybel'naia pesnia (Tchaikovsky)   p.22-23
Kontsert (1889)   p.4
Krysolov Op.38, No.4   p.59
Kvartet dlia dvukh skripok, al'ta i violoncheli No.2
   p.30, 372

"Let Me Rest Alone" Op.26, No.9, see Ia opiat' odinok
Letter to Stanislavskii (musical letter), see Pis'mo
   Stanislavskomu
"Let Us Leave My Dear" Op.26, No.5, see Pokinem
"Let Us Rest" Op.26, No.3, see My otdokhnem
Liebesfreud (Kreisler)   p.18-19, 126, 145, 162
Liebesleid (Kreisler)   p.18, 126, 145
"Like Blossom Dew-Freshen'd" Op.8, No.2, see Ditia,
   kak tsvetok, ty prekrasna
"Lilacs" Op.21, No.5, see Siren'
Liturgiia Sviatogo Ioanna Zlatousta Op.31   p.35, 111,
   253, 328
Liturgy of Saint John Chrysostom Op.31, see Liturgiia
   Sviatogo Ioanna Zlatousta
"Loneliness" Op.21, No.6, see Otryvok iz Miusse
"Love's Flame" Op.14, No.10, see V moei dushe
Lullaby (Tchaikovsky)   p.22-23

Manfred (1890)   p.27, 314
Margaritki Op.38, No.3   p.59, p.20-21, p.62
Mélodie Op.3, No.3, see Morceaux de fantaisie Op.3
Melodiia Op.21, No.9   p.49
Melody on a Theme of S. Rachmaninoff   p.28-29
"Midsummer Nights" op.14, No.5, see Eti letnie nochi
"Migrant Wind" Op.34, No.4, see Veter pereletnyi
Minuet from L'Arlesienne suite No.1 (Bizet)   p.18
Miserly Knight Op.24, see Skupoi rytsar'
Molitva Op.8, No.6   p.43
Monna Vanna   p.32, 41, 147
Morceaux de fantaisie (1899), see Fantasticheskaia
   p'esa
Morceaux de fantaisie Op.3   p.8, p.21, p.61, p.63-64,
   100, 145, 190, 209, 236, 244
Morceaux de salon Op.10, see Sem' p'es Op.10
"Morning" Op.4, No.2, see Utro
"Mourn of Life" Op.34, No.10, see Sei den' ia pomniu
"Muse" Op.34, No.1, see Muza
"Music" Op.34, No.8, see Muzyka
Muza Op.34, No.1   p.54-55
Muzyka Op.34, No.8   p.56
My otdokhnem Op.26, No.3   p.51

Nad svezhei̯ mogiloi̯ Op.21, No.2 p.47
Na smert' chizhika Op.21, No.8 p.49
Ne mozhet byt' Op.34, No.7, p.56
Neosushchestvlennai͡a simfonii͡a p.28
Ne poi̯, krasavit͡sa Op.4, No.4 p.40, p.60, 208, 230
Ne ver' mne drug Op.14, No.7 p.44-45
Nevoli͡a Op.15, No.5 p.34
"Night," see *Noch'*
"Night is Mournful" Op.26, No.12, see *Noch' pechal'na*
"Night, The" Op.15, No.2, see *Nochka*
Noch' p.47
Nochka Op.15, No.2 p.34
Noch'i͡u v sadu u menia͡ Op.38, No.1 p.59
Noch' pechal'na Op.26, No.12 p.53, p.21 (arr.), 208
"No Prophet I" Op.21, No.11, see *I͡a ne prorok*

Obrochnik Op.34, No.11 p.57
"Oh, Do Not Grieve" Op.14, No,8, see *O, ne grusti*
"Oh, Never Sing to Me Again" Op.4, No.4, see *Ne poi̯ krasavit͡sa*
"Oh No, I Beg You, Forsake Me Not" Op.4, No.1, see
   O net, moli͡u, ne ukhodi
"Oh Stay, My Love, Forsake Me Not" Op.4, No.1, see
   O net, moli͡u, ne ukhodi
"Oh Thou, My Field" Op.4, No.5, see *Uzh ty, niva moi͡a*
"Oh, Vanka, You Bold Fellow" Op.41, No.2, see *Akh, ty Van'ka*
"O Mother of God, Perpetually Praying," see
   V molitvakh neusypai͡ushchui͡u Bogorodit͡su
Ona, Kak polden', khorosha Op.14, No.9 p.45, 230
O, ne grusti Op.14, No.8 p.45
O net, moli͡u, ne ukhodi Op.4, No.1 p.38-39
Oni otvechali Op.21, No.4 p.48
"On the Death of a Linnet" Op.21, No.8, see *Na smert' chizhika*
Opi͡at' vstrepenulos' ty serdt͡se p.37
Oriental Sketch p.16-17, p.63
Ostorovok Op.14, No.2 p.43
Ostrov mertvykh Op.29 p.25, p.65, 2, 44, 75, 86, 93, 98-99, 123, 133, 210, 219, 285, 299, 318
Otryvok iz Mi͡usse Op.21, No.6 p.48, 129, 208
"Over the Little River" Op.41, No.1, see *Cherez rechku*

Pantelei̯-t͡selitel' p.34
"Panteley the Healer," see *Pantelei̯-t͡selitel'*
"Peasant, The" Op.34, No.11, see *Obrochnik*
Pered ikonoi̯ Op.21, No.10 p.49-50

Index of Rachmaninoff's Compositions

Pesniā (cello and piano) p.28
Pesniā razocharovannogo p.38
Piātnadtsat' romansov Op.26 p.50
Piece (1890) p.8
"Pied Piper, The" Op.38, No.4, see *Krysolov*
"Pine Tree" Op.15, No.3, see *Sosna*
Pis'mo Stanislavskomu p.54
"Poet, The" Op.34, No.9, see *Ty znal ego*
Pokinem Op.26, No.5 p.51-52
Polichinelle Op.3, No.4 p.8, p.61
Poliūbila iā na pechal' svoiū Op.8, No.4 p.42, 208
Polka de W.R. p.14, p.61, 53, 93
Polka italienne p.13, p.63, p.65-66
Pora! Op.14, No.12 p.46
Poshchady iā moliū Op.26, No.8 p.52
"Powder and Paint," see *Belilitsy rumenitsy vy moĭ*
"Prayer" Op.8, No.6, see *Molitva*
Preliūdiiā (1891) p.8
Preliūdiiā i vostochnyĭ tanets Op.2 p.29
Prelude (1891), see *Preliūdiiā* (1891)
Prélude et danse oriental Op.2, see *Preliūdiiā i vostochnyĭ tanets*
Prelude in C-sharp Minor Op.3, No.2 p.8, p.21, p.61-62, 4, 58, 129, 202, 208, 254, 307, 333-34, 336, 363
Prelude in D Minor (posth.) p.16
Preludes for Piano Op.23, see *Desiāt' preliūdiĭ*
Preludes for Piano Op.32, see *Trinadtsat' preliūdiĭ*
Prince Rostislav, see *Kniāz' Rostislav*

Quatrième concert pour le piano avec orchestre Op.40 p.6, 7, 68, 181, 207, 225, 340, 375
"Quest, The" Op.38, No.6, see *Au*
"Quickly, Quickly, From My Cheeks" Op.41, No.3, see *Belilitsy, rumenitsy vy moĭ*

"Raising of Lazarus" Op.34, No.6, see *Voskresenie Lazariā*
Rapsodie sur un thème de Paganini Op.43 p.6-7, 7, 44, 68, 83, 111, 148, 213, 274, 285, 323, 360, 364
"Rat-Catcher, The" Op.38, No.4, see *Krysolov*
Rechnaiā liliiā Op.8, No.1 p.41
Rhapsody on a Theme of Paganini Op.43, see *Rapsodie sur un thème de Paganini*
"Ring, The" Op.26, No.14, see *Kol'tso*
"Rock, The" Op.7, see *Utes*
Romance (piano duet) p.10

Romance in A Minor (violin) p.28
Romance in F Minor (cello), see *Pesniā*
Russian Rhapsody for Two Pianos, see *Russkaiā rapsodiiā*
Russkaiā rapsodiiā p.8-9, 35, 372

Scherzo from a Midsummer Night's Dream (Mendelssohn) p.19, 145
Seĭ den' iā pomniŭ Op.34, No.10 p.57
Sem' p'es Op.10 p.10, 93, 99, 209
"She is Lovely as the Noon" Op.14, No.9, see *Ona, kak polden', khorosha*
Shest' khorov Op.15 p.33-34
Shest' muzykal'nykh momentov Op.16 p.11, 41, 99, 100, 228
Shest' p'es Op.11 p.10-11
Shest' romansov Op.4 p.38-41, 108
Shest' romansov Op.8 p.41-43
Shest' stikhotvoreniĭ Op.38 p.58-59, 93, 173, 305
Simfoniiā d-moll (1891) p.23, 318
Simfoniiā No.1 Op.13 p.24-25, p.20 (arr.), 2, 19, 47, 78, 98, 116, 129, 177, 204, 207, 222, 253, 285, 295, 318, 346, 354, 359, 360, 366-67, 372
Simfoniiā No.2 Op.27 p.25, p.66, 83, 93, 160, 174, 204, 285, 299, 318, 365, p.299-300
"Sing Not to Me, Beautiful Maiden" Op.4, No.4, see *Ne poĭ, krasavitsa*
Siren' Op.21, No.5 p.48, p.20 (arr.), p.64, 46, 93, 208
Six Choruses Op.15, see *Shest' khorov*
Six moments musicaux Op.16, see *Shest' muzykal'nykh momentov*
Six morceaux Op.11, see *Shest' p'es* Op.11
Six Songs Op.4, see *Shest' romansov* Op.4
Six Songs Op.8, see *Shest' romansov* Op.8
Six Songs (Six Poems) Op.38, see *Shest' stikhotvoreniĭ*
Skertso (1887) p.23, 35, 228
Skupoĭ rytsar' Op.24 p.32, 90, 113, 140, 147, 342
"Slavery" Op.15, No.5, see *Nevoliā*
Slav'siā Op.15, No.1 p.34
Sleeping Beauty (Tchaikovsky), see *Spiāshchaiā krasavitsa*
Smerkalos' p.37
"So Dread a Fate I'll Ne'er Believe" Op.34, No.7, see *Ne mozhet byt'*
"Soldier's Wife" Op.8, No.4, see *Poliūbila iā na pechal' svoiū*
"So Many Hours" Op.4, No.6, see *Davno l', moĭ drug*

Index of Rachmaninoff's Compositions 329

Son Op.8, No.5   p.42
Son Op.38, No.5   p.59
Sonata for Piano No.1 Op.28, see *Sonate für Pianoforte Op.28*
Sonata for Piano No.2 Op.36, see *Deuxième sonata pour piano Op.36*
Sonate für Pianoforte Op.28   p.13, 99, 201, 223, 299
Sonate pour piano et violoncelle Op.19   p.30-31, 199, 237, 294
"Song of the Disillusioned," see *Pesniā razocharovannogo*
"Sorrow in Springtime" Op.21, No.12, see *Kak mne bol'no*
Sosna Op.15, No.3   p.34
"Soul's Concealment" Op.34, No.2, see *V dushe u kazhogo iz nas*
Spiāshchaiā krasavitsa (Tchaikovsky)   p.22
"Spring" Op.20, see *Vesna*
"Spring Waters" Op.14, No.11, see *Vesennie vody*
Star-Spangled Banner (Smith)   p.22
"Storm, The" Op.14, No.3, see *Buriā*
String Quartet No.1, see *Dve chasti iz kvarteta* (1889)
String Quartet No.2, see *Kvartet dliā dvukh skripok, al'ta i violoncheli*
Sud'ba Op.21, No.1   p.47
Suite in E Major (Bach)   p.17
Suite No.2 for Two Pianos Op.17, see *Vtoraiā siuita Op.17*
Sumerki Op.21, No.3   p.47-48
Symphonic Dances Op.45   p.27, p.21 (arr.), 15, 44, 98, 148, 207, 233, 285, 312, 316, 318, 350, 360
Symphony in D Minor (1891), see *Simfoniiā d-moll* (1891)
Symphony No.1, Op.13, see *Simfoniiā No.1 Op.13*
Symphony No.2, Op.27, see *Simfoniiā No.2 Op.27*
Symphony No.3 Op.44   p.27, p.66, 17-19, 160-61, 171, 175, 204, 225, 274, 285, 318, 340, 365
Symphony No.6 (Glazunov)   p.18

"Tears" Op.5, No.3, see *Fantaziiā. Siuita No.1 Op.5*
Tebiā tak liubiāt vse Op.14, No.6   p.44
"There Are Many Sounds" Op.26, No.1, see *Est' mnogo zvukov*
"These Summer Nights" Op.14, No.5, see *Eti letnie nochi*
"They Answered" Op.21, No.4, see *Oni otvechali*

Three Nocturnes, see *Tri nokturna*
Three Russian Songs (chorus and orchestra) Op.41,
  see *Tri russkie pesni*
"Thy Pity I Implore" Op.26, No.8, see *Poshchady iă moliu*
"'Tis Time" Op.14, No.12, see *Pora!*
"To Her" Op.38, No.2, see *K nei*
"To the Children" Op.26, No.7, see *K detiăm*
Trinadtsat' preliudii Op.32   p.13-14, p.61-62, 21,
  53, 93, 95, 179, 208, 213, 244, 289, 315, 336
Tri nokturna p.7
Trio élégiaque (1892), see *Elegicheskoe trio*
Trio élégiaque Op.9, see *Elegicheskoe trio Op.9*
Tri russkie pesni Op.41   p.35-36, 2, 207
Troisième concert pour le piano avec orchestre Op.30
  p.6, 68, 99, 107, 124, 134, 148, 180-81, 197, 199,
  232, 241, 249, 274, 320, 357, 365, 368, 371, 374
Twelve Songs Op.14, see *Dvenadtsat' romansov Op.14*
Twelve Songs Op.21, see *Dvenadtsat' romansov Op.21*
"Twilight" Op.21, No.3, see *Sumerki*
"Twilight Has Fallen," see *Smerkalos'*
Two Episodes à la Liszt   p.27
"Two Partings" Op.26, No.4, see *Dva proshchaniiă*
Two Pieces (violin) Op.6, see *Dve p'esy Op.6*
Ty pomnish' li vecher p.38
Ty znal ego Op.34, No.9   p.57

U moego okna Op.26, No.10   p.53
Utes. Fantaziiă dliă simfonicheskogo Orkestra Op.7
  p.24, p.20 (arr.), 24, 93, 108, 160, 236, 318
Utro Op.4, No.2   p.39
Uviăl tsvetok   p.38
U vrat obiteli sviatoi   p.36
Uzh ty, niva moiă Op.4, No.5   p.40, 108, 230

Valse and Romance   p.9
Variations on a Theme of Chopin Op.22, see *Variătsii ne temu Shopena*
Variations on a Theme of Corelli Op.42   p.17, 39,
  177, 360
Variătsii ne temu Shopena Op.22   p.12, 19, 39, 93,
  99, 133, 190
Vchera my vstretilis Op.26, No.13   p.53
V dushe u kazhogo iz nas Op.34, No.2   p.55
Vesennie vody Op.14, No.11   p.46, p.66, 110, 208, 230
Vesna Op.20   p.34-35, 249, 286
Vse otniăl u meniă Op.26, No.2   p.51

Index of Rachmaninoff's Compositions 331

Vespers Op.37, see *Vsenoshchnoe bdenie*
Veter pereletnyĭ Op.34, No.4 p.55
V moeĭ dushe Op.14, No.10 p.45
V molchan'i nochi tainoĭ Op.4, No.3 p.39-40, p.63-64, 208
V molitvakh neusypai͡ushchui͡u Bogorodit͡su p.33
"Vocalise" Op.34, No.14, see *Vokaliz*
Vokaliz Op.34, No.14 p.58, p.26 (arr.), p.62, p.65-66, 30, 191, 285, 334, 343
Voskresenie Lazari͡a Op.34, No.6 p.56
Vsenoshchnoe bdenie Op.37 p.35, 111, 184, 192-93, 253, 328
Vtorai͡a si͡uita Op.17 p.12, p.62

"Water Lily," see *Rechnai͡a lilii͡a*
"Waves Slumbered, The" Op.15, No.4, see *Zadremali volny*
"Were You Hiccupping?", see *Ikalos' li tebe*
"What Happiness" Op.34, No.12, see *Kakoe schast'e*
"What Wealth of Rapture" Op.34, No.12, see *Kakoe schast'e*
"When Yesterday We Met" Op.26, No.13, see *Vchera my vstretilis*
"With Holy Banner Firmly Held" Op.34, No.11, see *Obrochnik*
Wohin? (Schubert) p.21-22
"World Would See Thee Smile, The" Op.14, No.6, see *Tebi͡a tak li͡ubi͡at vse*

"You Knew Him" Op.34, No.9, see *Ty znal ego*

Zadremali volny Op.15, No.4 p.34
Zdes' khorosho Op.21, No.7 p.49

Subject Index

(N.B., Numbers preceded by "p." refer to page numbers; all other numbers are item numbers in the bibliography proper)

Appearance 19, 194, 223, 265, 276, 307, 317, 335, 364
Automobiles, love of 307, p.300

Bibliographies 5, 25, 30, 55, 167, 187, 222, 227, 239, 308, 319, 337, 348, 369, 375
Biographies 25, 33, 50, 70, 117, 157, 196, 203, 205, 222, 227, 239, 282, 308-09, 319, 339, 353, 358
Birthplace 48, 227

Choral Works 185, 192-93, 227, 253, 328
Comparison with: Borodin 318, 347; Bunin 356: Busoni 141, 235; Chekov 207; Chopin 359; Colonne 91; Glazunov 47, Grieg 55; Hofmann 304, 317; Kreisler 191; Mahler 91; Medtner 16, 47, 102, 124; Mussorgsky 31; Nikisch 91; Paganini 364; Prokofiev 119; Rimsky-Korsakov 318; Schubert 31, 136; Schumann 359; Scriabin 16, 47, 184, 235, 248, 329, Stravinsky 351; Taneev 47; Tchaikovsky 156, 174, 345, 373; Wagner 31; Zweig 142

Composing Career 15, 37, 99, 110, 154, 170, 177, 207, 228, 262, 278, 288, 318, 348
Compositional Style 16, 19, 21, 24, 27, 39, 47, 50, 55, 68, 70, 90, 101, 116, 123, 134, 136, 170, 173, 181, 184, 192, 204, 209-10, 214-15, 225, 232, 238, 253, 263, 283, 285, 289, 300, 316, 323, 327, 340, 348, 359-60, 366, 371, 373
Concert Seasons p.67-68, 13, 38, 155, 199, 268, 278, 332
Concerti 61, 68, 70, 105, 127, 170, 181, 227, 283, 320
Conducting Career p.68-69, 29, 43, 91, 93, 140, 151, 153-54, 187, 193, 245-47, 262, 264, 266, 274, 278, 302, 338, 348, 352
Conservatory Study p.67-68, 5, 35, 43, 52, 84, 158, 177, 242, 264, 282, 344
Creativity 5, 18, 36, 41, 89, 135, 176, 193, 275, 299, 319, 338, 348, 366, 373
Criticism of 27, 67, 68, 72, 74, 77, 115, 118, 138, 170, 188, 204, 243, 280, 283, 297, 303, 321, 360

Subject Index

Dies irae, use of 44, 116, 285, 315
Discographies 13, 33, 55, 70, 87, 146, 180, 196, 369

Eulogistic Articles 3, 84, 86, 234, 324

Film Music, influence on 289, 293
Flight from Russia 79, 266-67, 271, 278, 295, 327

Historical Status 57, 77, 84, 115, 137, 165, 188-89, 303, 335, 338

Imagery, use of 17, 24, 135, 230, 239, 263, 284, 315-16
Influenced by: Borodin 156; Chaliapin 288; Chopin 190; Cui 156; Dargomyzhskiĭ 185; Glinka 185; Kreisler 177; Liszt 210; Rimsky-Korsakov 156, 228, 230, 345, 373; Rubinstein, A. 261; Tchaikovsky 156, 174, 345, 373
Interviews 11, 13, 15, 51, 121, 161, 195, 200, 258, 261-63, 266-67, 284, 307, 313, 344

Letters 9, 13, 18, 19, 25, 33, 36, 37, 40, 41, 49, 75, 80, 89, 139, 144, 150, 163, 174-75, 186, 206, 224, 290, 295, 301-02, 308, 311, 348, 362, 367, 370

Loss of Desire to Compose 29, 40, 101, 161, 168, 176, 262, 271, 326, 345, 353
Lyricism 20, 107, 129, 136, 148, 160, 232, 256, 269, 288, 300, 316, 347-48

Modern Music, remarks on 51, 98, 129, 186, 194, 256-57, 263, 269, 271, 362, 366

Negro Music, comment on 307

Obituaries 17, 338
October Revolution 158, 178
Operas p.68, 24, 30, 76, 90, 113-14, 140, 147, 152, 156, 227, 293, 348
Orchestral Works 2, 70, 204, 227, 238, 314, 318, 348, 360

Paintings, *see* Portraits
Personality 52, 58, 62, 98, 105-06, 142, 144, 163, 184, 206, 217, 296, 311, 317, 330, 362
Pianistic Style 14, 65, 92, 95, 109, 128, 132, 141, 162, 165-66, 179-80, 187, 197, 210, 229, 236, 241, 244, 255, 258, 261, 268, 300-01, 303-04, 313, 320, 335, 336, 374
Piano Career p.67-68, 128, 154-55, 162, 222, 241, 252, 259, 262, 275, 278, 288, 301, 303-04, 332

Subject Index   335

Piano Works 7, 21, 70,
   100, 125-27, 179, 181,
   201, 222, 227, 300,
   306, 336, 348
Portraits 64, 150, 369
Psychological Studies
   23, 40, 142, 291, 310,
   359, 360

Radio broadcasts, aversion to 161, 200, 260
Recording Career p.93-94, 105, 191, 229, 260,
   281, 358, 363
Recordings p.93-94, 61,
   69, 112, 132-33, 145-46, 180, 197, 242,
   279-81, 325, 363, 369
Reminiscences 12, 13,
   19, 32, 35, 36, 40, 45,
   49, 52, 63, 66, 80, 81,
   87, 108, 122, 165, 169,
   175, 196, 207, 211-13,
   220, 229, 278, 287,
   296, 325, 330, 346,
   349, 352
Reviews 2, 4, 34, 54, 83,
   86, 90-93, 103, 109,
   112, 141, 151, 153, 156,
   160, 178, 223, 236, 242,
   244-51, 265, 268, 274,
   292, 312, 342-43, 350,
   357, 374-75
Revisions 55, 100, 198,
   225, 266, 340-41
Russian Chant, use of 116,
   192, 253, 316, 328-29,
   368
Russian Heritage 17, 20,
   24, 79, 84, 136, 144,
   157, 160, 174-75, 255,
   271, 307, 316, 327,
   346-48, 353, 358, 368,
   373
Russianism 17, 19, 56,
   130-31, 136, 160, 173-75, 230, 242, 307, 312,
   347, 353

Songs 70, 94, 110, 120,
   140, 143, 172-73, 208,
   227, 230, 270, 305
Song Style 46, 88, 120,
   147, 172-73, 185, 230,
   270
Soviet Boycott 96, 111,
   178, 184, 243, 308, 331
Symphonic Style 17, 116,
   130-31, 148-49, 160,
   204, 318, 320, 373
Symphonies 204, 227

Tours, *see* Concert Seasons

World War II 17, 54, 139,
   159, 243
Works, lists of 5, 13, 18,
   33, 70, 117, 157, 187,
   196, 222, 227, 282, 308,
   319, 337, 341, 348, 369

Youthful Years 5, 35, 36,
   40, 49, 50, 52, 129, 144,
   157, 160, 220, 222, 226,
   228, 258, 282, 284, 318,
   345-46